Signing in Puerto Rican

D0161907

A Carlos
Thanks for being
with us today
Abrazos, Andrés Torres
20 abril 2013

Signing in
Puerto Rican

A Hearing Son
and His Deaf Family

Andrés Torres

Gallaudet University Press
Washington, D.C.

Gallaudet University Press
Washington, D.C. 20002
http://gupress.gallaudet.edu

Library of Congress Cataloging-in-Publication Data
Torres, Andrés, 1947–
    Signing in Puerto Rican : a hearing son and his deaf family / Andrés Torres.
    p. cm.
    ISBN-13: 978-1-56368-417-3 (alk. paper)
    1. Torres, Andrés, 1947—Childhood and youth. 2. Torres, Andrés, 1947—Family. 3. Children of deaf parents—United States—Biography. 4. Deaf—Family relationships—United States—Case Studies. 5. Puerto Ricans—New York (State)—New York—Biography. 6. Deaf—New York (State)—New York—Biography. 7. Catholics—New York (State)—New York—Biography. 8. Puerto Rican Society for the Catholic Deaf. 9. New York (N.Y.)—Biography. I. Title.
    HQ759.912.T67 20099
    306.874092—dc22
    [B]
                                                                2009024417

∞The paper used in this publication meets the minimum requirements of American National Standard for Information Sciences—Permanence of Paper for Printed Library Materials, ANSI Z39.48-1984.

To Viveroni,
who is always there

Contents

Acknowledgments

I HAVE ACCUMULATED MANY debts of gratitude in writing this memoir. First to family, living and past, who shared their memories and answered my queries about early life in Puerto Rico and later years as migrant newcomers in New York City. These are my beloved late parents, and my *tías* and *tíos*, especially Blanca, César, and in memory Mariamelia, Olga, Magdalena, Carmela, and Celestino (Chelo). My dear cousin Mary helped re-create the time and feel of our experience as children of deaf parents. She has kept a firm presence in the deaf world, establishing a sign language school on her own. To the many family and friends who provided their recollections and who encouraged me to press on, my deep appreciation. Some knew that they would make an appearance in the narrative. I hope I have done justice to their stories as well. I have changed some names in this account.

I received help from readers and wordsmiths. Without their feedback this work would never have gone to print. Many thanks to those who gave comments at various stages: Jane Blanshard, Lady Borton, Juan Flores, Janet Francendese, Esther Kingston-Mann, Barbara Kivowitz, Demetria Martínez, Roberto Márquez, Susan Meyers, Judy Polumbaum, and Lisa Sánchez. Jacob Miller, to whom I am especially grateful, read and re-read the entire manuscript cajoling me to prune it of the flaws and excesses of a novice memoirist.

Along the way I benefited from material aid, professional advice, and inspirational support. The following have my lasting appreciation: Kevin Bowen, Doris Braendel, Junot Díaz, Martín Espada, James Green, Ernesto Malavé, Rubén Martínez, Jennifer Raab, Vita Rabinowitz, Jaime Rodríguez, and Pat Zorita. Participants in various writers' workshops encouraged me along the journey: The Iowa Summer Writing Festival, The William Joiner Center Writer's Workshop, and The Brookline Writing Workshop. My brothers and sisters from CODA (Children of Deaf Adults) cheered me on to the finish line.

Thanks also to colleagues at various institutions in which I was employed during the years this memoir was in process: The College of Public and Community Service (CPCS) and the Mauricio Gastón Institute, both at the University of Massachusetts Boston; and The Center for Puerto Rican Studies and Hunter College, at the City University of New York. In spending a third of your life at the job, you might as well enjoy the company you keep. Fortune has graced me with co-workers who took an interest in this story and who cared that I complete it. My thanks also to two publications that previously published portions of this book, the weekly newspaper *Claridad* and *CENTRO Journal*.

Ever the gracious and supportive editor, Ivey Wallace of Gallaudet University Press welcomed this memoir and responded attentively to my questions and requests. Deirdre Mullervy supervised the production process with care and proficiency. Serena Leigh Krombach was a thorough copy editor.

My family has always been the bedrock of inspiration for me. As an only child I turned to my cousins and in-laws for the emotional bonds one needs in life and they have more than compensated for my lack of siblings. My children and their spouses—Rachel and John, Orlando and Analía—give me more joy than I can express. My grandchildren Jaclyn, David, Jonathan, and Abigail, keep me looking to the future. Carmen Vivian, my wife and unsung heroine, keeps it all together, and then some. In loving gratitude I dedicate this work to her.

1

The A Train

"STEP LIVELY, STEP LIVELY." The conductor's command came sharply over the loudspeaker as they jumped aboard. Life had taught them to regard punctuality as a vital habit. Too often they had been overlooked or left behind, so they were already poised at the doors as the subway slowed to a halt. My parents were going downtown to the Friday meeting of the Puerto Rican Society for the Catholic Deaf. Together with their friends Isaura and Oliverio, they were riding the A train to the meeting hall, located in the central office of the New York City Archdiocese, near St. Patrick's Cathedral. I was with them as usual. The year was 1960.

Pop worked as a stock clerk in the garment center where his week-days were spent packing men's shirts into cardboard boxes. His hands were callused from the daily handling of those boxes, and the years of lifting and lugging molded his body into an athletic frame. He arrived home gritty and tired, but on those Friday evenings of the Deaf Society, of which Pop was president, he was a transformed man. In his grey suit and blue tie, his face sweetly scented with his favorite lotion, he could have passed for someone well beyond his true station in life. As president of an organization, he might as well dress up for the role. Like most Latin men, Pop sported a mustache, finely trimmed and clear of his upper lip. His thinning dark hair was combed back.

The five of us worked our way through the busy car and in the far corner Mom and Isaura, dressed up and perfumed, found seats. They fit snuggly in a double seat, while I grabbed an empty spot some distance from them. Mom, short and chubby, occupied more than her fair share of space, which presented no problems for Isaura who was slim as a rail. Fortunately, I had already convinced my parents that a twelve-year-old boy didn't need to be making a fashion statement for these meetings. With my blue striped polo shirt, unadorned cotton slacks and Converse sneakers, I was good to go. Pop and Oliverio stood nearby, holding onto a silver pole where there were already two men. As the train pulled out of the station Pop and Oliverio faced each other.

"Do you think there'll be many people tonight?" Oliverio wondered, in signs.

"Maybe twenty-five to thirty. It will be a good crowd," Pop responded with his hands.

Signing on a subway that alternates between a stop-and-go crawl and a bouncing sprint is not the easiest thing to do. Elbows and knees were in constant motion, as the men braced themselves against the gleaming silver pole. Each would've been grateful for the use of a third arm.

"We have a lot of business to discuss: the credit union and planning for the dinner, and Monsignor Lynch wants to talk to us. Then we will have the movie. I hope we do not waste time on silly arguments." Pop liked to run the meetings efficiently and leave time for socializing.

They kept the signs to themselves, trying to conceal the conversation like poker players sheltering their hands. Pop didn't like to verbalize loudly or put his gestures on display, as did other deaf people I knew. Nevertheless, the other two men at the pole were startled; they weren't sure what to do. I had seen this before and I knew what they were thinking: Is it wrong to look? Or do you just pretend they're not there? These two just stayed where they were, fidgeting and looking away. Pop had been through this often and he didn't care. He wasn't going to be a zombie on the subway. On he went, signing with Oliverio, discreetly, but without shame. Next to me Mom and Isaura were gossiping too, *chismeando* with their hands. As soon as we'd jumped aboard they'd gone straight for the corner seats, to avoid the view of other passengers. They conversed with their hands down on their laps, making only the subtlest of facial movements. I was accustomed to this scene: watching my parents sign in the subway, and watching the hearing people watch them.

Pop and Oliverio continued, as did Mom and Isaura, oblivious to the attention gathering about them. By now the other passengers, not just the two men at the silver pole, noticed the deaf people talking. Then, toward the center of the car, a group of young kids had noticed: "Hey, look over there," one of them said. "Look over there at the deaf and dumb people!"

Then came the bulging eyes and giggles.

"Oh yeah, look." Another chimed in, pointing at my parents.

A third one let out, "Hey I can do that, can't you?"

They threw their hands about, competing for the loudest laughs. Any exaggerated movement would do: fingers in acrobatic maneuvers, clownish faces, grunting noises. Standing and sitting, they were bunched together and making like they were trading signs. They pretended it was an inside joke, but they must've known my parents could see what was going on.

168th, 145th, 125th. The train raced downtown as the show continued. And in the audience I saw a variety of reactions: embarrassment, pity, and fear. I perceived varieties of anger as well. There was anger directed at the troublemakers. And there was another anger reserved for my parents, for starting the whole mess in the first place.

Up to now, I was a bystander, seated apart from them.

"Ahtay!" (I was known as "Andy" in the hearing world, but "Ahtay," with the accent on "tay" is how it sounded in the Deaf world.) Pop waved at me to get my attention. He said for me to get the time from someone.

Of course, Pop knew the time. What he wanted was not the time but for everyone else to know that I was with him. I asked an elderly lady sitting across the aisle. I always preferred approaching older people. I signed the time to Pop; he told me to thank the elderly lady; she told me to tell Pop he's welcome; Pop nodded his head at her, with the trademark grin that barely curled the corners of his mouth. He raised his hand in thanks and the lady smiled at me.

Then the passengers turned to me, interpreting the scene. The boy in the corner is with the deaf folks, but he can hear and speak. He's been observing the whole scene, and maybe he's been watching us too. Earlier Pop and Oliverio surprised the two men at the silver pole. And now the confusion deepened, the faces changed again, and I guessed at what they were thinking: "Hey, I don't get this. Don't deaf people have deaf children?" "Wow. What's it like to be a child in that home?" "Did that kid learn to speak with his hands, before he learned to talk?" "So he can curse all he wants? Hey, that's cool!"

I remember what went through my mind in these situations: "Sometimes hearing people, they get so stupid. Like the kids on this train, making fun of my parents with their phony sign language."

Once, earlier, on another subway ride when people were staring at my parents, I felt so bad for them that I got up and screamed, "Hey, what's the matter with you? You never saw deaf people before? They're just regular people, you know!"

Man, that blew them away! You should've seen them when they realized I could hear and talk *and* sign. How quickly their faces changed. But I knew when it was all over, and they were home, they'd laugh themselves silly. To think they were fooled like that! So yelling or making a scene every time wasn't worth the trouble. I learned that from

Pop. He might give a dirty look, but that was about it. But that Friday night, when I was an eighth grader and the kids were mimicking my parents and their friends, something else happened.

The subway pulled out of the 125th Street station. The A train had one extended stretch of nonstop travel. By itself, the ride from 125th to 59th street was worth the price of admission. The train zipped by local stations so fast that you could barely identify them. Also, there was a forest of I-beams that cluttered the view as we raced along the middle tracks of the tunnel. It was an ear-busting sprint and I doubt any train in the entire system sped along like the A train on that stretch. And I doubt any of them gave you as bumpy a ride. At top speed it felt as if the train wheels weren't made for those tracks, as if the manufacturers had miscalculated ever so slightly the proper circumference of the wheels. Each bounce and clash sent a charge up my spine. The clanging and pounding of steel on steel was so thunderous even Mom and Isaura, who were still sitting in the corner seats, covered their ears.

All that excitement just agitated the kids further, provoking them into kindergarten play: dancing fingers, twisted faces, animal voices. And worst of all, there was the laughing. My parents and Oliverio and Isaura looked away. The other passengers were upset and uneasy.

As the train screeched into 59th Street, where we would switch to the D line, we were ready to get off. Finally. On the way out, Mom poked at my shoulder: "Ahtay."

She pointed to the kids so they could see her then she angrily signed to me what she wanted them to know. Then she crouched her short, chubby body in their direction, flashed a menacing look that left no doubt what she thought of them, and threw them the middle finger of her right hand.

The kids recoiled, giggled nervously, then stopped laughing.

Mom poked again at my shoulder, ordering me to translate.

I relayed her words. "She says God will punish you for making fun of us; she says your children will be born deaf."

2

Early Signs

MY PARENTS, ANDRÉS TORRES and Bienvenida Ayala, were married in April of 1946, having met the previous year at a party at the Ayalas' apartment at 1494 Madison Avenue, near 103rd Street. The apartment had been a center of socializing for deaf people who had come to New York from Puerto Rico because the Ayalas had four beautiful deaf daughters, known as *las mudas*, and deaf men came from all over the city to ingratiate themselves with the Ayala elders. Andrés had fixed his sights on Bienvenida. It was a brief courtship steered aggressively by my father, who at thirty-two was nine years older than my mother. She resisted because she enjoyed the single life and didn't want to tie herself down to a man just yet. But her three deaf sisters had already been married off, and her parents pressured her to wed.

Several of Mom's brothers and sisters had already moved with their young families to the South Bronx, to a neighborhood only a mile of city blocks away from El Barrio, on Manhattan's East Side, where the Ayalas had first settled in the 1930s. My parents moved to join the

Ayala siblings, and there, on 140th Street and Brook Avenue in a fourth-floor walk-up, my parents began their life together.

Ten months later my mother delivered me onto the scene, after fourteen hours of hard labor culminating in a Caesarean section. She was big-boned, like all the Ayalas, but like her fourteen siblings, not too tall. Giving birth was not a whole lot of fun, Mom would say. The doctors and nurses didn't speak Spanish, let alone sign language.

Unveiling the memory of those early times in the South Bronx reveals the sights and sounds that I have carefully preserved throughout the years: echoes, silence, toys, music, a fire. And most prominently, signs. According to Mom the first two words she taught me were *Mamá* and *pee-pee*. She showed me the sign for *Mamá*, tapping the right thumb of the open right hand on the chin, once for each syllable, and she also taught me to say the word loudly, *"Mamá!"* Waving and yelling were back-up communication systems for the important signs. The more desperately I needed her, the more frantic the waving, and screaming too.

Another word that often called for frantic waving, *pee-pee*, was signed by sticking my thumb between the index and middle finger and shaking the clenched fist. Later in life, as I tried to figure out the origin of various signs, I assumed that the thumb represented the penis. There it is, dangling right between the legs. That must be how that sign evolved, I thought. Then I learned that it was based on the letter T, for *toilet*.

When I signed *pee-pee*, she pulled out the white metal pot from under my crib, or took me to the bathroom, and I took care of business. Nighttime was a different story. I was a bed-wetter until I was five or six. It was an unfortunate habit and no doubt began because my parents, dead asleep, couldn't hear me wailing for attention. My pee-pee signs, however well formed, however frantically waved, were of no use in the dark. Neither was the yelling.

Eventually I stopped wetting my bed. Mom used to say I was a "smart boy," because I learned how to stop wetting myself. But in truth it must have been the stench of urine, and not my IQ, that solved the dilemma. This was the crude origin to lifelong traits of mine: a tolerance for discomfort, and a boundless capacity for deferred gratification.

Other words I picked up early on from Mom were *ca-ca* and *leche* (milk). *Ca-ca* was simple. I just pointed to my butt, and mouthed the word loudly to her face, with a hard *c,* as in "ka-ka." Mom also taught me the standard shortcut terms, used even in the hearing world, for the bodily functions: one finger up for pee-pee, two fingers for ca-ca. The sign for *leche* was made by imitating milking a cow. The way Mom showed me, it was just rubbing the fists up and down against each other—this was the home sign she used growing up in Puerto Rico, slightly different than the sign used in America made by clenching a fist. I mouthed the word *leche* to make sure. Then she would get me my bottle.

Pop gave me my "name sign:" the right fist, forming the letter *A,* tapping the top of the left fist. "Ah-táy" was how he vocalized it, as close as he could get to saying Andy. I was named after him, with the nickname he had when he came to school in the United States. (Name signs are created individually, usually by a family member or close friend. I have run across other Andys who have different signs than mine. And I once met a deaf man named Albert who had my sign, the *A* tapping on the fist. We were identical in the Deaf world; different in the hearing world.)

"Ahtay! Ahtay!" Pop had a warm timbre to his voice. He would have been a baritone if he'd been able to sing like hearing people. It was pleasant to my ear and excited me when he called. I loved running into his arms when he came home from work calling out "Ahtay!, Ahtay!"

Mom whispered my name, putting the emphasis on the first syllable, blowing softly so that it sounded like "Hhhót-tay." She vocalized lightly, so she couldn't get my attention from the next room. If I was out of sight, she shrieked a sharp high tone and I came running. Mom called out from her throat, like a person in danger: *"Ahhh!"* I tensed up when she yelled for me.

In my early years I spoke a jumble of Spanish and English. Spanish was my parents' native language, which they used in a combination of spoken words, signs they learned growing up in Puerto Rico, and "home signs" they had invented for themselves as children. By the time they were each living in the United States, even before they met, they were gradually switching to a signed form of English. I learned this from them too. As I entered young childhood, five or six years old, and became more exposed to English-speaking people in the hearing world, English became my second language, after signed English. Spanish, the dominant voice among my hearing elder relatives, remained a tertiary language—a background noise throughout my coming of age—and re-emerged in later life.

Mom's younger brother César, who grew up with her in Las Piedras, Puerto Rico, once came to see us. He may have been the first to be disturbed by what my parents and I took for granted: the silence that penetrated every corner of our apartment. Without a television (my parents couldn't afford one) and without a telephone (of no use to my parents, even if they could afford one), our place must have had an eerie feel to his ears. Mom hardly had any volume in her voice. She vocalized quietly, gesturing to him with the primitive home signs. So the apartment would have seemed like a hollow chamber to him. César would have heard only the echoes of his own voice.

Maybe Uncle César wasn't the first to notice the reign of silence. But he was the first to actually do something about it, by purchasing a radio for me. He showed Mom how to operate it and even wrote down numbers on the dial where the best stations could be found. I was only three, so I don't remember what kind of music I listened to most. Mom would move the tuner until I heard music I liked, which I indicated just by raising my hand and nodding my head.

Somewhere in my brain is lodged a song that captivated me then, probably in 1949 or 1950. Each time it appeared, I stopped what I was doing to listen. It was soft and beautiful and poignant. I can't recall if it was a piece of classical or popular music. There were lyrics, but Spanish or English, I don't know. There were horns, not violins. Slow, not fast. Lilting, not rocking. I can't reproduce the melody, only a vague recollection that it was warm and sad. Hearing that song was a totally random event. I didn't know what station played it, or when it would come on. I could only stumble upon it by luck. There was no way I could access that enchanting sound myself.

One day when I was about four years old there was a loud pounding on the door of our apartment. The clamoring voices on the floor landing jolted me into a state of alert. I jumped up from the living room floor where I had been working on my Wild West book, coloring Lash LaRue and Roy Rogers. I was trained to get Mom immediately at the sound of knocking, and this pandemonium sent me nervously to her. I rushed into the kitchen, grabbed hard on her apron and pointed toward the front door, nodding my head rapidly. She saw the urgency in my face.

Hastening to the door, she opened it to find two immense men, helmeted and in glossy dark coats, armed with axes and red tin canisters. In an instant they were indoors, gently brushing us aside. Behind them was the next-door neighbor, an elderly woman. The firemen headed for the kitchen and pried open the dumbwaiter door. They peeked into the shaft and yelled downward.

In a second, one of the men pulled out a canister and fired away, splashing the contents down the chute. A moment later, it was over. The firemen thanked Mom for letting us in, and waved goodbye to us. One of them patted me on the shoulder and said, "Good boy."

Mom reminisced years later that someone's garbage had caught fire in the dumbwaiter chute. When the firemen reached our floor, the elderly lady told them we were a deaf family. Mom said that if I hadn't come to her in time they would have had to bash in the door, or, worse, we could have been badly burned.

When my parents married, my father earned thirty-five dollars a week and my mother eighteen. Both worked in factories. Pop was a stock clerk for the Love Shirt Company, in midtown Manhattan. While he was stuffing men's shirts into cardboard boxes, Mom was getting her hands all dusted with black powder as a worker in a Brooklyn firecracker company. These jobs didn't require much education, or the ability to hear; even deaf people could hold them.

Soon after getting pregnant my mother quit work. Her boss was a peculiar guy who made her feel uncomfortable. He liked to grab his Puerto Rican female employees and lift them up off the factory floor and dangle them in the air. The boss wanted her to return later, but the family said she should stay home and take care of me.

We lived on a tight budget, relying on hand-me-downs from my mother's family, the Ayalas. Several cousins lived in my building, so I had plenty to pick from. The rent-controlled apartment cost only thirty-eight dollars monthly, but with just one income we weren't quite living in the lap of luxury.

From the beginning I had a preference for Pop. It could not be otherwise. Tradition had assigned Mom the role of disciplinarian. It was her job to change the wet bed sheets and to coax me through the minutiae of daily life: tidying up my things, eating the canned vegetables, and brushing my teeth. The only times I got whacked for bad behavior were by Mom, with a slap across the rear end. Pop never hit me, not once.

So Pop got to play the good guy. The best part of my day began at supper. That's when Pop came home from work bringing stories, jokes, and sometimes a surprise gift. Since she depended on him for news about the outside world, Mom looked forward to his arrival too. At dinnertime Mom and I were his students, asking for the meaning of words and signs.

Some nights Pop would sit with me, crayons in hand, and assist me as I worked on my Wild West coloring book. He suggested the appropriate hue and shade as I filled in the figures of cowboys astride their horses. He followed my efforts at connecting the dots, coaching me in the right direction.

He transfixed me with his precise oralizing of "A, B, C, D . . ." His voice sounded different from the speech of my hearing relatives. He produced a foghorn's version of the alphabet, hollow and deep, something my cousins and I called "deaf talk." Some hearing people could understand Pop if he spoke, but he only talked to people he trusted: family members; Father Lynch, who married everyone in the family and baptized me; and neighborhood friends. If he tried communicating with a stranger, the sound of deaf talk often jolted his listener. But with me, in the privacy of our home, he was free to intone loudly in deaf talk. With me he never had to worry about the strange noises from his throat. And I was never confused by Pop's alphabet.

Pop also tutored me in the number system before I entered the first grade. He bought math playbooks and drilled me on the exercises. He showed me how to write out each numeral accurately and the order they followed. The figure eight was my nemesis. Try as I did, I could never get it to flow from my pencil in an uninterrupted circuit. The other digits were easy; the figure eight I could produce only by piling one zero on top of another. Pop easily detected my falsely constructed eight and insisted gently that this was not the real thing.

"Make believe the line is like a train track, and that it crosses over itself," he would say.

"And do not lift the pencil; never lift the pencil."

Pop meticulously recorded the milestones of my early years. My book of "Baby's Treasures" registers the key steppingstones: birth, baptism, first words, first tooth, and first haircut. In a tiny plastic envelope is preserved a sample of curly brown hair, thanks to Mom. My father's graceful handwriting registers my accomplishments from birth through my fifth year, when I entered the first grade at PS 169. Like an accountant updating the ledgers, he fastidiously recorded the money I received on each birthday.

For the most part, I received gifts of one and two dollars. This wasn't a whole lot, but between my father's and my mother's families, I boasted twenty-one *tíos* and *tías*. In a good year, those small denominations would add up to a significant sum. Besides, as my father's notation faithfully documented, there were other tangible donations to my welfare: white pajamas, a blue sweater, a blue sailor's outfit with matching shoes, a green woolen blanket for the crib.

In the centerfold of my baby book is the family tree. At ground level several immense roots emerge from the earth's surface, migrating toward the base of the trunk. The giant plant is anchored deeply into Creation. On the thick branches jutting out from each side of the rippled trunk, Pop carefully filled in the names of my Torres and Ayala predecessors, starting with my great-grandparents and ascending to the present. In blue ink, etched in at the tree's leafy pinnacle stands my name "Andrés Ismael Torres, Jr." Years later, I would study my family tree obsessively. Pop's work enabled me to visualize my place in the natural order, from whence I came.

Then there were the photographs that Pop had carefully preserved. My favorite was of the Torres family on the Highbridge rocks. Pop said it was an Easter Sunday, soon after they had been reunited in New York City and my grandparents were living on Amsterdam Avenue. One son, Miguel, who stayed in Puerto Rico, was missing from the group. Nine people tied by blood, my grandmother Ita at the bedrock center, grasping each other as if for dear life. And other favorite pictures: of my parents' wedding day, and another of my Ayala grandparents with their deaf daughters.

No doubt I revered him. Since Pop wasn't always around, absent during the workday and often with his friends when the weekend came,

I was thrilled to be with him whenever I could. Like a rare baseball card that commands a premium because only a few specimens survive, Pop's scarce presence only intensified my love for him. Mom was reliably present, affectionate, my safe harbor. But it was Pop, teacher and authority figure, to whom I mostly showed my love. I didn't know to disguise this bias very well, for Mom figured this out eventually.

In retrospect I know I had unfairly stacked the deck against Mom. In fact, she doted over me and lavished me with much caring and hugging. I have dozens of photographs as evidence of this. Later Mom confessed sheepishly that when I was still an infant she daydreamed she was the Virgin Mary and I her Baby Jesus. Surely, that should be good enough for me.

From Pop I developed a desire for learning. Knowledge for the sake of knowledge. Mom bequeathed to me a fascination with the natural world, especially the animals that inhabited her childhood in rural Puerto Rico.

Sitting around the kitchen table Mom made me laugh describing how cows munch on grass. "Look at Elsie Cow," she signed to me over breakfast, pointing to the carton of Borden's Milk. "They are so funny when they eat." She rolled her jaws and circled her fists on top of each other to mimic the cow's grinding mouth. "They eat slow and happy. In Puerto Rico when I was small Mamá (my maternal grandmother Eufrasia) showed me how to milk the cow. It was the same as if it was my job on the farm."

She described her method. "Our cow was very big. I almost could not see over her back. But she let me grab her *tetas* (vocalizing in Spanish and pointing to Elsie's udders) and I squeezed them. It was fun. I could feel the warm milk going from the bag and through the *tetas*. I pointed the milk into the tin pan."

And then, she continued, the cats would come, two of them, with spots in different colors. The sound of the milk dropping into the pail immediately attracted them. They let Mom know, not with meows she couldn't hear but with staring eyes, that they wouldn't mind if she directed some of the white liquid their way.

"I shot at them and watched them trying to catch the milk. They loved me because I was their friend and gave them something to drink." But after a few times Mom's Mamá noticed and scolded her, telling her to not squander milk in foolish games. No more squirting the cats after that. It was also Mom's duty to walk the cow to a nearby pond. There, in a spot surrounded by trees that shaded the fresh water pool, the animal would drink. Mom said she was warned by her Papá not to go into the water. It was not the place for a seven-year-old girl to play games. People had been swallowed up in there.

She also had to collect the chicken eggs, and my grandmother Eufrasia had a special sign for this. She held out her left palm and dropped her right fist on it. An egg falling from the chicken. With this sign, Mom went about rounding up any available eggs. Mamá also taught her how to tell if a chicken was going to lay her eggs soon: stick your pinky up the birth canal and feel for a shell.

"I asked Papá if we could have our own dog. I was lonely and bored. The other brothers and sisters went to school, but the *mudas* (the four deaf sisters) had nothing to do, only work." Papá Catalino, father of the fifteen Ayala offspring, brought home a short-haired black-and-white mutt. Peligro ("Danger") became the family guard dog. All the children loved Peligro, but according to Mom, she convinced the others to let her be the dog's master.

"One time a man came to the farm. Papá said the man had to cut Peligro in his pee pee, so he would not chase after girl dogs. This was needed, or one day the dog runs away. For Peligro to be a good dog, we needed to cut his pee pee."

I cringed as Mom described that afternoon for me. The amateur surgeon wrestling the squirming Peligro to the ground, slicing his razor into the poor pet's testicles. Blood sprouting all over, the dog yelping and squealing in the man's arms until he finally calmed down, and the man applied gauze to the wound. Like Mom, I was horrified.

Of all the creatures in her early days, there was no doubt which was the most impressive. There were no *caballos* on Don Catalino's farm, but people often came by on horseback: relatives, government people, merchants, and men of God.

Tutín Piñero was one of Mom's many brothers-in-law. His stern demeanor softened when he was with the young *mudas*, and he loved seeing the girls' excitement as he rode in on his magnificent horse. Mom was overwhelmed by the horse, which was simply too big and intimidating. Tutín eased her anxiety.

"Tutín let me pet the horse on his neck. The skin was smooth and wet," Mom signed, slowly brushing one palm over another, her round white face in fond reminiscence. Mom said she was content with this, that the horse let her stand beside him and stroke his sleek neck.

Mom's sister Carmela was not at all frightened. Tutín's visit was the highlight of the week because, as a special treat, he would let Carmela mount the horse. With her brother-in-law slowly circling the horse, and the other kids watching in envy, Carmela basked in the glory of her courage. Carmela was "*bien brava*," Mom voiced. (This was how Mom talked to me. Sometimes speaking in Spanish, sometimes signing in Spanish; sometimes speaking in English, sometimes signing in English. Pop too.)

But once, Mom recalled, the horses brought tragedy, not fun. The family knew a Protestant minister who often visited, bringing the Scripture and some company to the Ayalas' rural outpost.

"The man visited Mamá and Papá, and they drank coffee and talked about God. Carmela and me, we stayed outside watching his horse. Then the man said goodbye and rode away."

Some minutes after the minister left, Don Catalino heard a desperate call for help from his friend. He rushed toward the sounds of alarm, the kids in quick pursuit, and found the minister plunged in a mud hole. The mud hole was near the same watering pond that Papá had warned Mom to avoid.

Mom gasped as she saw the two, animal and master, sinking gradually into what seemed like quicksand. The minister recovered and pulled himself free, but the huge horse was stuck deep and plummeting. The men grappled frantically to control the animal. Mom and Carmela ran about clapping and yelling, begging them to save the horse. But to no avail.

Papá sped back to the farmhouse and returned with his revolver. The girls watched, crying and screaming, as the minister brought his horse to a merciful end. The sight of the horse drowning stayed with both girls for a long time. For months Carmela, the brave horse-lover, had nightmares of that horrible day at the pond.

"Carmela became sick, and did not eat for months; she became skinny and sad," Mom signed. To signify the word "skinny," Mom showed an upright pinky. To signify "sad" she tilted her head to one side and blanketed her face with a palm. She looked like the Sorrowful Virgin. Intently following her description, I too was there in Las Piedras, Puerto Rico, in the 1920s. I saw them shoot the horse in the head, as the earth engulfed him.

By the time Mom was describing her animal adventures, we were living in upper Manhattan, on Amsterdam Avenue near 171st Street. The South Bronx, where the Ayala clan had concentrated, had been our home for four years. But by 1951 Pop wanted us to be closer to the Torres family, and they lived in Washington Heights. There, near his six sisters and my grandparents, is where he wanted to make our life. Of his six sisters, three were deaf.

The building, a solid four-story brick structure that looked like it could withstand an earthquake, was located on 169th Street and St. Nicholas Avenue, not very far from Columbia Presbyterian Hospital. It was there, at Public School 169, that my educational career began.

From the first grade, I loved school. It was exciting to sit in a busy classroom reciting the alphabet and times tables in lively chorus with my friends. Being called upon to read from a story book and to write sentences on the blackboard: that was my idea of fun. In the play periods of 1955, I found the counterpoint to the unrelenting quiet of our apartment. To chase and be chased was heaven. I marvel at the class photos from those years. We were boys and girls of all backgrounds— Jewish, African American, Irish, Italian, Chinese, and Puerto Rican— packed together, smiling and mugging for posterity.

Mom walked me to school each day, delivering me punctually. PS 169 reminded her of the Lexington School for the Deaf, she later told me, where she had been a student. She loved school too, but she was already fifteen when she came to New York. She had no schooling in rural Puerto Rico and was placed in the first grade here. She was a young woman practically, learning her ABCs side-by-side with kids half her age. She made friends and picked up signs in English from other girls her age but did not receive classroom instruction with her girl-friends. She continued for three years, and then was told she had to go to work. That was back in 1941. Compared to her three older deaf sisters, Mom was fortunate; they had even less schooling than she.

In the third grade our teacher Mrs. Leighton informed us of Parents' Night. She looked forward to speaking with our parents about our schoolwork. Mrs. Leighton was a pleasant, plump blonde, whom we occasionally drove crazy with our antics. When she had enough of our whispering and note-passing behind her back, she would literally put her foot down to restore order. We were never in fear of her, though; at day's end she dismissed us with a bright smile and a reassuring "See you tomorrow, children."

I accompanied Mom to Parents' Night. When we arrived, I found it odd that none of my classmates were there. Mrs. Leighton seemed surprised to see me, sitting with Mom in the waiting area outside the classroom. When our turn came, Mom and I entered the classroom where we were welcomed by Mrs. Leighton, sitting behind her desk.

"Good evening, Mrs. Torres. I'm glad to meet you. Have a seat."

Mom smiled at her, politely, but fidgeting. Unlike Pop, Mom was out of her element dealing with hearing people, especially *americanos* with any authority. Mrs. Leighton waited a few empty moments, then:

"Hello, Andrés. I didn't expect to see you. You didn't have to come you, know. Mrs. Torres"—she said, directing herself to Mom—"it wasn't necessary to bring your son, but that's OK, he can wait outside, if you don't mind."

I interjected. "I'm here to talk for my mother; otherwise she can't understand you."

"Ah, but of course; now I understand, excuse me, Mrs. Torres."

Again Mom nodded, as if she knew what the lady was talking about.

Mrs. Leighton began. "Well, Andrés, tell your mother that, mostly, you are doing well in class. You are quite punctual with your homework. And your workbook is neat and clean and up to date. Go ahead, tell her that."

I relayed the teacher's remarks. Slowly and methodically I signed the sentences to Mom. I didn't know the sign for "punctual," so I came up with, "She says I almost always hand in my homework on time." Even if I had known "punctual" it wouldn't have mattered, since it was a foreign word to Mom. If Mrs. Leighton was perplexed by my display of handiwork, she didn't let on. She continued.

"And, Andrés, tell her that it's good that you arrive every day ready to work. You are usually one of the first students at your desk." I was pleased to be the bearer of good tidings and once again passed the information to Mom in signs.

Mom responded. "I know. Tell her. I make sure to bring you in early every day. I wake you up early and make your breakfast fast, and get you here good time every day. And I always wait here in the afternoon to bring you home, and . . ."

"Wait, wait." I interrupted Mom and signed anxiously. "Slow down, you go too fast for me to explain to teacher."

The surprised Mrs. Leighton interceded:

"Wait a minute, my child, you aren't translating into Spanish? I thought your mother speaks Spanish."

"No, my mother is deaf; she speaks in sign language."

"My goodness, I had no idea . . . and your father?"

"He's deaf too; I'm the only one in the house who talks regular."

She glanced back and forth between Mom and me. Mom nudged me on the shoulder; that was her way of saying, "What are you and her talking about"? I explained the teacher's confusion.

Mrs. Leighton composed herself and continued. She started all over, and watched attentively, squinting her eyes occasionally as I translated for Mom. She praised my participation in the classroom and my friendly ties with students. Mom was pleased to know this, and she assured Mrs. Leighton that she would continue to get me to school on time. She added that I should tell the teacher about Pop helping me with my homework. Then, confident in her growing rapport with Mom, Mrs. Leighton changed her tune slightly. Apparently, she didn't want to paint *too* rosy a picture.

"Now, Andrés, I do have something else to say, something that concerns me. Tell her that there are times you disrupt the class with your loud laughing. Tell her that I have told you this, that I want you to stop this and be more serious in class."

Hold your horses, Mrs. Leighton! I thought. Do I have to tell her this? Didn't you just finishing saying what a good kid I am? I was tempted to avoid Mrs. Leighton's complaint with an end run. I could have translated her words into something harmless. Neither she nor Mom would ever know. I knew other hearing kids of deaf parents who would do this. But not me. I obediently divulged Mrs. Leighton's criticism to Mom. Her response was not surprising.

"Why? Why are you being wild in class? Your teacher is nice woman; you must obey her. Wait till I tell Father. Tell the teacher we will punish you if you laugh loud again."

Dutifully, I translated into spoken English for Mrs. Leighton. But she didn't really need my help. She got the gist of Mom's message on her own. After that she and Mom got along just fine.

One day when I was six, Mom and I were walking along Amsterdam Avenue. Her curiosity got the best of her and she asked me, out of the blue, "Whom do you love more, me or Father?" Where she got the idea for this question, I never figured out. When Mom asked me to choose between her and Pop, I spoke freely. I looked up at her, as we walked side by side in the street, and signed my answer to her in four simple gestures: "I love Father more."

When we got home, she let loose. "What do you mean, why do you love Father more? I do all the work in the house. I cook and feed you, I wash your clothes, and I watch out for you. Father comes home late; you see him only sometimes. Do not forget, I suffered a lot when you were born. You see how small I am? I was in much pain when you came out. The doctor had to cut my stomach for you to come out. There was blood all over. It hurt and I was crying for a long time."

She lowered the front of her pants down her belly. I could see part of the scar from the Caesarean.

"See? See? This is how I suffered when you were born. So why do you say you love Father more?"

She had done this before, in affectionate moments between us. She would direct my eyes at the battle wound then point to me, as if to certify an unbreakable bond between mother and child. I would stare in awe at the line of raised flesh, and run my finger up and down. But this time there was anger in her signs and bitterness on her face.

I trace back to that day an ingrained habit of carefully weighing my response to personal questions. There comes a moment in life when the child's spontaneity is quashed. From that moment of Mom's reaction to my gushing truthfulness, I began to grow up.

The next few years we bounced around from apartment to apartment. We had hit a bad time financially and I never knew why. For a while we lived on 179th Street near Audubon Avenue on the top floor of a two-story wooden house. Its only redeeming feature was a balcony that looked out onto the street, but inside everything was packed into a single room. My parents' sleeping quarters was a meager space cordoned off by a ceiling curtain. My mornings were announced by the clanging metal rings coming around the rods that dangled from the ceiling. That was Pop pulling the curtain aside and getting up for work. The bath tub was next to the kitchen sink, but the toilet was in the outer hallway and we shared it with another family. I slept in a corner next to the balcony door. Our meals became the barometer of our fortunes. On good days Mom made white rice mingled with chunks of salty Spam. The times of desperation were signaled by a bowl of Cheerios and milk for dinner. This period, in 1954 when I was about seven years old, lasted less than a year, but it occupies spacious regions of my consciousness. That period of hunger and uncertainty became a constant reminder of a time I wished never to repeat.

Our difficulties were solved the old-fashioned way: separation. In the summer of 1955, Mom and I were shipped to southern New Jersey to live with her sister, Carmela. Pop moved in with my grandmother Ita. I guess the plan was that Pop would save up enough from work to eventually bring us back to New York City. My mother's sister Carmela was an Ayala *muda* and lived in southern New Jersey with her family. They had settled in a rural area, not too far from Camden, and there were deaf friends in the region. Fortunately Carmela had two sons, Victor and Willie, who were my playmates. But I ached for Pop, who could make the long trips from the City only occasionally. The plan must have worked because two years later Mom and I were on our way back to New York City. We were returning to the Highbridge section of Washington Heights to be with Pop again, and no one was happier than I was.

3

A Signing Village

IN MY TENTH SUMMER, 1957, my parents found our new home, 514 West 176th Street, not far from my grandmother's place on Amsterdam Avenue. On the fourth floor of a five-story walk-up we settled in. Apartment 43 consisted of a bedroom, a kitchen, a bathroom, and a living room, each sprouting off of a tiny hallway. After Mom and Pop conducted me on the maiden tour, which took all of five minutes, I asked the obvious question: "So where do I sleep?"

"In the bedroom, that is your room."

I followed up with the next most obvious question. "Then where do you two sleep?"

I followed them into the living room, where Pop unfolded the couch displaying its other feature. "Here; see, we bought a sofa bed for us." My parents were ceding me the only private room; besides the bathroom, it was the only room with a door.

My room had been furnished with a brand-new bed, a headboard and mahogany frame propping up a sturdy spring mattress. In the corner next to the window were a used wooden desk and a lamp. Pop made sure I was going to have a place to pile my books and do my schoolwork.

The room also had a built-in closet that reached to the ceiling, and a three-drawer bureau with a mirror. My privacy wasn't total, for this is where Mom stored her personal items and clothing and would come in anytime to retrieve her things. She would also ask me to leave the room when she needed to change.

Each room, the bathroom too, was equipped with a special light bulb that was wired to the front door. Pop got one of his deaf electrician friends to install a customized lighting system. Visitors would press the button on the front door of the apartment (for my parents), and as a fallback, pound on the door (for me). As soon as someone pressed the white button, all four internal bulbs flashed simultaneously.

Flickering lights triggered nervous energy in apartment 43. Did we have company? The landlord? Immediately Mom started sniffling (her sinuses went into overdrive with the least bit of excitement). Pop started shuffling, and I started for the door.

Every inch of my new home was lead-painted–over or buried under linoleum. I suspect that people then associated wood with poverty, for there was no surface evidence of Mother Nature's contribution to the construction of apartment 43. Perhaps the original immigrant inhabitants of these tenement buildings wanted to be as distanced as possible from their Old World origins. In any case, we Puerto Ricans from the New World followed suit and embellished the walls, trimmings, and borders in layer after layer of paint. We interred the original floors under man-made carpets of dazzling design—in our case, a blue-green floral print.

People in Washington Heights could be classified into two groups: those whose windows opened out into the sun-drenched, peopled streets, and those—like us—whose view consisted of shadowed back alleys and the cats who prowled the spaces between buildings. The front-dwellers were exposed to public life. They observed humanity in their daily comings and goings and in socializing on the stoop. They kept an eye on the kids scrambling about the sidewalk below.

But the private domain was reserved for the back-dwellers. From my living room I could see into the bedrooms of the buildings of 175th Street. These people I never knew, never even recognized on the street. They inhabited a world totally distinct from mine. Hidden behind the window drapes, the voyeur could peer into their lives. On steamy summer evenings when the back-dwellers of 175th left windows open and curtains apart, I stared at the women changing their clothing, the couples lying half-naked in bed. I bought a pair of plastic toy binoculars to improve the view.

Anonymous to each other, back-dwellers were linked by a complicated system of clotheslines. These cords reminded me of those sky-high footbridges you saw in old movies like *Lost Horizon*. There were dozens of these lines strung across the back alley, connecting our buildings on 176th with those on 175th. I wondered who originally put up these cords and how they extended the line from one end of the alley to the other.

The cords ran through pulleys that were anchored in the brick wall at each end of the line, and from them everything from towels to underwear was hang-dried. I thought it was a pretty bold thing to do, to dangle bras and panties in the open air like that—to see them floating in the wind like that provoked thoughts about the bodies that wore them.

It became my job to retrieve articles that had fallen from our clothesline. This happened frequently since Mom had difficulty maneuvering the lines with her short arms. Complicating matters were the metal security bars, which were designed to keep children—and other tiny humans like Mom—from tumbling out apartment windows. It drove her insane trying to wiggle the clothing off the line and through the openings of the rusted gate.

Inevitably, something would be lost to the abyss below. Mom then commissioned me to descend five flights to the basement and retrieve the fallen articles, usually socks, which gave her the most trouble. "And do not forget the clothes pins," she would remind me.

Pop had the least privacy of the three of us. He rarely came into my room. He could be found in the kitchen only for dinner (he left so early for work, I only saw him breakfasting on weekends) and those times when Mom successfully coaxed him into drying dishes. He looked ridiculous in her apron, but he went through the motions if Mom badgered enough.

The bathroom was the space most in demand, and Mom soon achieved a monopoly over it. She could spend hours in there and what she was doing was anybody's guess. There was a peach-colored hot water bottle that hung permanently from the shower curtain rod. The tub was a monstrous craft supported by iron lion claws, and took up most of the floor. Next to the door sat the toilet. We flushed it by yanking a chain that dangled from a water box suspended high on the wall.

There was an inch-wide gap between the bathroom door and the floor, which was fortunate because I could reach Mom in an emergency. All I had to do was jam the *Daily News* through the crevice at the bottom and wiggle it. If Mom was sitting on the toilet, it caught her attention and she knew to finish up her business. If Mom was in the tub, I was out of luck. That's when the kitchen became the latrine of last resort, and I would go there and piss into the sink, then turn on the hot water full blast. Under no circumstances would I *ever* let Mom go into the bathroom if there was a remote chance of my needing to do "number two." I learned to anticipate these things.

The living room contained two armchairs, a sofa bed, Pop's rolltop desk, and the TV. There was also space enough to fit Mom's Singer sewing machine, a wedding gift from her sisters. The machine was hidden beneath a thick cotton covering that Mom made herself. She would never expose the beautiful wooden casing for fear of someone scratching it. Propped up on four legs, curved like swans, it also served as a lamp desk. Two windows led out to our fire escape, where Mom rested her potted plants.

The *pièce de résistance* of the parlor was our Zenith black-and-white. Centered against the wall between the windows, the bulky box with long antennae dominated the room's landscape. Since it lacked its own legs, we bought a wooden TV stand that was just four skinny sticks attached to a flat platform. This poor excuse for a TV stand was expected to prop up something many times its weight. Seemingly tired from shouldering that burden, it trembled when we accidentally bumped into it. Even clicking the station dial—which wasn't easy, so hard was it to turn—would cause the stand to quiver.

Once my friend Walter Martínez and I were wrestling on the floor, and our entangled legs tripped the TV stand over. The Zenith came crashing down, one of its sharp corners zeroing in on Walter's buck teeth.

"Look out, the TV!" I shouted.

He dove aside, and the monster box rattled the floor. (Walter was unharmed; lucky for him, and lucky for our neighborhood baseball team—we would have had to find another third baseman as no one had Walter's arm at that position.) We quickly restored the TV and stand to their proper place. Mom was in the kitchen fifteen feet away, and didn't hear a thing.

With the bathroom as Mom's turf and the kitchen and my room of no interest to my father, the living room afforded Pop the only possibility of privacy, if only to sit quietly and erase the world's distractions with a catnap. It was there that he had his favorite armchair, from which he could rule his castle.

He had but two places to store his worldly possessions: a closet that he built in the hallway for his clothes, and the chestnut-colored rolltop desk. The desk had three drawers to keep his underwear and paperwork. Lifting the cover revealed a warren of tiny shelves and cubicles containing his ballpoint pens, stationery, and cigarettes. As president of the

Puerto Rican Society for the Catholic Deaf, he needed a place to store the organization's records. In the desk he also kept records of his main vice, gambling.

Mom's base of operations was the kitchen, which had a window facing the side alley of the building. It comprised the sink, a gas oven, a Frigidaire taller than she was, and a GE washing machine. Flush against one wall was a metal dining table surrounded on three sides by wooden chairs. A religious calendar, provided each January by the parish, and a clock were the only decorations on the walls. The washing machine was equipped with wooden rolling pins through which Mom passed the wet clothing for wringing. She warned me never to stick my fingers near the pins.

Fricassee de pollo was my favorite meal, which she would make from scratch. She prided herself on cooking with fresh carrots and potatoes, and on using real garlic and onions, not the powdered stuff that came in plastic jars. She would buy dried beans, not the canned variety, and soak them for hours to go with her rice dishes. Beef stew (*carne guisada*) was right up there with the *fricassee*. Her pork chops were an exception to the normally flavorful cuisine. She always overcooked them, saying you had to kill any worms that might have worked their way into the pig. By the time they were served the *chuletas* were squeezed of any taste, and it was a struggle to break the meat down into edible portions. Pop, who had bad teeth from so much smoking, said it was like chewing on shoe leather.

I could tell from Mom's cooking what kind of mood she was in. Blandness, in the form of potato pancakes or fishcakes, signaled a bad day. TV dinners did, too. Any deviation from the principle of fresh ingredients indicated that something was bothering her. It was her form of protest. Sometimes Pop and I would be seated waiting for the food, and she would unceremoniously shove the plates onto the table. We knew she was upset. We just ate and got out of there quickly.

Mom was not a fast worker. I caught Pop and other relatives making her the butt of jokes and snide remarks about her snail's pace. She was slow, but she was unfailingly punctual in her timing. She took twice as long as others to make a meal, but it didn't matter because, working backwards from the deadline, she accurately calculated when she should start. By 5:30 supper was served, and we had better be in our chairs.

Once, after a stretch of late arrivals, she lashed out at my cavalier attitude to house rules. I walked in nonchalantly, accompanied by my friend Tachy. Mom reached up and grabbed my left earlobe, pulling me firmly toward the kitchen clock that hung on the wall over the dining table.

"No! No!" she yelled, simultaneously pointing at the time and clutching a handful of flesh. Normally, as I said, Mom didn't "speak" loudly when accompanying her signs with verbal sounds; she just sort of whispered. If she was angry, though, she raised the decibel level, and you would have no doubt about her emotional state. Screaming "No! No!" in a tone that screamed through her throat, anyone knew she was pissed. Tachy exited apartment 43 discreetly.

Like all the deaf mothers I knew, Mom was fastidious about keeping her apartment clean. She swept the rooms daily, like a sailor swabbing a ship's deck. She prized open spaces, never cluttering the living room with coffee tables or benches. Hard as she tried, though, she could never achieve the pristine cleanliness that she dreamed of. No matter how thorough, how meticulous her efforts, there was that ubiquitous adversary that challenged her at every turn. This was the dreaded *Blatella germanica*, otherwise known as the common cockroach, present everywhere in New York City's tenements, and descended from a sturdy line of insects dating back 350 million years, to the time when dinosaurs were just beginning their earthly reign. If these diminutive crawlers survived the mega forces that destroyed *Tyrannosaurus rex*, how could Mom expect to tame them?

The fault wasn't in our hygienic practices. It was simply that the roaches bred easily inside dark damp walls that enclosed the bathrooms and kitchens of old buildings like ours. Within those decaying walls there was a vertical shaft of plumbing, hidden from us, that connected the toilets, bathtubs, and sinks of all the floors of building 514. All it took was one weak link in the chain, just one carefree undisciplined family who didn't share Mom's policy of vigilant tidiness and perpetual drying. One such household and the whole building was subject to infestation. Crumbs, tiny pools of cooking oil, and leaky faucets were the combustible ingredients. The six-legged bugs multiplied ad infinitum.

Mom tried to make their life intolerable within the confines of apartment 43, with daily sprayings of Black Flag and strategic placements of Roach Motels. But she had no control over the cockroaches' maneuvers in other regions of the building. During the daytime they nested securely out of reach in a less tidy apartment; then, with the rising moon, they would conduct nightly raids for tasty morsels and water in our apartment. When the lights went out, we implicitly surrendered the kitchen to them. If I went for a midnight snack it meant bracing myself for the inevitable: a dozen glittering brown critters making a mad dash to safety as soon as I switched on the light. I was the only child in a deaf household. At home solitude and silence were my faithful if dull companions. But those frisky brown shadows made sure I never felt alone.

Being the hearing one in the family, I had advantages. I could sneak up to my parents undetected and watch them talk, if I wanted. At night, I could cast a glimpse into the doorless living room to see what they were up to.

I tried not to be obvious or obtrusive. But there was no way, in our small quarters, that I could avoid being caught from time to time. When our eyes met in this way, the air was silenced for a few frozen moments with a quiet more profound than that even most deaf people usually know. It was a fleeting reminder that even though I was of their blood, we were divided by a chasm of difference. I was the outsider in their midst.

From time to time, I conducted tests, even macabre experiments. Just to make sure. From my room, I would yell toward the living room,

"Hello! Can somebody come here? I need help, please!" or, *"¡Mira, mira, el agua está bajando del techo!"* (Look, look, the water's leaking from the ceiling!) or, "Mom, look what I found in your closet."

Nothing.

Sitting with them in the living room, watching TV, nonchalantly covering my face with the newspaper, "Shit! Fuck! *¡Mierda! ¡Pendejo!* Asshole!"

Nothing.

In this manner I eliminated any shred of doubt about my situation. No, this wasn't a sick joke somebody was playing on me.

Pop was a gambler. Small-time, but big-time-enough to drive Mom crazy. She constantly complained that he wasted our money on betting and cigarettes. His method for playing the numbers intrigued me, but I never could decipher it because he shielded me from his schemes for wealth accumulation.

With dark-rimmed glasses sitting on a broad nose, there was a professorial air about him, as he leafed through the newspaper in search of the clues that determined his "pick." If not for the cigarette hanging limply from his mouth and his rolled-up sleeves, you might have imagined he was grading student papers. But that's not what he was up too. Seated in his armchair he was working out his pick for the next day. His rectangular head seemed directly attached to his thick shoulders, with just a hint of a neck in between. The broad forehead was cleared of hair, as his wavy black top was always combed back. On the upper right edge of his forehead was his trademark scar, the size of *una habichuela roja* (red kidney bean), which he attributed to a fall from a palm tree during his childhood Puerto Rico.

Pop always carried a notepad and ballpoint pen in his shirt pocket. He kept dozens of palm-sized pads in his desk, relentlessly consuming them like an allergy sufferer going through boxes of tissue. He liked the kind that had spirals so you could flip over the sheets, or tear them off easily. It looked like the pad used by Sgt. Friday (Jack Webb) on *Dragnet*, only smaller. The notepad enabled Pop to write things down when dealing with hearing people, such as an address, a price, a name, or the time.

He also used the spiral pad to divine his pick. From the corner of my eye, seated on the sofa and pretending to be engrossed in the TV, I casually spied on him as he worked out his secret formula. This is the way his system worked, more or less: First he inspected the attendance figures at Yonkers Raceway, which were published in the back pages of the *Daily News*. He started with the last four digits, then kept adding and subtracting numbers from other sports statistics—scores, more attendance figures, and baseball batting averages. Whether he followed a defined protocol or just kept shuffling data around until he felt good about a number, I could never tell.

The residue of his complicated effort was dumped in the tin basket at the foot of his desk, crumpled balls of notepad sheets containing the evidence of his calculations. Once he settled on a number, he wrote it neatly on a sheet. The next morning, on the way to work, he took it to his bookie, the *bodeguero* across 176th Street.

Returning to Washington Heights, and settling into the apartment at 514 West 176th Street, had the advantage of reuniting me with my closest cousins, Jimmy and Mary. They belonged to Titi Olga, my father's sister, and her husband Seymour, who were both deaf. Jimmy, Mary, and I were close emotionally and chronologically. I was the "oldest" of the trio, having been born a week before Jimmy. (I often wondered if our parents had vacationed together on Memorial Day weekend of 1946.) Mary joined us sixteen months later. The photos of us three together dominate my picture albums. Jimmy's sandy brown, straight hair was a counterpoint to my dark and wavy locks. Mary, who shared

Jimmy's hair color, is squished between us in the pictures. The three of us sport huge, toothy grins. Out of view are our parents cajoling us with clownish faces and index fingers lifting the corners of their mouth ("smile, smile") and rotating palms against each other ("cheese, cheese"). Once, when Jimmy was a toddler, he somehow got his head stuck between the bars of the crib in the middle of the night. His crying was of no use until it alarmed Margie, an Irish woman who had befriended my family and who lived in the apartment directly beneath Titi Olga. Hearing Jimmy's wailing calls through the open windows Margie went across the second floor to wake up my grandmother Ita who had keys to Titi Olga's apartment. Jimmy was a risk-taker and was prone to getting himself into jams like this. The head-in-the-crib incident was prophetic in another sense, for later he was nicknamed "Jimmy Cabeza" (Jimmy the Head) around the block.

Jimmy's propensity for mischief only increased the family's vigilance of his sister. All the adults, deaf and hearing, conspired to contain her movements and associations. Mary's best friend was Nancy Chin, who came from a large Chinese–Puerto Rican family that lived in the same building. Nancy showed Mary how to get into the street without getting caught by Ita who, from her second-floor window, could see everyone entering or leaving the building. The girls would sneak up to the roof of building 2372, climb over the divider onto the roof of 2374, descend the stairways and exit onto the street, out of my grandmother's view. One day, though, Ita spied Mary on the street and yelled for her to come home.

"*¿Mary, que tu haces allí en la calle? ¡Súbete ahora mismo!*"

"*Pero Ita, Mami dijo que puedo jugar aquí.*" Mary defended herself, saying her mother (Olga) gave her permission to be downstairs.

"*¡Te dije: súbete ya!*"

"*Pero, Mami dijo . . .*"

"*¡Mary! Yo soy la madre de tu mama, y te digo que súbas ya!*" Ita wasn't hearing any more of it: "Mary, I am the mother of your mother, and I'm telling you to come up now!"

On the Torres side there were twelve cousins, including three who lived in Puerto Rico, the children of Pop's only brother Miguel. I had forty-five Ayala cousins, thanks to Mom's fifteen siblings. *Las mudas*— Mom, Pancha, Diosa, and Carmela—were each married to deaf men, giving me nine other cousins who were children of deaf parents. Most of the Ayalas lived in the South Bronx, clustered near St. Mary's Park. All told the Torres-Ayala "clan" consisted of twenty-three nuclear families, eight of which were deaf. Those deaf families yielded twelve hearing children, including me, who grew up learning Sign as their first language. On the Torres side, my Titi Olga took it upon herself to instruct *all* her hearing siblings and *all* their children (my cousins) in sign language. The Torreses were the center of my family life growing up. The ancestral land was Puerto Rico, but the home base when I was young was 2372 Amsterdam Avenue.

There are remote villages in the Amazon and among the Bedouins of the Middle East where deafness is so prevalent that hearing and deaf people cohabit and communicate as one community. From the eighteenth century to the twentieth century a similar community existed in Massachusetts, on Martha's Vineyard. I grew up in such a "signing village," a Puerto Rican version, right in New York City.

As soon as we moved back to Washington Heights, Pop put me into Catholic school. He would have enrolled me there in the first grade, but this was precluded by our sorry financial situation. I had heard that Incarnation School, a parochial school, located just one street away on 175th, was a no-nonsense place run by nuns and brothers. As of the sixth grade, when I started at Incarnation, the boys and girls were in separate classes. The teachers assigned a lot of homework and didn't put up with kids fooling around or coming late to class. Too bad, because I liked the controlled informality of the public schools I had attended through the first five grades. I had to forgo something else—instead of calling me by the name that appeared on my birth certificate, Andrés, the teachers began to call me Andrew, which stuck with me until my early 20s.

My initial exposure to the Christian Brothers, who were responsible for educating the boys, was not promising. It came at the hands, literally, of one Brother Benedict. I don't recall a moment of intimidation from my public school teachers. A year as Brother Benedict's pupil confirmed the rumors I had heard about Catholic schools; they were where parents sent their children to learn the three P's: punctuality, penmanship, and punishment.

Brother Benedict did not suffer fools gladly, especially the ten- and eleven-year-olds in his charge. He was a stocky young man with a volatile character. The slightest infraction, or even minor errors on student assignments, turned his face red with anger. He frequently resorted to yelling and rebuke. Arriving late to school, submitting incomplete homework, chatting during class: all were violations subject to corporal punishment. One word captures the atmosphere in Brother Benedict's class: terror.

One day a sizeable group forgot to bring in a particular textbook in a collective oversight that maddened him to no end. Huffing and puffing, he lined us up in a semicircle in front of the classroom. There were as many guilty individuals standing as innocents sitting. Ruler in hand, he proceeded to whack our outstretched palms, making several rounds. His one concession to mercy was dispensing a noticeably lighter thrashing to the smaller boys like me. But that didn't prevent tears from welling up in our eyes, tears from pain and indignity.

Once at Sunday Mass, when it was my turn to handle the collection basket, Brother Benedict thought I was doing my job less than enthusiastically. He came up behind me and clasped my neck in a firm one-handed grip. My awareness wilted as the air was cut off from my brain.

"Pass the basket *all the way* into the pew, Andrew."

Brother Benedict was not well, to put it mildly. In later years I heard that he had been released from the Order.

After surviving the hot-tempered Benedict, my class was promoted to the next grade, and we were assigned to Brother Casimir who taught us the next two years. Brother Casimir was a striking figure, tall and well built, with close-cropped sandy hair and a ready smile. He looked magnificent striding through Incarnation's hallways, his ankle-length tunic cinched at the waist and swirling about. Somehow his virile physicality meshed seamlessly with the holiness of a reclusive monk.

He enforced discipline with a firm but gentle voice and rarely descended to Brother Benedict's measures. In the classroom he was always on his feet, racing up and down the aisles to accentuate a point in a lecture or nudge a fading student back into consciousness. He was someone you could actually go up to in the street and engage in conversation, as I did. At Sunday Mass I observed him silently kneeling, his eyes closed in meditation. I was sure he communicated directly with the Almighty. To an impressionable adolescent like me, Brother Casimir was someone to emulate. And there were deeper origins of my admiration for this man of God.

My family's religious lineage traced back to their days in San Germán, on Puerto Rico's west coast. When my grandparents, Moncho and Ita, came to New York in the mid-forties and settled in Washington Heights, they became parishioners of The Church of the Incarnation, a grand cathedral that was described as "the St. Patrick's Cathedral of Washington Heights." They were among the earliest Latino families in the area and were disheartened by the strange looks and cold shoulders of their fellow worshippers. No welcoming words or glances, not even from the priests. Month after month, my family filed into the church, enough of them to occupy an entire pew on their own. Devotedly they sat through the prayers and sermons, even though the hearing ones—such as Ita, Titi Nereida, and Titi Mariamelia—couldn't understand the English, and the deaf ones—such as Pop, Titi Tata, and Titi Olga—couldn't hear the English. Faithfully, they took Communion and contributed their weekly alms. When Mass was over, they emerged from the magnificent cathedral and perched on the corner of

175th and Audubon, anticipating an overture from someone, anyone. But welcoming words or glances never came, until years later.

They were proud Catholics and trusted that God loved all His children equally. But these *americanos* can be awfully stiff and conceited, my grandmother Ita thought. Clearly, the generosity of heart that Puerto Ricans were known for was being tested in their new place. This must have been what my *abuelo* Moncho was referring to when he advised his children *"Escojer lo bueno de los americanos, y botar lo malo"* (From the Americans, take the good and throw out the bad).

Still, my family was devotedly Catholic, so it was expected that I'd be a good Catholic boy. Besides, I had a role model in Pop. The crucifix hanging from his neck, the rosary in his pants pocket, the sight of him on the living room couch signing his prayers silently to himself: these were constant reminders of his religiosity. To me, he was an imposing figure, handsome and husky, looming large over his sisters. Closing his prayers with the Sign of the Cross, faintly kissing his thumb, it was the sacred meeting the sensual.

It was different with Mom, though. When the Ayalas arrived in New York they converted from the Protestantism of their days in Puerto Rico to Catholicism. But Mom was never attracted to the ritual and formalities of the Church. She was bored stiff by Sunday Mass, a sentiment manifested in her body language. She never could summon up the self-control for that most elementary of sacrifices: kneeling upright at prayer. Mom would rest her behind on the bench, so that she was bent over with her elbows on the back of the pew in front of her. It was a slackening of discipline that would get you a terrifying scowl, or worse, from Brother Benedict.

I followed Pop's spiritual tracks, treading even deeper than he did. During one stretch of time in the seventh grade I attended Mass *daily*. In the dead of winter, I woke up at six-thirty each day and shuffled off, zombie-like, to the seven o'clock service. That early in the day Incarnation Church was almost empty, and I derived solace from having the place practically to myself. I didn't have to compete with so many others—as on Sundays—for God's attention. We were assured that God listens to you wherever you are; but I suspected He preferred to see you at *His* place.

I followed the thirty-minute Mass from my missal book, reading along as the priest solemnly recited the prayers. Weekday Mass was a sermon-less affair, the entire experience in Latin. It wasn't quite so dead a language to me, since I glimpsed the meaning of terms similar to the Spanish I had been exposed to. I felt a privileged intimacy with this ancient vocabulary of worship.

There was no point in going to Mass, I believed, if you didn't take Communion. To partake of the Eucharist, the high point of the Mass, meant fasting one hour before and, also, being free of mortal sin. The later condition was more difficult to meet than the former, because my pre-teen hormones were beginning to vigorously assert themselves.

Impure thoughts and "self-abuse" were a regular preoccupation, so by going to daily Mass I was engaged in a frontal assault on the vices of imagination and flesh. Sometimes I was victorious in this struggle against evil. But more often than not, my wandering mind and keen libido made me an easy target for the Devil. Fortunately, there was always Confession on Saturday nights.

It was eerily comforting to take Communion at the dawn of a winter day. Outside the great neo-Gothic structure that is Incarnation, the sun was just beginning to lift into view and break through the city chill. Inside the candle-lit church, all was warm and subdued. Unlike on Sundays, when organ music and choir songs filled the air, there was just the barely audible prayer of the celebrant and his congregants. After the moment of Transubstantiation, when the bread and wine of the Eucharist were transformed into the body and blood of Jesus, we approached the altar to receive the sacrament.

Alongside the other communicants, I waited, kneeling, then closed my eyes as the priest neared me. Intoning the Latin for "Body of Christ," he rested the white wafer on my tongue then stepped to the next person on my left. I rose and returned to my pew, praying hands interlaced at my chest.

Kneeling, I meditated on this supremely sacred moment. I accepted Church teaching that the host is indeed the Son of God, not just a symbolic representation. I contritely petitioned His forgiveness for my sins and vowed to overcome my weaknesses. I was humbled that Jesus was sacrificed out of God's love for me.

Still, it was difficult to achieve total focus every time. The materiality of the host distracted me from thoughts of the transcendental. The thin yeasty coin would stick to my tongue, sometimes the roof of my mouth. It would curl and melt on contact with my saliva. I preferred to wait till it practically dissolved, then swallow the remaining bit. I didn't understand how some people could actually chew on the wafer. What if a dry particle got wedged in my teeth? I wouldn't dare go out into the cold with a piece of Jesus still in my mouth!

It consoled me to have this peaceful interlude with my Lord and Savior. Being one of the few to daily take the Eucharist made me feel special. I was now ready to take on the real world.

I had many such moments as a daily practitioner of Catholicism. Toward the end of the seventh grade, I became an altar boy and participated at every religious function, from daily service to Sunday High Mass. The most challenging test of my religious zeal came in the form of six o'clock mass at the Convent. Only the most reliable among the altar boys were invited to serve at the Convent of the Sisters of Mercy, the nuns who taught at Incarnation School.

At 5:45 AM I would tap the door of the quaint, two-story red brick building that housed the sisters. An elderly bespectacled nun in black habit would greet me with a smile and show me to the small sacristy, where the priest would be donning his vestments and preparing the vessels for the service. Serving Mass at the Convent was unlike anything I experienced at Incarnation Church. Here I gained entry into an intensely private world, an exclusive community of women. Kneeling in the chapel were the nuns I would see later at the school. In the morning, their pink, scrubbed faces appeared sublimely pliant. Later I'd see the same women, stern-faced, barking commands at their students. Here they seemed so accessible to me; later they'd affect a distanced seriousness. I wondered: why the need to trade one image for another as you transit from the private to public arena? Which persona is the real you, Sister?

My role at Communion was to accompany the priest as he dispensed the host from the chalice. I held the silver plate under each nun's chin at the moment of acceptance. If there were to be a mishap, a failed exchange between priest and nun, I'd be there to intercept the fall. The sacred moment was not without a touch of sensuality. From this vantage point I could see the nuns' moist tongues as they emerged to receive the host, and I can't deny I felt a certain excitement. Not all the sisters fit the stereotype of the spinster. I had to stifle such thoughts, though, for they were unbecoming to an acolyte of the Church.

Beyond my early spiritual awakening, I was a kid who also loved letting off steam and often did so with my cousins Jimmy and Mary. We spent many Sunday evenings at my aunt Isaura's third-floor apartment. Since the late forties she and her husband Romeo lived right next to my aunt Olga and her husband Seymour, with cousins Jimmy and Mary. One floor below lived my grandmother Ita.

Isaura, my father's sister, was Ita's first-born and had unusually effective command of oral Spanish. She could lipread and knew sign language well, English too. She was slightly taller than Mom and slim. She wore tinted eyeglass lenses that I had never seen on anyone else in the family and they complemented her small build. Most of my elder relatives liked thick dark frames on their glasses.

When we were little my aunt was an affectionate protector and interceded on behalf of her nieces and nephews whenever we were disciplined harshly by our parents—she herself had no children. Then as we got older, she changed into a somber and withdrawn woman. At New Year's Eve parties she walked about as if in a daze, her eyes teary. I would ask Pop what was wrong with his sister.

"Nothing, she is just sad; do not worry about it."

Isaura's nickname was Tata, which means we called her Titi Tata. Clamoring excitedly to get her attention, we screamed out "Titi Tata! Titi Tata! Titi Tata!" By the time of our Sunday evening get-togethers at Titi Tata's, we knew to be very careful around her; for Titi Tata worried constantly that, behind her back, people were mocking her, and even stealing from her.

Nine of us would be cramped together. The adults—Titi Tata, Titi Olga, Romeo and Seymour, and also Mom and Pop—sat wherever they could: on the plastic-covered sofa, the two roomy armchairs, or the one metal folding chair. Jimmy, Mary, and I would sprawl on the floor. In one corner stood an enormous *aguacáte* (avocado) plant, which Titi Tata had lovingly cultivated over the years. After climbing freely for some years it was slowed down by the waiting ceiling, only to resume progress by bending inward. The *aguacáte* wanted to behave like ivy, crawling across the ceiling of the living room to the other side. How could this leafy giant be rooted in such a small pot? And how could it thrive in such an unnatural setting, without sunlight and invigorating winds?

Mom had shown me how to grow my own plant. I stuck toothpicks into an *aguacáte* pit, rested it on the lid of a coffee can, and then supplied it with enough water to nourish the brown ball of seed. Before long a green stem emerged from the pit. It was easy. The leaves sprouted and the stem gained altitude. Eventually I lost interest in it, so that I never got around to potting it. I used to ask Titi Tata why her plant didn't produce its own *aguacátes* so we could eat them.

"These plants are hard to grow inside buildings. You have to watch them carefully and water them a lot. But inside these rooms they do not make baby *aguacátes*, like they do in Puerto Rico."

On those nights we watched *The Ed Sullivan Show, Gunsmoke,* and wrestling. Wrestling was our favorite. We loved the flamboyant characters: "Haystacks" Calhoun, who was a six-hundred-pound behemoth; golden-haired Buddy Rogers; muscular Antonio Rocca; and Ricky Starr, who finessed his opponents with the leaps and twists of a ballerina. Wrestling appealed to the kids for another reason: we didn't have to do much translating for our deaf parents. They could follow the action easily, as opposed to drama programs with lots of dialogue that needed interpreting.

Romeo was a diehard fan. Our uncle, who was born in France, had a slight body frame and filled the room with noisy grunts when irritable. He was a frenetic signer and when he and Tata argued everyone stayed clear. Romeo couldn't tolerate cheating wrestlers. When the "bad" guy kicked his rival in the groin or poked him in the eye, or when the hero was being pummeled by *both* members of the enemy tag-team, Romeo got livid. Uncle Romeo reserved his deepest contempt for incompetent and lax referees, who failed to see the violations or let off the bad guy with a weak reprimand. Once, in a rage over what was happening on the screen, he picked up a folding chair and slammed it to the floor of the packed living room, almost hitting us. Mostly we shrugged off Romeo's tantrums. We kids suspected that the wrestling matches on TV were theater, rigged performances between good and evil. None of us could persuade Romeo that it was just entertainment. Like his wife Titi Tata, Romeo wasn't all that well.

Titi Olga and Seymour were similar to Romeo in being aggressive and vocal signers. They competed intensely to get in their signs. Hearing people, staring face to face, can pretend to be listening to one another. But let your eyes wander off when an angry deaf person is addressing you and you're asking for trouble! There's no feigning attention—you're likely to get a firm tapping on the shoulder if your attention seems to drift. Try to cut off Titi Olga in the middle of a sentence and she would grab your forearm or hand to let you you know she wasn't done.

My father, who was of a more moderate temperament than the others, had trained me to wait until he had said what he wanted to say. Completing a train of thought, he would pause, then look me in eyes and flick both outstretched hands around a few times. That was the sign for *finished,* and the go-ahead for me to talk. Mom and Pop were the most passive of the three couples. Mom, who had only a third-grade education from the Lexington School for the Deaf, simply could not keep pace with the rest of them. Pop had a wait-and-see attitude, preferring not to jump into the middle of a heated dispute.

One Sunday night in particular, in the spring of 1958, my cousins and I were in a jolly mood, half watching TV, half teasing each other with riddles and jokes. At one point, Jimmy blurted out the word "Chinese," causing the three of us to break into raucous screams. To this day, I don't remember what led us to crack up over Jimmy saying "Chinese." All I recall is that we busted out laughing, rolling on our sides.

As they say in Spanish, *Pa' que fue eso!* As they say in English, Man, all hell broke loose!

"Why are you laughing? Are you making fun of me again? I'm not blind, you know; I see you sneaking laughs and joking about me! What for? What for?"

Titi Tata, our sweet but troubled Titi Tata, was furious again. She told the others she spied us getting thrills at her expense. Now we were really in for it. This was not the first time we stood accused, not by a long shot.

Mary rushed to the defense, signing and vocalizing back at Titi Tata, still glaring down at us from her armchair. "What are you talking about? We're not making fun of you or nobody."

Titi Tata persisted, "Oh yes you are; I can see. Always playing around, joking, and making fun of us. You think because I am deaf, that I do not know what is going on? You think so?"

The smacking hands pealed louder; the arms hardened, thrusting sharply forward and back. Her emotional state was obvious to us. These were not the slow, flowing arcs of casual talk. These were the brusque, geometric slashings of anger and exasperation. I joined the fray, signing excitedly. "Titi Tata, you're wrong, you always do this. We're not making fun of you; we're just having fun with ourselves. This has nothing to do with you. Please!"

The adults stared uneasily at the back-and-forth between us. Then Titi Olga jumped in to take her sister's side. "That's enough. Stop picking on your aunt. No more laughing and making faces like that. Do not disrespect."

The others nodded. Pop, too, but half-heartedly. When this had happened before, Pop and I would talk, and he took my word that we weren't teasing his sister, or anyone.

We stayed on the floor, crossed-legged, eyes up at our accusers. Several competing emotions overtook me. Pain, that they would think us capable of making fun of them, like other people do in the stores and the subway. Futility, that we were powerless to prove our innocence. Even bemusement, that we could be in such a comical, absurd situation.

Then Jimmy tried explaining. "Look, all we were doing was fooling around and I said 'Chinese.' That's all. Understand? For example, if you're talking a long time, then somebody—out of nowhere—says 'Chinese,' that's funny. Right? It has nothing to do with you. See, 'Chinese!' 'Chinese!' 'Chinese!' It's just funny!"

¿Pa' que fue eso?

Jimmy's rapid-fire mantra, "Chinese!" "Chinese!" "Chinese!" launched us into uncontrollable hollering. The sound of that word, repeated again and again, on the emotional borderline between tragedy and farce, ignited an epidemic of giggling, then all-out shouting. Helplessly, we rolled over each other in a jumble of clapping hands and laughter.

The elders were horrified. Right there before their eyes, we had ridiculed them again!

"That's it! That's it!" Titi Tata exploded. "I'm getting Blanca up here," and she stormed toward the door.

"No! No! Titi Tata, Titi Tata, Titi Tata! It's nothing. Forget about it!" Frantically, we tried to change her mind. But she was gone. Down to the second floor she went to fetch . . . Titi Blanca.

My Aunt Blanca, the last of the children of Ramón and Amelia Torres, lived with Ita. In her late twenties and single, she worked as a secretary in a downtown office building. She was petite, vivacious, and beautiful. Her Rita Moreno–like looks attracted a swarm of men. But Ita was not about to give her last daughter away to just anyone. She had already dismissed several suitors.

Blanca was Ita's principal caretaker, and my grandmother was grooming her to be the next matriarch, the one to carry on family tradition. She was also perfectly tri-lingual, in Spanish, English, and Sign. Blanca's older sister Mariamelia, also beautiful and also trilingual, had previously been the one to reconcile differences between generations. She often took our parents to medical appointments and dealt with the schools that we attended. Titi Mariamelia taught my catechism for First Holy Communion. Mariamelia was sweet and I loved her. But Mariamelia had married and was no longer living in Washington Heights. This role was now assigned to Titi Blanca.

Blanca became the sole adult able to interpret for the deaf Torreses. She was smart and a proud *puertorriqueña*. And she didn't care about signing in public with her siblings. She would stare down the starers.

But by now my cousins and I were on the threshold of teenager-hood, and we saw Blanca in a different light. She was the enforcer. She was often brought in, as on that Sunday night, to discipline us. Titi Tata returned with Titi Blanca.

"*¿Caramba, que pasa aquí? ¿Están portándose mal, ustedes?*" our youngest aunt demanded to know.

Nervously and in every detail, we gave our side of the incident—this time without a tinge of levity. Sincerity, truthfulness and accuracy would win over Blanca, we hoped. And it was easier to explain in spoken language. We already knew many more words in English than in

Sign. Standing in the living room, with all of us observing, Blanca consoled her sister. In Spanish and Sign, she cooled off Titi Tata. We were still sprawled on the floor, when Blanca turned to us and announced: "OK, OK, that's it; now everybody just forget it," she announced. "From now on, just watch TV; and no more laughing. I don't care about what, just no more laughing when you're here like this."

In moments like these I learned the fine art of reticence, of calibrating my responses in every situation. You can never assume that your words or deeds are received in the same way you intend them. You can save yourself a lot of trouble if you just think things through clearly in advance. But habitual self-censure exacts a high price.

In the same way I learned to evaluate when it was safe for me to laugh, I learned to be cautious about the future. Pop had a plan for me. I should say: Pop had a plan for us. We never talked about it in those terms, but years later as I looked back at that time, I could figure out the general idea. I realized that my father had hoped I would always be close—physically, as well as emotionally—to him and Mom. I can't blame him, really, for envisioning a future in which I would be their provider and caretaker until the end. Whom else could they count on? They groomed me to be the loyal son, their communicator and advocate in the hearing world. And following family tradition, they expected me to father grandchildren whom they could fuss over and spoil.

I'm convinced, too, that as soon as he saw his first-born was an Andrés and not an Andrea, he opted to put all his eggs in one basket. He would invest all his energies and resources in the one child, who would eventually be the head of a household. He had computed the simple math. Having a large family in the city would be counterproductive to a happy and secure future.

Like any ambitious mastermind, Pop had the main elements of his plan in place: a strategy, a timetable, and critical resources. The strategy was education. He would make sure I got the best schooling possible so that I could become a professional of some kind. The timetable was measured in four-year stages, high school, then college, and maybe even beyond. By the time I was ten years old, in 1957, he was already projecting my future. The critical resources? This was the tough part, for Pop's wages as a packer in the garment center, a job a deaf man could hold down, were not ever going to cover the grade-A education he planned for me. And he had no reason to assume his son was bright enough to qualify for fancy scholarships.

No, Pop could not count on internal resources to finance his plan. The one critical resource Pop could pin his hopes on was extraneous to the family. Enter Mr. William Eckenrode, a millionaire from Baltimore.

"We are sending you to Maryland for a few weeks in June. There is a summer camp that Mr. Eckenrode told me about, and you'll have a good time there."

My father was shrewd in his dealing with hearing people, focusing on those who could make a difference for him: bosses, priests, landlords. He had no problem making friends with anyone who had the slightest access to power. That's where Eckenrode came in. William Eckenrode, who was hard of hearing and could fingerspell quite rapidly, was a businessman and a devout Catholic. He was especially interested in the Deaf community and had taken a liking to Pop, having met him at a function of the International Catholic Deaf Association. He was an executive with the Paulist Press, a publishing house affiliated with the Paulist Fathers. During his trips to New York City, he visited us at our apartment.

I could tell Pop had charmed the older man, bringing him to howling laughter with descriptions of his exploits as a boy in Puerto Rico and at St. Rita School for the Deaf, the residential school in Cincinnati, Ohio, where Pop went to high school. They argued about sports and frequented Yonkers Raceway together. A big man with a gut, Eckenrode spoke in a raised tone, as if he wanted to hear himself clearly. No one ever dared tell the millionaire, it seemed, that he was talking much louder than he had to.

I found it amusing to watch him and Pop in action. The deaf man conversing in a hybrid of signs and fingerspelling with the boisterous giant. If the dialogue got stalled from a confusion of signals, they would revert to lipreading or scribbling on a notepad. At times Eckenrode abruptly held out his hand in a halting motion and stopped the conversation so he could adjust the hearing aid in his left ear. This had to be an instinctive reaction because he certainly didn't need it talking with Pop.

In the spring of 1957, my father told me his rich friend had offered to sponsor my attendance at a summer camp in Maryland. Camp Gabrielle, located in Hampstead, fifteen miles northwest of Baltimore, boasted a lake, baseball fields, and plenty of activities for boys. It was run by the same religious order that operated Saint Gabriel School for the Deaf in Santurce, Puerto Rico, which Pop had attended with his sisters.

"You will like it very much," Pop signed. "And after the two weeks at camp, Mr. Eckenrode invites you to stay at his home in Baltimore. He has a big, beautiful house. I was there."

"But I don't want to go away this summer. I want to stay here, with my friends on the Block. We already have a baseball team for the summer. Who are the other boys at the camp? I don't know anyone in Baltimore." ("Baltimore," like many cities in sign language, was denoted by the first letter. All you did was make the letter "B," shake it up and down a couple of times, like you were chopping a log, and there you had it—"Baltimore." For "Boston" you curled the B downward in front of you, like you were drawing a large question mark in the air. The only time I ever used these signs was talking baseball with Pop. If it weren't for the Orioles and Red Sox, I never would have known the signs for these cities.)

Pop knew my friends on the Block, and he approved of them. After work he would snoop around our usual spots along Amsterdam Avenue between 177th and 178th and in Highbridge Park. He knew we were a pretty good crowd and we loved hanging out together. Smoking, cussing, and sounding each other out were our worst crimes. We weren't a street gang and there were no drugs on the scene yet.

Compared to other parents in the late 1950s, who nervously wondered what their kids were up to during those New York City summers, he didn't have all that much to be concerned about. But there was no use my resisting. The deal was done, and that July of 1958 I was a long way from apartment 43, my family, and the Block.

Pop promised there would be lots of activities at the camp and he was right. Each day was jam-packed with athletic programs and other diversions like hiking. It was there I learned how to swim. After supper the boys turned to more sedentary pursuits: checkers, reading, and ping-pong. A tiny wooden booth served as the canteen where, after dinner, we lined up to buy candies. Then it was off to bed to close the day. Our sleeping quarters looked like an army barracks. The rows of double-decker bunk beds reminded me of the war movies we watched.

Before long I figured out that most of the kids were schoolmates or neighborhood chums. In suburban Baltimore there were no blacks or Chinese, it seemed. Everyone was white and had a scrubbed-down look, like the kids on the Cheerios box. They were different even from the Irish and Italian kids in Washington Heights. Apparently they found me as strange as I found them.

One day, after a dip in the lake, several of us were drying ourselves on the pebbled strip that served as a beach. A few kids came up to me. I could tell they wanted to say something yet felt awkward addressing me. Then one of them broke the ice:

"Hey Andy . . . are you colored?"

"Whaddya mean?" I had never been asked that before.

"You know . . . are you a Negro?"

It took a few moments before I said anything. "No, I'm Spanish, why?"

"Oh." I guess they had never heard an answer like that before. They looked at each other and walked away.

I think my broad nose, bronzed summer skin, and unfamiliar last name set them wondering about my background. Maybe it was my unruly hair. I could excuse them somewhat if they were bewildered by my appearance. Titi Tata often greeted me by pinching my nose with her left hand and simultaneously signing the word for a black person, which was done by tapping her own nose with her middle right finger. The maneuver was accompanied by a grimace on her face and her salutation.

"Pareces un moreno," she said in Spanish.

Once, Mom put me through a peculiar routine. She severed the foot end of a worn nylon stocking with her scissors and converted it into a skull cap. Then, she told me to put it on. "Titi Tata said to wear this to sleep every night so your hair becomes straight." The head-in-the-hosiery stratagem lasted a week before I convinced Mom it was ridiculous.

After Camp Gabrielle, I spent a week at Mr. Eckenrode's house in suburban Baltimore. "House" is a misnomer, for his home looked like a mansion and it was by far the largest residence I had ever been in. It had numerous rooms and each was impeccably kept. Portraits of another era hung from the walls. In the second floor hallway, intricately carved model sailboats perched on shiny wooden cradles.

I had a room to myself on the second floor, containing a queen-size bed, dressers, closets, and plenty of floor space. It was big enough to absorb all of apartment 43. Two windows let the sunlight in each morning and gave me a terrific view of the front yard and street. I slept late and had my own TV. Meals were a solitary affair in a large dining room, dominated by a huge table that could have accommodated King Arthur and his knights. The food wasn't so memorable, but I had never been surrounded by such fine china, such gleaming utensils, and such intricately embroidered napkins.

Responsibility for overseeing household operations was in the hands of two elderly, gentle ladies: Miss Grable and Miss Gertie. Mr. Eckenrode entrusted the maids with every last detail in the mansion, including guests like me. They treated me kindly and with respect. They served my every meal, took care of my laundry needs, and made my bed. I was living like a king.

But a king *sans* a kingdom. Unfortunately I had no one to play with; not even toys or a ball and glove. I had a mansion to myself but didn't know what to do with myself. Mr. Eckenrode the businessman was not around very much. He spent an afternoon asking me about Pop, school, and my sports heroes. He promised to send me a Christmas gift if I got good grades at Incarnation. But he kept his distance and corrected me whenever I failed to address him as "Sir."

It was a quiet neighborhood, without the busy traffic and street noises I was accustomed to. I missed the shrieking transistor radios emitting my favorite songs out from neighborhood windows, girls skipping rope, guys splayed out on the sidewalk shooting marbles, screaming kids chasing each other into the showering rains from open fire hydrants. I didn't notice a grocery store or supermarket. Inside the grassy yard, cordoned off by a thicket of shrubbery so tall that it topped me, I played hide-and-seek with imaginary hunters, concealing myself behind a pair of oak trees or on the wrap-around porch.

There were moments that summer when I wondered what exactly I was doing in Baltimore. I couldn't complain about Eckenrode's distant hospitality. Miss Gertie and Miss Grable certainly seemed helpful and amicable, and the kids at Camp Gabrielle were civil enough, even if a bit aloof from the swarthy, broad-nosed stranger from New York City. Still, I was definitely out of my element.

When Christmastime came, Mr. Eckenrode made good on his promise. I received a hefty package in the mail, wrapped in brown paper and corded with twine. My parents smiled as I tore that package to shreds to get to the contents. It was a box of G.I. Joe toy soldiers, compliments of our friend from Baltimore. I prized that collection of miniature infantrymen and artillery pieces, especially the helmeted soldier with the bazooka hoisted on his shoulder. In one blast he neutralized the enemy position. On the living room floor I conducted many battle scenes with those olive green figures of hard rubber. If only I could enjoy the millionaire's bounty without having to spend a big chunk of my summer in Maryland. But Pop reminded me that this was the reward for being friendly with Mr. Eckenrode. He told me I would return to Baltimore next summer, but all I could think about was how to get out of it.

"Andresíto, quieres una china?" The reassuring voice reached me from the kitchen, summoning me to join her with the offer of an orange (*china* is a Puerto Rican term for the fruit).

I was stationed at the front window of my *abuela* Ita's apartment, observing the languid march of Sunday traffic along Amsterdam, when she called.

In kitchen chairs, we faced each other across the rectangular dining table. She took an orange from the glass bowl sitting on the plastic-covered table, and held it firmly in her palm. Her hands were wrinkled, her arms lightly streaked with blue veins. What a contrast to my young, textureless skin. Old and worn were her hands, but *Abuelita's* grip on the orange was as sure as her hold on our family.

I can imagine the scene today, can see it as if I am back in that kitchen with my grandmother now. I watch her go to work, removing the skin with her paring knife. Starting at the top of the fruit, she carves out an uninterrupted stream of orange peel, a long, continuous, rippled strip that coils into a ball when fully detached from the juicy core. No spraying, no sticky residue. Only the tangy sparks shooting from the orange rind into my nostrils. I marvel at her skill. She might have been a sculptor in another life, or a master carpenter. She quarters the skinned fruit, and hands me the pieces on a small saucer.

"Toma, míjo."

I dig into my treat, trying not to make a mess. Unlike Ita I haven't perfected the art of orange-partaking. She hands me a napkin to dry myself off, and I keep munching my citrus.

Under the graying wavy hair, Ita is sad-faced. Through her glasses I can see the shadows of time under her small brown eyes. Subtle lines make their imprint on the cheeks and around her mouth. I've watched her in family gatherings and she rarely shows intense emotion, either of joy or grief. She's a stern woman, but won't lose her temper easily or lash out at you. She doesn't break into loud laughter, either. At her happiest, she'll raise her cheeks slightly and giggle softly. She doesn't dominate the scene with boisterous comment or display. Yet, for all her reticence and elegant composure, no one confuses her place in the family. She's the boss.

My thing is oranges. Ita's thing is coffee. Having taken care of me, she pours herself a cup. As for proportions, she much favors boiled milk over liquefied bean. The odor of steaming milk makes me nauseated. Ita likes her sugar too, a major vice in our diabetes-prone family. She dips the white bread that she buys in the Cuban bakery into the topped off cup, and this inevitably sends the coffee spilling onto the saucer. After a few slices, the small plate has collected enough coffee to justify a separate ritual: the final stage of saucer-slurping. Our matriarch is not above the habits of commoners.

She's looking me over now, like a drill sergeant with new recruits on the first day of boot camp. Ita zeroes in on the familiar spots, checking for flaws. Usually my cousins Jimmy and Mary are with me at inspection time, but today I'm alone in the limelight, and I'm uneasy.

"*Ay, niño, porqué tu eres tan flaco?*"

Whenever I visit she interrogates me about my skinny arms. Reaching across the table, she grabs my left hand with her left hand. I want to pull away, but it's no use. With the right hand she circles her thumb and middle finger around my wrist. If thumb and finger meet, that means there's been no progress. The look on her tired round face, her pressed lips and head swaying sideways like a pendulum, shows disappointment. She doesn't frighten me because I know she loves me dearly, like she loves all her *nietos* and *nietas*. But who's to blame for my lean frame? Maybe she thinks I'm not getting enough rice and beans at home. The scrutiny continues with further questioning.

"*Fuíste a la Misa hoy, mi niño?*"

Of course I went to Mass today. "*Sí, Ita, sí.*"

For Ita, missing Sunday Mass is unthinkable. She's reminding me that nothing is more important—not even our family—than loyalty to God the Father and His Holy Roman Catholic Church.

I'm enjoying the chunks of tart orange but the questioning continues. Next she asks, "*Y eres un buen muchacho en la casa, míjo? Te estás portando bien con tu Papá y Mamá?*"

"*Sí, Ita, sí,*" comes the automatic response. Yes, I've been a good boy at home, and, yes, I'm behaving right with Pop and Mom.

I'm anticipating the next question.

"*Y el español, Andresíto; estás hablando el español?*"

"*Un poquíto, Ita, un poquíto.*" She wants to know if I still speak Spanish, and I reply yes, a little bit. I've learned to charm Ita with a boyish grin, revealing my two sizeable front teeth, and my patented response, *un poquíto, un poquíto.*

Invariably she hugs me, chuckling, "*¡Ay, que lindo, Andresíto!*" She doesn't realize, though, that the only time I speak Spanish is when I'm here, and that I'm more of a listener than a conversationalist. She reminds me of the importance of speaking the family's language, of not forgetting the Spanish.

"*Sí, Andresíto; es bien importante que hables español. Es el idioma de tu familia. Queremos que no te olvídes el español.*"

How often have I dwelled on that exchange and so many others just like it over the years with the benefit of hindsight. Why didn't Ita ever broach the obvious issue of my parents' deafness? Why didn't she ever acknowledge my peculiar condition as the only child of deaf adults?

I've also wondered what I would say if I could address her today. If *abuela* and *nieto* were meeting across time, sitting at her kitchen table this very moment. I could imagine my words if I were the one asking the questions.

"Please, Ita, how could you expect me to speak Spanish like you? You gave me a father who was born deaf. What was I supposed to do? I had to speak sign language at home with Pop and Mom, speak English in school; and you wanted me to speak Spanish here in your kitchen, too? It's not my fault I didn't speak Spanish like other kids. What was I supposed to do?

"Ita, I know now that you suffered much, and you worked so hard to keep our family together. But why weren't you more expressive with me? Why didn't you hug me and laugh with me more often, like an *abuela* is supposed to do? And most of all, why didn't you ever show sympathy for my predicament? I can't believe you didn't notice my dilemma. Mom used to say being deaf isn't fun. Well, being the child of deaf parents isn't fun either! Why didn't you ever say anything? Were you pretending obliviousness? Were you afraid that sympathy would open the door to self-pity? Were you worried I would fall into religious doubt, finding no use for a God that could allow this curse on our family?

"And, Ita, why did you insist on me speaking Spanish? Did you fret that I would lose my roots, my Puerto Rican identity? Were you afraid I would be gobbled up by the decadent American culture? Didn't you understand that was the risk you took when you and Abuelo left your beloved island? Didn't you realize that was the bargain you struck when you brought the family to the "promised land" of New York City?

"Why did you repeatedly remind me to behave with Pop and Mom, and to watch out for them? Did you expect me to be with them always, like your children who stayed always with you? Couldn't you imagine how that would frighten me, dedicating my whole life to their well being, never being able to chart my own path? Don't forget, you had *eight* children to look after you. And you weren't deaf. Ita, didn't you see that all your questions were beside the point, the point being that I needed you to sympathize with me and to assure me that everything would be okay, somehow?"

I'll never know her response to these queries. In retrospect, I realize I have spent much of my life trying to interpret my grandmother's silence on the questions that most mattered to me, the ones I never asked.

Hours after my orange snack, hours after the conversation that never took place, there is a knock on the door. Squinting through her rimless glasses, Ita recognizes her son through the peephole.

"*Llegó Papá, Andresíto.*"

It's Pop, come to pick me up. Before long, I will be back at our apartment on 176th, where Mom is preparing Sunday dinner. The three of us will be having fried chicken with white rice, a Mom specialty. Then I'll finish my school assignments. Disney is showing the movie on Davy Crockett. I can't enjoy TV if I have homework hanging over my head.

In the second-floor stairwell, outside my grandmother's apartment, Ita asks Pop about his day. "*Y todo bien, hijo?*"

She "speaks" in "home" signs, using the gestures invented during their early days in Puerto Rico: circling her hands in front of her to mean "*todo*"; then pulling her fingers away from her lips, as if blowing a kiss, to mean "good." She mouths the words in an exaggerated way so he can read what her lips are saying. Somehow, Pop knows that she's asking him if he's okay.

Ita's system didn't work when she had to explain something that required a few sentences. That's when she would need me to bail her out and interpret for Pop. Half of her eight children were deaf, but she never learned the *real* sign language, the one I knew. Necessity gives birth to language, as it does invention. *Abuelita* didn't need to know sign language as long as her hearing children and grandchildren knew it.

Pop answers Ita.

"*Bien,*" he says in Spanish, reinforcing the affirmative response with a nod of his head. When Pop speaks it doesn't come out exactly right; more a high-pitched shriek, with too much emphasis on the second part, "*-en.*"

After a few more exchanges with Ita, Pop looks down at me and signals that we're ready to go.

"*Vamos,*" is what he's trying to say; accompanying this with a hand movement that looks like he's brushing a fly from his face.

I leave as I arrived, reaching up to hug my grandmother around her plump waist and asking for her blessing.

"*Bendición, Ita.*"

"*Dios te bendiga, Andresíto.*"

One last reminder from her, as I descend the stairs with Pop:

"*Pórtate bien, niño, y que seas un buen hijo.*"

Yes, I say to myself. I'll behave and be a good son.

4   Hearing Streets

WHAT I MISSED IN Maryland was the neighborhood and my friends. As mentioned earlier, in the summer of 1957 Mom and I had been reunited with Pop after a two-year stay with my cousins in southern Jersey. I was eleven when we moved back to Washington Heights. There I was introduced to the young crowd with whom I would form my core relationships for the next fifteen years. Many of them are close friends to this day.

The center of gravity for our activities and relationships was a modest parcel of concrete and blacktop bracketed on two sides by five-story walk-ups. This was where 177th Street met Amsterdam Avenue. It was a corner, really; but we called it the Block. The Block was the epicenter of our existence, that domain from which flowed all activity and aspiration, and its open terrain—counting sidewalks, stoops, and street—was no larger than the infield of a baseball diamond. If you included the buildings attached to that open space, our turf was really two square city blocks, from 176th to 178th, between Amsterdam and Audubon avenues.

A block was not a block unless you had numbers. In any given year, we had a few dozen, easily. And a block was not a block unless you had the appropriate terrain: elevator-less tenements that subjected kids to daily contact, a street corner (177th and Amsterdam), a bodega (Santos'), a main stoop (belonging to the Bolton building), and a nearby park (the gravel field and adjoining rocks on the other side of Amsterdam, and cordoned off from the street by a block-long chain-link fence). We knew of other neighborhoods in the city that were dominated by twenty-story public housing projects. But these overwhelmed the kids with dense anonymity. Then there were the areas marked by two-story private homes. But these sections were too sparse, not the best conditions for a "real" block. Washington Heights had plenty of blocks. This was in the late fifties and early sixties, B.D.E. (Before the Dominican Era; that is, before the influx of immigrants from the Dominican Republic in the late 1960s).

The Block provided numbers and terrain, necessary for a good game of Ring-a-Leevio. It was an urban version of Cowboys and Indians, but with everyone getting to play both roles. Every game we played, not just Ring-a-Leevio, was like theater. We had the stage, the (unscripted) drama, and characters—mostly the characters.

My first friend on the Block was Irving Ghigliotty, not your most Spanish-sounding name. His father's family had immigrated to Puerto Rico from Corsica in the 1800s, and when his parents came to New York they, like many new arrivals, gave their son an American-sounding name. Lucky for him, someone in his family had the good sense to give him the nickname Butchy.

Butchy lived at 2372 Amsterdam Avenue, the same building that my grandmother Ita lived in. He was around my family for as long as anyone could remember. He was my age and height and, like me, an only child. I had an open invitation to his apartment, on the fifth floor of 2372. When I got bored with life in apartment 43, I went to Butchy's. I had to use caution getting up to his place since I had to circumvent Ita's surveillance. From the corner of 177th I could detect my grandmother's graying hair and pudgy nose as she gazed out over Amsterdam Avenue from her second-floor window. If she noticed me I would have had to explain what I was up to, and, worse still, probably have to stay with her. I loved the warmth of Ita's place, but I preferred hanging out at Butchy's.

In just about every adventure of my youth—baseball, football, Ring-a-Leevio, Boy Scouts, and basic hanging-out—Butchy was there. He was slightly taller than I was, not as fast, but in possession of long, sturdy arms. He could throw a hardball faster and further than most of us, which entitled him to be the lead pitcher for our baseball teams.

Butchy's father, Bing, ran a garage near Columbia Presbyterian Hospital, and he sponsored our baseball team. His mother Hilda, tall and graceful, knew my family well and I'm sure she sympathized with my situation as the only hearing child of deaf parents. I felt privileged to be included in the Ghigliotty family outings upstate, all-day affairs of swimming and ball playing. All I had to do was bring my bathing suit since Hilda always prepared a sandwich for me. On these picnic days, I arrived early so they wouldn't leave without me. They were barely awake when I knocked on their door, but I didn't care, because I didn't want to be left out. I quietly waited in their living room, playing with their mixed spaniel, Champ.

The first time Butchy showed me to the roof to his building it was a revelation. Looking directly over Amsterdam Avenue I could observe the Harlem River, which flowed along the east edge of Washington Heights. On the other side of the river valley was the Bronx. In effect this part of the Heights sat on the eastern slope of upper Manhattan. From Butchy's roof we had a perfect view of the main landmarks in the vicinity of the Block: the gravel field, Highbridge Pool, the Water Tower, and the High Bridge itself, which spanned the Harlem River. Until then I had never had such a broad view from above.

Not until my twenties did I comprehend the curious geography of that area. We occupied the northern edge of a world-famous island, precariously appended to the mainland by a network of bridges. Washington Heights was our solar system, the Block our Earth. But in reality, we were but a tiny provincial star, light-years away from the center of the universe, downtown Manhattan.

Butchy's roof had another interesting attraction. It was home to a colony of pigeons that belonged to the Connollys, who also lived on the fifth floor. The caged birds came in every shade of gray. We watched as the Connolly brothers opened the wire mesh gates and released them skyward. On that day, and many times after, I admired them flapping in large circles and then disappearing out of view. To where, who knew? It was curious to me that the pigeons always returned to the coops. They had entered into an implicit bargain: freedom for the secure comforts of seed and shelter. I wondered too why I never saw pigeon chicks in that rooftop colony or anywhere else. Where did they nest? How did they survive the New York winters?

Up on the roof—a place so special that a hit song was composed about it, beautifully rendered by the Drifters—Butchy and I forged our friendship in countless moments during the summers of the late fifties, when we were not yet teenagers. One of our favorite rituals involved that most basic and banal of activities: chewing gum. We carried a ration of Bazooka gum, which we picked up at Santos' bodega on the corner of Amsterdam and 177th. With milk crates for chairs, at our safe haven on the top of the world we sat leisurely gazing over the Heights and working on our Bazookas.

The pink squares of sweet viscosity packed a lot for the price. For only a penny, you received three treats in one. First, it gave you an unbelievable sugar rush to kick off the day. Secondly, it contained the raw material for serious bubble-blowing contests. Masters of the art, we were adept not only at creating huge pink balloons, but also at popping them cleanly without leaving a sticky mess on our faces. Finally, the blue-and-red wax-coated wrapper contained a comic strip, peopled by Bazooka characters. The stories and jokes were goofy, causing us to parody them.

When a Bazooka character chuckled, the boxed dialogue with the arrow pointing to the character said, "tee-hee." That was how people laughed in the Bazooka world. We had never heard a real human say "tee-hee!" "Ha-ha" was what laughter sounded like, not "tee-hee." Bazooka-language entered our vocabulary. Whenever Butch and I were on the verge of laughter for whatever reason, we would catch ourselves and blurt out, "tee-hee." This would only provoke more giggling and laughter. So there naturally evolved a higher form of laughter, if we were really on the verge of busting out: "Tee-hee *and a half.*" Then, "tee-hee *and three quarters.*" And so on.

The Chin family, with eight children—split evenly between boys and girls—lived on the fourth floor of 2372 Amsterdam, one flight above my cousins. Their mother, Marina, was Puerto Rican, and their father, George, Chinese. Anyone who ever lived around the block, even for only a few years, knew of the Chins. Years later, running into old friends, the question invariably came up: "Hey, remember the Chins?" "What ever happened to Rosie?" Since I lived around the block as long as anyone, I knew the Chins well, except for Francine the oldest and Yorgy, the youngest. Their tawny faces—containing traces of their Asian and Latin origins—grace my photo collection from those years. The two oldest boys, George and Henry, were stocky and of medium height and resembled martial arts masters: built solidly with a thickness in body frame that made them seem firmly entrenched in the ground. The rest of the Chins covered the gamut of physiques, thin to plump.

I was overwhelmed by the idea of Chin-hood, of so many siblings. I couldn't imagine what it was like living in that household. Where did everyone fit? How did they feed everyone? I approached the Chins like a smorgasbord, relating to individual members depending on my mood, or stage in life. George, the oldest son and also known as Junior, was the comic and always ready for some fun. He married a girl, Joanie, who was at least a foot taller than he was. Henry, my age, was the contemplative one, a partner in what we imagined to be intellectual conversation. Margie noticed me before I noticed her, and became my first girlfriend. Nancy, Rosie, and Willie gave me the chance to play big brother and adviser.

There were others among the cast of characters in those days, kids I would be dealing with for years. Alan "Tachy" Dávila, another Puerto Rican, also seemed to have been with us since day one. No one ever bothered to find out where his nickname came from (*tachar* means "to scratch out" in Spanish). Tachy was the essence of laid-back cool. He didn't effuse angst or panic. His caramel face and dark hair were the backdrop to a permanent smile and pleasant disposition. And he was fast on his feet. Tachy was one of those guys whose presence you always expected, indispensable for a game or a party. Like Butchy, he was a familiar and comforting presence to my parents.

Teddy Power was one of the better handball players around the block, which was strange because he was a big, top-heavy dude on skinny ankles who looked like he could fall over any minute if he wasn't careful. Teddy was memorable for another reason. He was hard of hearing and a lipreader. His speaking voice had the tone of a hollow echo. It wasn't pitched exactly right, but it was a familiar sound to me, like deaf talk. A deaf person with excellent command of speech, that's how he sounded. When you talked with Teddy, the conversation always turned LOUD! With extra volume he compensated for the insecurity of not knowing if he was being heard. In the same way that we unconsciously raised our voices during a long-distance phone call, everyone kicked up the volume as soon as Teddy showed up.

Once, grabbing the side of a parked car to support myself after slipping on a puddle of car oil, I ripped open a nasty gash on my left pinky. The car I reached for had a metal stripping that jutted out and caught my finger, unleashing blood all over me. Teddy brought me up to his apartment in the Bolton, where his mother helped control the bleeding then got a cab to take me to Columbia Presbyterian Hospital. The pinky was patched up and the 18-stitch scar is a permanent reminder of Teddy P.

I can still correlate the names and faces of these characters, and so many others, like Walter, Alfalfa, Teddy Z., Dooley, Bernardo, and Waldy. For others the connection is less robust. I remember a face, dimly in a fog, but not the name. I retain names in old telephone directories—"Barbosa," "Porky," "Catarro"—but less so the faces attached to them.

For some there are preserved the lineaments of a specific incident, perhaps a one-time conversation, a flirtatious glance, or a rumor. I stay connected to these one-time friends by a slim thread of recollection. I refuse to abandon them, much as I refuse to discard my wallet-size telephone directories, battered and faded.

There was an initial core group around the Block in the late fifties when I was not yet a teenager. Then came successive waves of newcomers, replacing some of the originals. I was a constant thread, living in apartment 43 until my early twenties. The roll call spans the alphabet from Arzán to Ziffer: Báez, Baggio, Barris, Camacho, Cameron, Chin, Coch, Colarte, Connolly, Coyle, Dávila, Figueroa, Ghigliotty, González, Hernández, Jones, Joseph, Karalis, Kelly, Laracuente, Medina, Menzella, Pacheco, Pérez, Peláez, Peppas, Piñero, Power, Ramírez, Rivera, Santiago, Senkif, Shapiro, Toohey. In that stew of identities and personalities, another part of me was being formed. These were the characters in my hearing world.

The November after I survived my Maryland summer and started seventh grade, I was with my buddies on the gravel field. We had chosen sides for a game of touch football. The fall weather was perfect, blanketing the gray-pebbled ground with enough of a chill to keep the air clear. Touch football was about all the gravel field was good for. When we played baseball on that same field during the hot and humid summer months, it was farcical. The ground balls and base-running kicked up a minor dust storm, practically choking us. More than once my appearance was rearranged by a screaming grounder that crashed into my face. An afternoon on the field, and socks and pants were saturated in grey soot, much to our moms' chagrin.

Two sides, five guys each team. John Connolly and I had emerged as competing leaders in the early years of the Block. At thirteen he was two years older than I was, and his family had lived in Washington Heights for a long time. The Connollys were among the last of the Irish families to remain in the area. John's closely cropped red hair stood out in the crowd, and he wasn't particularly fond of the sounds of Spanish punctuating the street talk around the block. He felt the encroaching strangeness in his life but wasn't about to relinquish space or authority to the new. As the oldest, toughest one in our little crowd, he still was in charge.

It might have also bothered him that I was challenging him at the quarterback position. I learned how to pass the football accurately and for a good distance. I could drill a bullet line-drive or heave the Hail Mary. And I had my timing just right, anticipating where my receiver would be so the ball would be there in time.

One day, John's frustration came to a head. We faced each other at the line of scrimmage: me in the middle, Butchy and Alfalfa to my left, Jimmy and Tachy to my right. John stood in front of me with the ball. The four other guys on his side positioned themselves to defend each of my receivers. Carrot Top flipped me the ball to start the play.

"Here ya go, spic."

He threw both arms up in front of me, waving to disrupt my view, and began counting:

"One thousand, two thousand, three thousand . . ." I had five seconds to release the ball. If I didn't get it off in time he would rush at me and end the play by grabbing me. According to our rules, I could keep trying to find a receiver as long as I evaded his two-handed "tackle."

I scanned the field looking for an open teammate, but they were all covered tightly by defenders. Jimmy's man, knowing the speed demon that was my cousin, played him deep and just waited; no chance for the bomb. Then, out of the corner of my eye, I saw Tachy break loose from his guy, hitting a sharp right angle outward.

"Four thousand, *five* thousand!" I anticipated John's leap at me, dropping back a few yards to avoid his grasp, and threw a pinpointed pass that hit Tachy, just before he went out of bounds at the right sideline. A completed pass, for a fifteen-yard gain.

"Yeah, way to go Tachy!" I cheered.

"Lucky play, spic, lucky play," John grumbled, loud enough to be heard by everyone.

Back in the huddle, I gave the next play. "OK, this time, Jimmy and Alfalfa criss-cross over the middle; Tachy and Butchy, you both go long. Tachy's the prime receiver. Break!"

Again, John tossed me the ball to start the next play.

"All right, spic, let's see you do it again."

Enough was enough.

"Hey, man, cut it out! What's the matter, huh?" I stood facing him, bouncing the ball nervously on the tips of my fingers.

"Oh? I can't talk like that, spic? I can talk anyway I want."

The rest of the guys, on both sides, watched awkwardly, not knowing where this was going. None of them liked John's taunting, which had been going on for months. It seemed whenever he was in a bad mood or just wanted to put us in our place, he would bark that ugly four-letter word.

Spic. Spic. Spic. I hated the sound of it. To complicate things, there was ambiguity about the word; I didn't know where it came from or exactly what it meant. Someone said it came from Americans hearing Hispanics say "I no *speek* the English." But what about the cleaner Spic and Span, which Mom used daily?

I heard the white kids calling each other "mick" and "wop," but it didn't seem they used it as an insult. It came out like a fraternal salute when they said it. When they yelled "spic," though, I heard animosity and derision. Once a classmate at Incarnation said to me, "The only thing spics are famous for is Zorro." I didn't know enough about my heritage to counter with anything.

That day at the gravel field, anger broke through the confusion. I had to do something. The problem was that John Connolly could kick my ass, and I wasn't ready to offer up a bloody nose in defense of an amorphous identity. In fact, I was definitely not the fighting type. Being the only child, I had no one to practice with. Physical violence was a rarity in my home. Mom could mess with my mind occasionally, but she spanked me only a few times in my life. Pop never laid a hand on me.

I tried diplomacy. "Look, John. You can't do this anymore. You're pissing us off royally." (Yes, "us," I quickly reasoned; in numbers there was strength). "You gotta quit that, or you can go play by yourself, dammit."

This threw him off guard. He stared quizzically at me, pondering my words for a minute or two. Then he surprised us. "Aw, forget it," he said. "Let's get on with the game."

And that was that. It was over before it started. We finished the game and many others after that. Among my buddies we never really discussed the incident, though it seemed they looked at me a little differently from then on, maybe out of pride that we won some respect. Maybe out of amazement that a few words skillfully strung together could get the same result as a broken nose or punched-out teeth.

In any case, I became something of a leader, although not the kind we knew about in other neighborhoods. We weren't a street gang flouting the law, or defending our turf. That would have been a waste of time to us. Nevertheless, we were ever aware that we were different from most of the kids in Washington Heights, white, with European backgrounds. In the Highbridge area where we lived, the Dávilas, the Medinas, the Pérezes, the Riveras, the Torreses were the coming majority.

But John Connolly, who unwittingly helped to create our sense of identity, never used the four-letter word again. Later, I often thought, "Man, after all that, he wanted to keep us as friends." I wondered: did he change because he realized Highbridge was changing, that we were outnumbering the old Irish families? Or did he genuinely come to realize the foolishness of using words that hurt? In John's case, I came to see that it was the latter. At heart, the kid with the thick red hair was a good guy. Our friendship persevered and we never discussed the incident on the gravel field. For years afterward, we kept in touch, until young adulthood sent us separate ways.

With the approach of spring 1959, Pop received word from his friend William Eckenrode that he would sponsor me for another stay at Camp Gabrielle.

"Ahtay, Ahtay," he called me into the living room. (I never told him that he was way off with his pronunciation of "Andy." Besides it sounded nice to me. In the whole world, he was the only one who called me by that name.)

"Mr. Eckenrode wrote me. He invites you to camp again this summer."

Before he could get another word in, I cut him off. I was prepared for this moment. "No I don't think I want to go anymore." By now I had decided to hold firm to this decision. I was not going back to Maryland in the summer.

"Why not? You like it there. It's better than staying here in New York. Here it is boring for you."

Pop had a way of sweet-talking me into things. He could be very persistent but I wasn't going to yield this time. "I don't want to go. I have plenty of things to do here. We have the baseball team going and I don't want to miss any games; and I have the Boy Scouts too, we're planning some hikes. I definitely want to stay here in New York."

"Mr. Eckenrode is good to you. He paid for you the last summer; and he sent you the toy soldiers for Christmas, remember?"

"Yes, he is kind to us, but I don't feel comfortable there in Maryland. The kids are different. The old women are nice but in his house there's nothing to do. I want to stay here with my friends." I was holding my ground.

"Mr. Eckenrode is an important man. He helps deaf people and maybe helps you too. If you say no, then he feels hurt and won't help. Think for your future."

Oh, so was that the idea? Was Pop trying to hook me up with the man from Baltimore so that he would be a patron of sorts? Was this Pop's way of looking after my future, and maybe *his* future too? Maybe so, but that's not what I wanted. I was uncomfortable being in debt to the man from across the Mason-Dixon line.

"I don't care. I made up my mind. I'm not going to Camp Gabrielle. I'll stay here." And that was it. It was the first time I had overtly countered Pop's will. Pop couldn't physically extradite me from the Heights; he had to acquiesce. But this was not the end of his plan to secure my—or should I say, our—future.

By the seventh grade I found myself in the Boy Scouts of America. Besides Butchy and I, other guys like Tachy, Raúl, and Alfalfa joined. We somehow ended up in Troop 797, which was sponsored by the Temple of the Covenant, a local synagogue located on 180th Street near Broadway. Our meetings were held at PS 132, the grammar school attended by many of the kids on the Block. Along with guys from several local neighborhoods we formed what might have been the most ecumenical troop in the country.

Fred Zenker was our Boy Scout Master, a great guy. Every other Friday night we suited up in our pressed olive green uniforms and red neckerchiefs and presented ourselves to Fred. Being a Boy Scout was akin to being in a paramilitary organization, without the guns. As teenage soldiers we swore total loyalty to our comrades and country and pledged unquestioning respect for authority. Troop 797 was a brotherhood with a clearly defined philosophy and structure. The Boy Scout Handbook was our Bible.

Our leaders trained us in the rudiments of martial culture, civic participation, and outdoors survival. At Troop assemblies we were drilled in marching formations and tested in our knowledge of Scouting rules and traditions. Fortunately for us, Fred wasn't one for letting the Scouting image go to his head. A man of gentle common sense, he knew we were there for one reason: the weekend hikes to Ten Mile River and Bear Mountain.

I think Fred had another purpose, which was to bring together the Catholics and Jews from each side of Broadway. It was in Troop 797 that I made my first Jewish friends. Wise-cracking Denis Fiedler didn't seem to have a care in the world, and he remains in the recesses of my memory as Washington Height's greatest spitting champion. I have never seen anyone who could send saliva hurling through the air like he could.

Henry Korzinyck was a sad-faced, chubby boy whose home I visited a few times. Of all the kids in the Troop, I found him the most perplexing. I wondered what made Henry, of Polish background, so subdued and forlorn-looking. Years later, I read about the Polish Jews during the Holocaust. Only a few thousand had survived, and I thought of Henry Korzinyck.

I was an upwardly mobile Boy Scout, climbing the ranks and piling up merit badges galore. I learned skills quite unconventional for a city kid: wildlife management, pioneering, nature, civics, and basketry! Each time a new badge was awarded me, Mom proudly sewed the colorful insignia onto my sash.

In his late twenties and physically fit, Fred had no trouble keeping up with us on camping trips. He taught us how to pitch a tent in the snow, cook meals over burning logs, and identify animal tracks. After he showed us how to bake a potato in a mud pack, no one dared using aluminum foil or bringing A&P's canned Irish Potatoes. He led us on "forced marches" over hill and stream and spooked us with midnight stories around the campfire.

Fred's favorite saying was, "A little dirt never hurt nobody." Out in the woods, we shouldn't expect pristine cleanliness; some of Mother Nature was bound to filter into our food and drink. How liberating to hear these words, since our mothers fussed so much. Unfortunately, none of us reached the pinnacle of Scouting achievement, which was the rank of Eagle Scout. It may have been simply that time ran out on us and we aged out. Or perhaps it was one December night that did us in.

One winter we gathered at the community room of the Temple of the Covenant for our annual party. Parents were invited but ours, being Catholic, didn't feel comfortable attending. (And forget Mom and Pop; they rarely went to social events if they were going to be the only deaf people.) Each year the troop staged a talent show with comic skits and musical performances. Promotions and new merit badges were announced. No doubt Fred wanted to put his boys on display for the Temple congregation. This was a great bunch of kids, deserving of continued sponsorship.

On this occasion, the official program was followed by informal socializing. It was a festive atmosphere and everyone—Jews celebrating Hanukkah, Catholics celebrating Christmas—was in a holiday mood. Then, out of nowhere, the guys from the Block launched into Christmas carols. There was no harm done, certainly, with "Jingle Bells" and "Rudolph the Red Nosed Reindeer." But then we switched to the traditional religious songs, "Oh, Holy Night," "Silent Night," and "Come All Ye Faithful," invoking Baby Jesus and the Virgin Mary.

The impromptu performance left the adults uneasy; we detected them whispering and staring at us. Did we know we were upsetting them? I think so. Still, we persisted with song and chant, letting our mischievous side get the best of us. Church teaching had infused in our young minds, however indirectly and subtly, the idea of Jewish culpability for Christ's death. I, for one, had accepted this notion. The night ended in cold silence as we all departed for home.

After that, things were never the same. There were rumors that the Temple of the Covenant was disassociating itself from Troop 797. Fred was caught in the middle, wanting to preserve the special community he had created. Some time after, his Assistant Scoutmaster, Mr. Shenck, died unexpectedly of a heart attack, leaving Fred to carry the load by himself. Fred came around the block to see me, to give me news of Mr. Shenck's untimely death. He asked me to round up the guys to attend the funeral service.

It was the first time any of us had attended a Jewish service. The Temple's interior was simple, devoid of the ornate architecture and stained-glass windows that characterized Incarnation church. The pews were without knee rests, and the ceremony substituted Hebrew for the Latin we were accustomed to. I fidgeted in my seat, confused about the proper decorum for a Catholic in this situation. Should I respectfully observe Jewish convention, sitting and rising with the congregants? Or should I stay seated as a passive onlooker throughout the tribute? My upbringing dictated loyalty to my Catholicism, and I sat throughout the service, and so did the other guys from the Block.

5   Juvenile Maneuvering

IN LATE FALL OF 1959, I was an eighth grader at Incarnation grammar school. The elementary grades were ending and it was time to plan for high school. We received leaflets describing the various schools, including what grade average each school required for admission and the tuition charged. An A student would have a shot at the elites: Xavier, Manhattan Prep, Fordham Prep, Mount St. Michael. Students with a B average could expect to get into Power Memorial or Cardinal Hayes. Below that, you would hope for Rice or Bishop DuBois. Then there was the matter of the Diocesan tests. Basically your test scores on these entrance exams, along with your grade school average, determined which schools you were eligible for.

I showed the blue information sheets to Pop. We looked over the papers, but mostly it was Pop looking at me while I looked at the sheets. He studied my face for signs of my reactions; this was the reliable way for him to grasp the real meaning of those flyers. As I pored over the documents laid out on the kitchen table, he scanned me for telltale signs: a nodding head and smile, furrowed brows, a grim façade. The expressions revealed to him the range of emotions instigated by the data, from confidence to quiet desperation.

The data were neatly arrayed in columns: school, grade expected for admission, and tuition. There was nothing arbitrary about the decision process. When it came to getting into a Catholic high school, you either had it or didn't, it seemed. Grades, test scores, and tuition. In Washington Heights, Catholic boys who didn't make the cut were left with one alternative and that was George Washington High School, "GW."

The goal of every serious student in Incarnation, so the Brothers taught us, should be graduation to a Catholic high school. Public schools were for non-believers and the unruly. Ending up in GW, it felt to me, was grounds for expulsion from the Faith. The religious aspect played a big part in Pop's thinking too, but mostly he was being practical. He simply believed I would get a better education in the Catholic school system.

Tuition ranged from $25 to $50 per month, depending on the quality of the school. That was a tidy sum back in 1959, at least for us. I nervously inspected the blue sheets, making sure I understood all the terms, so I could break it down for Pop. I could find no mention of special considerations, negotiation, or appeals. At least I wasn't aware of any such exceptions. And I certainly didn't think of asking the Brothers at Incarnation about them. To me, parochial schools were around since the time of Jesus, an unchanging system with fixed rules and regulations.

"If I get good scores on the entrance exams," I signed to Pop, "I get a choice of which school to attend. If I get low scores then I wait to see which one will take me." He stared at the sheet, then signed to me.

"You think you will do well on the exams?"

I told him I wasn't sure, but that I was confident of getting into a middle-level school like Cardinal Hayes or Power Memorial. Lots of my classmates were hoping to get into one of these. He nodded his comprehension, glancing at the papers on the table.

Since the fifth grade Pop had refrained from monitoring my academic progress, letting me worry about it. I took over, even to the point of forging his signature on the quarterly report cards, so I wouldn't have to get into long, complicated conversations about my classes and grades. Not that he would have been unhappy with my performance; I was a consistent B- student. He just assumed I knew what I was doing and trusted me to do my homework. He wouldn't have had much to say anyway, because the material I was learning was already beyond what he had learned at St. Rita School for the Deaf in Ohio. He was twenty years old when he left after his sophomore year there. The gap between Mom and me was even greater.

By the seventh grade I was already "teaching" my parents from my schoolbooks: major events in American history, the meaning of specific words in English, and basic mathematics. It felt silly having Pop sign off on the report card, when I was the one explaining what the grades and courses were all about. And if I did poorly in a given quarter, what was he going to do, reprimand me? Give me advice on how to improve?

Pop and I reviewed the materials again. He asked me what I knew about each school: Is it a big or small school? Are the teachers Christian Brothers like the ones at Incarnation? Where is it located, and how will I get there, by subway or bus? Do they have good sports teams?

He sat pensively, taking in my responses, and showing few clues as to what he was thinking. His expression was dazed, his face directed at me but not fully interlocked with my signing. He was reading my signs and thinking at the same time; half in, half out of the conversation. I knew he was already thinking about the next—and biggest—question. He decided to hold that one off until another day.

"OK, I will speak with your mother, and we will talk more later this week."

Several days later, after dinner, Pop wanted to talk more about high school. This time Mom joined us at the dinner table. This is where all the important family discussions took place. I again displayed the information about the application process. We settled into our chairs, Pop avoiding eye contact with me. Mom, more spectator than participant, gazed in Pop's direction waiting for him to begin. I slowly rotated a pencil between my fingers, imitating the baton-twirling cheerleaders at a college football game.

"Yesterday, your mother and I, we discussed high school for you," he began, still avoiding my eyes. "I explained everything to her, the same way you showed me. We talked a long time." He paused briefly, then continued. "I am sorry, but we cannot afford the tuition fee. We do not have enough to pay twenty-five or thirty-five dollars every month." Finally, he aimed his sights at me, waiting for a reaction.

"So what does this mean?" I signed to him. "I can't go to any of these schools? Even if I do good on the exams?" Instinctively, I began assessing the significance of this turn of events. If we couldn't afford a Catholic school, then I was headed back to the public schools, where I had been before Incarnation. GW wasn't what I had in mind, but at least it was nearby, and I knew other kids from around the block would be there. It seemed like a foregone conclusion. But Pop had another idea.

"Why not ask Mr. Eckenrode if he will help you? Write him a letter and explain. He always wanted you to go to Catholic school."

Mr. Eckenrode? What's Pop trying to concoct *now*? The previous year I had turned down Eckenrode's invitation to return to Camp Gabrielle in the summer. I didn't think the man from Baltimore would lend me a hand now, after I ungraciously declined his offer.

"I don't think Mr. Eckenrode will help me, and I don't feel good asking him." I hated it when Pop cajoled me into asking for favors.

He pleaded with me, insistently. "You do not want to go to public school, right? You have to try with Mr. Eckenrode. Do not worry. It is OK. He will help you. I know him. He is a good man."

He may be a good man, I thought, but how did he take my decision not to return to Baltimore? Pop hadn't heard from him since writing him that I preferred staying in New York for the summer. I doubted that Mr. Eckenrode, who instructed me to address him as "Sir" in our conversations, took my rebuff lightly. On the other hand, I didn't want to jeopardize Pop's friendship with him. Maybe if we appealed to his sense of charity, Eckenrode might be willing to patch things up. What better way to support my dreams than to foot my school bills? Reluctantly I agreed to try Pop's strategy. The next day I sent a letter to Baltimore, asking Mr. Eckenrode for help. Would he cover my tuition fees so I could attend a Catholic high school? I promised I would eventually repay the debt.

A month later the answer arrived in a small white envelope. Inside, a single folded sheet contained the typed response:

"Dear Andrew,

"Mr. Eckenrode has instructed me to say that he has disassociated himself from you. He cannot assist you financially or otherwise.

"Yours, Miss Grable."

My plea for help had been summarily rejected. He didn't even bother to write me himself. How can an adult hold such a grudge against an eleven-year old? When Pop came home from work that night I angrily showed him the bad news.

"You see!" I signed emphatically, "I told you he wasn't going to help me. Now what am I supposed to do?"

Pop's plan for securing my high school education through the Eckenrode option, which probably had been germinating in his mind for a few years, had come to naught. He was caught between the desire to send his son to Catholic high school and the absence of financial means. But I identified an alternative solution on those blue forms that described the various high schools.

Barrytown, in upstate New York, was home to a preparatory seminary of the Christian Brothers, a religious order founded in the seventeenth century by a French priest, St. John Baptist de la Salle. For youngsters who felt a calling from God to join the community of Christian Brothers, this was the point of entry.

Like many of Incarnation's boys I thought, at one time or another, about becoming a Christian Brother. This was not a far-fetched idea, for the men in the long black, button-down cassocks and white bibs inspired us with their religious passion and devotion to our education.

Toward the end of the eighth grade, as I was attempting to salvage something positive after Eckenrode's letter of rejection, I seriously considered the notion of joining the Christian Brothers.

What does a twelve year-old know about devoting oneself to the spiritual life? Nothing, of course. But it seemed reasonable that I should consider a religious vocation since I had spent the last three years with the Christian Brothers. The vicious Brother Benedict I dismissed as an aberration, the exception to the rule; the kind Brother Casimir was someone after whom I could model myself.

The years at Incarnation and the spiritual piety inherent in my family had conditioned me to consider life in a religious order. Pop was taken aback when I brought up the idea of enrolling at Barrytown, the first step toward being a Christian Brother.

"You want to be a Brother, same as the teachers at Incarnation School?" The quizzical look on his face indicated his first reaction. The whole idea came out of nowhere, as far as he was concerned. "You understand it means you will not marry and have children. Maybe they send you somewhere far away from here. You will not be near your family."

I explained I had been thinking about it for a while, that I perceived a calling from God and that I liked the idea of a life of teaching. Pop had assumed that I would always be with him and Mom. He wanted a future in which I would start my own family and live close to him and Mom. He dreamed we would live together in the same house, a double-decker in Queens, he would say. And after he was gone Mom would benefit from the insurance plan he had signed onto. That was why Mr. Covello, the Prudential agent, visited us every few months to collect the premium. If Andy Jr. were to become Brother Vincent—the religious name I was planning to give myself—that would kill that idea.

In the end, it was impossible for Pop to deny my proposal. In Catholic homes it is a mark of honor for a child to accept a religious vocation. And how could he, president of the Puerto Rican Society for the Catholic Deaf, object? Besides, my cousin Jimmy had simultaneously been considering the Brothers too. We would both be entering at the same time. Pop had no choice but to go along with the idea, and left it up to me to follow through on the application process.

All seemed to be in order for Andy Jr.'s transfer from 514 West 176th Street to Barrytown, New York. And because there were no tuition costs at Barrytown, as I had noticed on the blue information sheets, I had solved the problem of enrolling in a good Catholic high school without Pop's help. The original problem I had to deal with, getting a free Catholic high school education, was now solved. Or so it seemed.

In the next months the drama of how to get a free Catholic high school education unfolded in an unforeseen manner. Soon after I was told that the Christian Brothers did not accept an only child directly into the seminary. Parents should not be deprived of their only offspring at so early an age, not even for a religious calling. I would have to wait until *after high school* to seek entry.

The news brought down the curtain on my visions of studying at Barrytown. It slipped me back to the original dilemma. I panicked at the thought that time was running out on my quest for a Catholic high school. But just when it seemed I was reaching the end of the line, yet another possibility was brought to my attention.

If I was serious about a religious vocation why not consider the *priesthood*? I could enroll at Cathedral College Prep, the high school run by the New York Archdiocese that prepared young men for life in the clergy. I could commute daily to the school that was located on Manhattan's West Side. I wouldn't need to leave my family until after the sixth year, after my sophomore college year, when I would enter Dunwoodie Seminary in Westchester County. There, I would begin the most serious phase of my preparation, a six-year period as a novitiate culminating in my ordination as a Roman Catholic priest. Or, I could even switch to Barrytown after four years of high school, and pursue my original vocation as a Christian Brother.

I assessed every angle, debated every pro and con, and consulted with no one. Not Pop, not my grandmother Ita, not Titi Blanca, not Brother Casimir, not Father Lynch. No one.

My logic was airtight and my motives pragmatic. I wasn't completely self-serving, I don't think; but neither was I driven by unalloyed commitment to God and his Church. It was the best option this thirteen-year-old boy could come up with.

"The more I think about it, the more it makes sense. As a priest I can serve God's will even more effectively than as a Brother, because I won't be limited to teaching. I might eventually be in charge of my own parish. I have some leadership qualities. I know I can give inspiring sermons and I think I'd be good as a confessor, too. Look at how the kids around the block come to me for advice. Also, being a priest will make my family proud of me, even more than if I'm a Brother. Maybe I'll even end up being assigned to minister to the deaf. That would be something. I might even be the first priest born of deaf parents. If it turns out this is not right for me, I can always change my mind. I have twelve years before being ordained."

I was also aware—thanks, once again, to the blue information sheets—that I wouldn't have to pay for tuition. The Church took care of that.

For days I evaluated everything, finally deciding I wanted to be a priest. I broke the news to Pop.

"A priest! Where do you get these ideas?"

Once again, I had thrown him for a loop. In the end, Pop went along with my decision. He was content, at least, that I would still be living at home. It also meant we wouldn't have to pay tuition.

I enjoyed the solitude of my room, when Mom wasn't using it to put on her make-up. It also served as my satellite station to beam in the melodies, rhythms, and lyrics from the musical firmament. The Zenith TV in the living room I had to share with my parents. The RCA radio, a gray-and-white plastic box that plugged into the electric socket under my desk, was all mine. In the privacy of my room I played that box hour after hour, as loud as I wanted.

Even when Mom was in the room, applying her skin cream or fixing her hair, I could leave the music at full blast. She would put her palm to the box and ask me what kind of sound was coming out. She liked the feel of the vibrating radio when I turned up the volume for her. I left the radio on when doing my homework, and well past my bedtime prayers. I could pretend I was deep in my dreams and keep listening, even with my door open.

After Mom and Pop bought me the RCA, I quickly found the stations that played my favorite sounds, like WABC and WINS. Rotating the transparent plastic dial I switched frequently between these and other stations. I was in constant, almost frenetic, pursuit of the songs I liked. On the Block, I traded impressions with the others, debating which singers had the best sound. We updated ourselves on the "Top Ten" hits, and told each other about new songs from favorite artists and entries from unknowns.

For some time I was under the illusion that all radio stations were located in a single building downtown, and that singers simply went from one station to another to perform their songs. I had seen old photos of radio programs with artists surrounding a microphone and assumed the radio was delivering live shows, just like TV. The songs came to me directly and intimately, and I could not imagine they were anything but live. The Penguins harmonizing on "Earth Angel," the Five Satins delivering "In the Still of the Night"; they were *right there* on the other side of the wavelength. It could not be otherwise, so beautiful and palpable were their voices! I never revealed this ignorance to my friends.

Poised in the cramped space that separated the foot of my bed from Mom's bureau, I mouthed the lyrics into the mirror. On a lucky evening

I might get to hear Little Anthony and the Imperials three, four times doing "Tears on My Pillow." It was thrilling to mimic the plaintive cry in the opening lines: "You *don't* remember me, but I remember you." I didn't dare compete with the soaring beauty of his voice, I was happy enough verbalizing in silence. The imaginary audience that I performed to never knew the difference. Since many of the songs received repeated play, I mastered them and developed a unique delivery for each one, complete with choreographed steps and routines.

What bits of jazz I came across on the dials did little for me, and my tastes were not yet attuned to Latin music. I suspect that my parents' deafness cut me off from this genre, even though it was popular among my hearing relatives, especially the Ayalas. In the late 1950s it was rock 'n' roll that excited me.

I reacted to the visceral, emotional effect of particular sounds. I wanted to be moved, not pleased. I wanted a swelling in my throat, a prickling in my spine. Not for me cabaret or Broadway tunes, or foolish novelty songs. My songs had to *mean* something, and if I could shuffle, jump, and finger-snap to them, all the better. That's what I wanted from my music; and invariably my RCA came through for me.

I wasn't going steady with anyone, but the songs conveyed all the passion and romance I could handle. Each night, along with Jackie Wilson ("Lonely Teardrops"), I moaned over lost love and rejection. Just as easily, my spirits could be buoyed by the raucous vibrancy of Ray Charles on "I Got a Woman," or the hopeful plea of the Dubs on "Could This Be Magic?"

Sometimes I was in search of another, more passionate yet indescribable emotion. I was particularly attracted to haunting, echoing sounds. When the Drifters sang "There Goes My Baby" and Roy Orbison pined away on "Only the Lonely" they were not just emoting over love. I heard a stark call for attention and recognition. They were saying it was okay for me to admit to my melancholy. They said I was entitled to ask the big questions: does anyone out there know about Andy Torres, only child of deaf Puerto Ricans, living in this crazy, impersonal city?

And the more dangerous question: does anyone out there feel sorry for me? They sanctioned the cathartic descent into private self-pity.

Fortunately for my mental health, the radio would rescue me from dwelling at length on these questions. Suddenly, the haunting sound would be replaced by waves of sheer beauty, thanks to Sam Cooke on "You Send Me." If not the shimmering virtuosity of Sam Cooke, there was the violent onslaught of rocking energy delivered by Chuck Berry ("Johnny B. Goode"), Elvis Presley ("Hound Dog"), or Little Richard ("Good Golly Miss Molly"). There was no room for melancholy after they sang.

Popular culture transmitted through the radio or viewed in movies can have a powerful impact on a kid just coming of age. And just as I loved the music of my youth, I was a fan of the movies. But how was I to know, at the age of thirteen, that the men who perished defending the Alamo were really the *bad* guys, or at least that their motives were questionable?

While sitting through *The Alamo,* Hollywood's 1960 version of that struggle, I wished I too could have died as an American hero. The 187 defenders were the underdogs, outnumbered ten to one. When Colonel Travis, played by Lawrence Harvey, drew a line in the dirt with his sword, I saw myself crossing over with everyone else. John Wayne, playing Davy Crockett in his coonskin hat, stirred me when he said that the Alamo was a symbol of freedom and that the Mexicans were the oppressors. I believed him.

The scene of the final onslaught by General Santa Anna's men, overtaking the last holdouts, devastated me. My heart sank as Colonel Travis and Jim Bowie, depicted by Richard Widmark, met their end. And the climax, in which Davy Crockett is speared bloodily to a door, affected me like no other movie scene. The overwhelmed volunteers, who had come to save Texas from the Mexicans, were massacred to the last man.

Such was the power of American mythology in those days. Before John Wayne's version, I was already a fan of Davy Crockett from the Walt Disney series on TV. Pop bought me a coonskin cap, a plastic rifle, and a hunting knife. Inspired by the heroic frontiersman from Tennessee, I wrestled with imaginary grizzlies and scalped a few Indians too. The first time I saw the movie was in the enormous Loew's theater on 175th Street and Broadway. I went alone, and sat through it three times. I came out wishing I had a cause to die for, like the men of the Alamo.

A year later, another movie had an effect on my subconscious search for identity. This time Hollywood offered me a polar opposite to *The Alamo* in the form of *West Side Story*.

Never had I adopted such a partisan attitude to the characters in a movie. I immediately sided with the Sharks and their charismatic leader, Bernardo, played by George Chakiris. Just like me, it seemed, he was an outsider trying to establish a footing in a new, hostile environment, and seeking respect for his family and people. Unlike me, he was clear about his identity and determined to fight violently, if necessary, for his rightful place on the West Side. The beautiful Rita Moreno, who reminded me of Titi Blanca, played Chakiris' *mujer* Anita; loyal to her nationalistic man, yet attracted to the freedom that could be enjoyed by Puerto Rican women in this country.

In the months following, I adopted a new persona that was evident in my dress. I purchased the same outlandish lavender shirt worn by 'Nardo, and wore it whenever I could. I had a thin black tie to go with it which, firmly undergirded by metal collar snaps, protruded like a phallic symbol. "Matching" the shirt was a pair of gray continental slacks with horizontal pocket openings. The pants were so snug I didn't mind that it came without belt hoops. The *pièce de resistance* of the wardrobe was my footwear and hosiery: pitch black, patented leather cha-cha boots, with zippered sides, accompanied by *red* socks. I credit Bernardo for inspiring me with the lavender shirt and black tie; where the rest came from, I don't remember.

At school long hair swished back into a "duck's ass," or D.A., at the nape was out of the question. So were sideburns. These were images unbecoming to young men who would make a vow of lifetime celibacy. So I lived a double life: during the daytime, a neat part along the left side and simple comb-over, at night and weekends, the full 'Nardo treatment, including the D.A. For this to work, I had to leave my wavy dark brown hair long enough for my street look, but not so long that it would violate the classroom code.

West Side Story affected me in less obvious ways. It was the first time I had seen on the big screen a full-scale depiction, in living color, of Puerto Rican life. Granted, it was replete with stereotypes: slums, street gangs, and heavily accented speech. Nevertheless, it was *something*. My Puerto Rican-ness had finally been legitimized. For young Puerto Ricans it was understandable, this feeling that something—anything— is better than nothing. Being feared was preferable to being ignored. Finally seeing characters I could relate to, I felt emboldened to go forth into the larger society with an identity of my own. The actor Russ Tamblin played the leader of the white gang, the Jets. I equated him with everyone who ever called me "spic," with the kids who pushed me off the basketball courts where I didn't belong, with the shopkeepers who eyed me suspiciously whenever I walked into their store. To *West Side Story* I owe the first awakenings of my Puerto Rican identity. Even if it meant downplaying my roots in Deaf culture—downplaying not because the two cultures were antagonistic to each other, but because I didn't have the emotional wherewithal to manage two "outsider" iden- tities simultaneously. At least that's how it felt then. If this was the price of making it in the hearing world, then so be it.

This was an ironic consequence, for I doubt the film's makers in- tended to raise the self-esteem of young Puerto Ricans. At the time I was ignorant of the themes elaborated in the story. Little did I realize that the movie was a modern adaptation of Romeo and Juliet, with al- lusions to the perennial themes of youth rebellion, ethnic conflict, and newcomer aspiration. The tragic romance involving Tony (Richard

Beymer) and María (Natalie Wood) was of minor interest to me. What *I* saw was a Puerto Rican story. Finally I had someone to replace Davy Crockett with. 'Nardo became my new hero. There was no end to the ironies, though: George Chakiris, who played 'Nardo, was of Greek American background.

A circuitous route landed me in Cathedral College High School, the preparatory seminary for New York City's parish priests. In the fall of 1964, at the ripe age of thirteen, I took the first steps of a projected twelve-year journey toward ordination in the priesthood. The Good Lord did not tarry in presenting me with the first test of fealty to my new calling.

It didn't take long before I was rudely disabused of the idea that kids studying for the priesthood were of a special moral breed. One day in my first semester, three hundred students waited impatiently in the auditorium for general assembly, whispering and fooling around in our seats. Suddenly someone cracked a joke that brought me to a roar of laughter and I could barely contain myself. Stifling myself as much as I tried, my voice nevertheless soared above the others around me. Then, from the row in front of me, I heard the hated four-letter word.

"Shut up, spic."

A portly bruiser with a crew cut turned around to glare at me, and I went from joviality to humiliation in one second flat. I was surprised that James Cahill was even aware of my existence, much less that he would send a slur my way. I sat back in my seat, deflated and silenced.

I didn't think of retaliating, verbally or physically; I was out of my element, unlike in the gravel field incident with John Connolly. In fact, I was the sole Puerto Rican in our class, comprised mostly of Irish and Italian working-class kids. But I was stunned that this could happen at a school with a sacred mission. How could someone who supposedly had a religious vocation speak that way, to a fellow Catholic no less?

And that was not to be the last time. "Let's go, spic, you're clogging up the stairway." "Carrying your knife today, spic?"

To complicate matters there was quite a bit of ambiguity attached to the four-letter word. Sometimes good friends would salute me: "Hey spic, how's it goin' today?" and "How's it hangin' today, spic?" Was I to interpret these in a spirit of camaraderie and endearment?

Surrealism took over. Every time I heard the four-letter word, it was the context that determined its meaning and intent. Who's the speaker? What's the situation? How's the tone? The word meant nothing by itself, it seemed. Brought up in Deaf culture, where body language and tone of voice is everything, and where context dictates the meaning of specific signs, it was easy to figure out the message behind the word. But still, it was a drain, this constant divining of other people's words and intentions.

Unlike what 'Nardo might've done, but as Jesus would have counseled, I adopted a turn-the-other-cheek philosophy. Just ignore the transgressors, and maybe they'll tire of it. Don't let on that it hurts. Don't retaliate with "mick" or "wop." Gradually the word lost currency in our interactions, but I was conscious that it could surface now and then.

Fr. Niebryzdowski was a tall and fit man with sandy blond hair combed in a part. He wore silver-rimmed glasses and his face rarely broke into a smile, which complemented his personality as a no-nonsense taskmaster who assigned lengthy readings. But he was so knowledgeable about his subject, and came in so prepared each day, that I was inspired to be a good student. He infused me with a permanent love of history, especially of faraway places and distant times. He escorted us through the Egyptian dynasties, Persia, the Greek and Roman eras and into medieval Europe. Along the way, I marveled at the various peoples who made a brief, if momentous, appearance on the world stage. They disappeared leaving behind a chapter, maybe only a few paragraphs, in our textbooks: the Assyrians, the Scythians, and the Ostrogoths.

One day he ordered four boys to the front of the classroom, posting them about ten feet apart along the front of the blackboard. He gave the one on the far left a small booklet then proceeded to unfold it, giving each boy a segment to hold up as he walked along the front. At the end was revealed a long strip of panels with intricate patterns of men in battle, court scenes and colorful landscapes. This was the Bayeux Tapestry in miniature, an embroidered chronicle almost a thousand years old, which depicted the Norman Conquest of England in 1066. "The real one," Fr. Niebryzdowski intoned, "is in a museum in France, and would go around this room twice."

From Cathedral I have permanent memories of the black-clothed men who instructed us. Our English teacher for several years was Fr. Rae, ruddy-faced and lanky, who, students said, helped himself to an extra portion of wine at Mass. Describing the moment when young Oliver Twist pleaded innocently for some extra gruel—"Please, sir, I want some more"—you would have thought Fr. Rae had an earlier career in Broadway theater. As he delivered that line, voice quivering and hands outstretched, my throat clogged up.

I picked up a fourth language, Latin, thanks to Fr. James Griffin, who displayed gleaming white teeth. Faced with the daunting task of conveying a dead language to active young boys, the priests of Cathedral found the perfect solution: *Caesar's Helvetian Wars*. The text, only eighty pages and small enough to put in your back pocket, had maps of battle zones, illustrations of weaponry and armor, and extensive notes on military strategy. *"Gallia omnis in tres partes divisa est."* All Gaul is divided into three parts. I would always remember that first sentence.

The next imparter of the dead language was Fr. "Big Jim" Byrne, big and blustery like John Wayne, but a gentle man at heart. Melded within his lectures were informal homilies on the meaning of life and personal sayings ("Don't be a mouse mind!") cajoling us to grand ideas and the higher things. This was practical wisdom for all young people. Surely he knew in his heart that not all his listeners were destined to reach the priesthood. Why not avail us all of the transcendental wisdom a man of his maturity possessed? "Big Jim" made me into a disciple of Cicero, the great orator—so much so that, in my sophomore year, I boldly decided to compete in Cathedral's annual elocution contest. Participants selected their own material and I chose the chariot scene from Lew Wallace's *Ben-Hur*. (The book was enjoyable, but I *loved* that movie!). When the judges announced, in front of hundreds of students, that I was the first-place winner among the underclassmen, my heart pounded. I competed in my junior and senior years, winning second-place medals both times. Andy Torres, a child of the Deaf world, a public speaker?

Unfortunately, the time of that first victory in my sophomore year not everyone was as happy as I. Leaving school that day, a student, stranger to me, came up and sulked, "Hey, you know, you didn't really deserve to win first prize." Then he walked away. I had no idea why he said that. The incident just confirmed for me that, as in the case of James Cahill, even those claiming a spiritual vocation are capable of injustice.

A few months after winning that contest, I was called in to an interview with a speech specialist. According to him some of my teachers concurred that I had a mild lisp. He asked me if anyone had ever pointed this out to me. After recounting my family history he went to work on me, evaluating my pronunciation. Sitting face to face, I read pages of materials out loud, in alternating speeds and volume. He recommended steps to correct my speech patterns, saying I should practice at home. The key was to speak slower and be conscious of how I enunciated my words. I met with him two or three more times. If that lisp did exist it must have been a remnant of early years when my only co-conversationalists were Mom and Pop. If it survived into high school, I wasn't aware of it.

We received our Spanish instruction from a bona fide Spaniard, Padre Mayoral. Padre was at an advanced age by the time we studied with him.

He walked haltingly and bent over. He was a few inches shorter than I was, and I was one of the shortest in my class (by my mid-teens I was close to the five and a half feet that I would ultimately be allotted). His physical condition should have elicited Christian empathy on our part, but we didn't know any better. Within the first month of class he lost control of us, our antics obliging him to warn us again and again: *"Mira,* boy." Like a pack of hyenas that will gang up on a frail old lion, we mercilessly disrupted his lectures with whispered jokes and spit-ball fights.

At Cathedral High religious instruction was the most important part of the curriculum. Monsignor Cohalen marched us through the Baltimore Catechism with his stern and inflexible manner. There wasn't much questioning or quibbling over the standard interpretation of the Faith. We were drilled in a strict, literal reading of the Bible. There was little free discussion of the less credible stories. Did the Garden of Eden truly exist? How could Noah possibly accommodate so many species on his Ark? Was Moses' parting of the Red Sea bona fide history? It was presented as the revealed word of God, transcribed by the Prophets. The Old Testament was a compendium of thrilling events and anecdotes, but the New Testament, especially the Epistles, bogged me down in a morass of numbing theological controversy and nit-picking. Except for the Gospels, of course, the greatest story ever told. Still, there were grave inconsistencies in the four versions of the life of Christ, and I was disturbed by a gnawing doubt: How do we know all these things really happened as they appear in print?

In the four years of biblical study, I remember only once raising my hand to voice an opinion about the scripture. I forget the specific issue, but I can recall nervously trying to get Father Murphy's eye. It must have been a doozy of a question, because the good father looked at me as if I had committed sacrilege. He brushed me aside with a few curt words and a grim look on his cheeky face. And Father Murphy, who taught us for three years, was a *nice* guy!

At home, in apartment 43, I privately celebrated mass in my room, the *St. Joseph's Missal* as my guide. Facing the mirror that sat on Mom's bureau, I recited the prayers and instructions in Latin, playing the parts of priest, altar boy, and faithful in their pews. I had even prepared my inaugural sermon, the one I would deliver at my first Mass, on ordination day. It wouldn't be delivered until I was twenty-five years old, but I was ready. I rehearsed it again and again, a rant of fire and brimstone, reminding my listeners of Jesus' excruciating demise on the Cross, offered as a sacrifice for our sins. It would be a diatribe of pain and guilt.

At Cathedral there was robust political indoctrination as well. In our history and social studies classes, we spent an awful lot of time on J. Edgar Hoover's *Masters of Deceit* and Whittaker Chambers's *Witness*. These books warned about the danger of a communist takeover of America. George Orwell's *Animal Farm*, it was explained to us, was a parable of the kind of totalitarian state we risked if we lost the cold war. The libertarian Ayn Rand was in vogue among the students, and we consumed *Atlas Shrugged* and *The Fountainhead* on our own. Down the street from Cathedral, on 86th and West End Avenue, an organization of Eastern European exiles established "Freedom House," a center of anticommunist propaganda. Their brochures and publications always found their way into the school's cafeteria and library.

No wonder then, that when the presidential election of 1964 came around, I favored Senator Barry Goldwater. I liked his emphasis on individual freedom and his patriotic call to fight communism. He was a dynamic leader, stirring me with his famous saying: "Extremism in the defense of liberty is no vice . . . and moderation in the pursuit of justice is no virtue." In another time he would have been a hero facing a martyrs' end at the Alamo. Goldwater's opponent was Lyndon B. Johnson, who failed to move me. To me, Johnson was just a hack politician. Our president had to be a man of principle and passion.

There were two special friendships I sealed during my high school years. Louie Shapiro, of Ukrainian Jewish descent on his father's side and Venezualan on his mother's, lived around the Block, but he was peripheral to its social life. We knew each other since the sixth grade at Incarnation but didn't really bond until Cathedral. No guy should go through life without at least one nerdy close friend, someone who challenges you intellectually, who couldn't be bothered with sports, who jolts you out of mundane gossip. For me that was Louie, though he would never have accepted that designation. He was a connoisseur of horror movies and loved raw hamburger meat. These are traits that might well suggest an eccentric personality. If he was eccentric, he was not off-putting or arrogant, just a great friend.

I don't know what his mother—widowed by the time I met Louie—was thinking when she convinced him that the priesthood was for him. I spent many nights at his place watching old films, passing on the raw hamburger meat and pretending to work on our boring homework assignments. After finishing his mother made us say the rosary, kneeling on her living room floor. Mom and Pop loved Louie and welcomed him into apartment 43. His thick eyebrows and glasses reminded them of Groucho Marx.

Louie had a sinus condition that interrupted class repeatedly. From the school's hallway, "Big Jim" Byrne, our Latin teacher, was heard to yell:

"Shapiro, *proficere!*" (Shapiro, get out!)

I wasn't much of a participant in classroom discussions, preferring to take notes and reading on my own. At Louie's I would bring up questions and doubts about theology, history, and politics that perplexed me. It was much more interesting than doing our homework.

Bobby Webster, a working-class kid from the Chelsea public housing projects, was my other great companion at Cathedral. He came from an Irish-Greek family that, like Louie's, had great expectations for their priest-to-be son. He had other cousins who were being coached into the religious life, as future clergy and nuns. As in Louie's case, these hopes struck me as off-kilter. Bobby had a sarcastic, cynical wit and a vocabulary steeped in the profane that I wouldn't expect could thrive in the church hierarchy. While everyone parted their hair on the left side, Bobby's was parted on the right. It was his way, apparently, of skewering convention. Something would have to give, sooner or later: the wisecracking jokester or the pretender to the pulpit.

Bobby was simultaneously gifted in the intellectual and athletic realm: a straight-A student in class, and a medal-winner on the race track. I envied that perfect combination. He had light blue eyes and a wiry, muscular frame. He was the only classmate, besides Louie, who knew of my parents' deafness. He found that interesting and eventually got to know my family very well.

Unlike most high schools, at Cathedral parents were not involved with their boys' education; it was understood they were transferring authority over their sons to the Church. Rarely were our families invited to school events, and parent-teacher conferences were unheard of. This was fine by me, because it allowed me to compartmentalize home and school.

I could just imagine a conversation between Pop and Msgr. Cohalen or "Big Jim" Byrne. Pop would have loved it; but with my schoolmates staring at us as I interpreted, I would have been squirming with embarrassment. Thereafter I would be getting weird looks from my friends. At least that's what I thought would happen. So I told my parents very little about what was transpiring on West End Avenue. As was my practice in grammar school, I forged Pop's signature on my report cards and official documents.

There was also a dividing line between my seminarian life and my life around the Block. By day I was attired in white shirt and tie and shiny black shoes, my wavy dark brown hair in a part. In the Heights I switched to a greaser look, hair slicked back with dabs of Brylcreem. As the kids around the Block got older and bigger, pursuing new adventures, I went along, not missing a beat—hanging out at the Bolton, sitting on the rocks next to the gravel field, experimenting with smokes and liquor, and flaunting our mastery of the latest dance steps. If your parents were away, you could throw a secret party—a "set"—dimming the lights with a dark-colored pillow case over the lamps. I tried not to miss those either. That's why, around the Block, they called me the "Hoodlum Priest."

It was during this time that I picked up another best friend around the Block, Salvador Coch Caballero Jr. Sal was one of the tallest Puerto Ricans I had known, about five-ten. He was two years older than I was. Perhaps I saw him as a protector; or maybe I thought hanging with him would get me to grow faster, through osmosis.

The Coch family lived on prime real estate, a second-floor unit in 502 West 177th Street, the building adjacent to the Bolton. With windows actually facing the street, they had a perfect view of everything that happened on the block. Everyone else lived in apartments that were too high, so their parents didn't like them peering out the window, or, like me, they were backdwellers. No one had a better view of the block than Salvador Coch Jr.

Sal and I became fast friends, but not right away. One day I arrived on the block to discover that a segment of 177th Street had been worked on by a municipal maintenance crew. An area of the gutter had been cordoned off with wooden planks to allow newly laid tar to dry. We couldn't resist: some of us picked up sticks that lied around and began puncturing the tar covering. Tar dries pretty quickly so we were unable to inscribe ourselves into history, like we would in a flooring of slowly hardening cement.

Our artistic aspirations frustrated, we turned to more mischievous designs, spooning up droplets of tar on the stick ends and flinging them at each other. This was living dangerously because I would have to face Mom's wrath if I got my clothes stained. In the skirmish that ensued no one was left unscathed by the hailstorm of hydrocarbons.

From his second-floor perch Sal was observing the action and took special delight every time I got splattered with the oily substance. He laughed loudly and seemed to be applauding each time I got hit. This didn't surprise me because we had been rivals for the attentions of Margie Chin, and lately I was losing out. In fact, the year before I had left an anonymous note under his apartment door; the message, carefully etched in block lettering, made a veiled threat to stay away from Margie. Sal's taunting riled me, so I grabbed sticks, dipped them in tar, and started pitching them at his face at the second-floor window.

"Hey man, whad'ya do that for?" he yelled.

"Why you laughing at me?" came my response from the street.

"Who says I'm laughing at you, and so what if I was?"

"Just mind your own business, fool!"

"Look who's talking; you're the fool, look at your shirt!"

A few more long-distance exchanges and the verbal warfare ended. Not long after, we began hanging out. We played handball feverishly and he soon became a regular on our various teams. We also pored over *Sports Illustrated* and the *Sporting News* to catch up on our favorite players. He stayed loyal to the Giants, years after they abandoned the Polo Grounds and moved to San Francisco.

Sal was an infectious optimist, always cracking jokes and coming up with ideas for things to do. My parents were especially fond of him because he was so gregarious and demonstrative. He was one of the regulars at my home and was not at all intimidated by my parents' deafness. He would ask me the signs for words so he could engage in baseball conversations with Pop.

I could tell when Pop was relaxed with a hearing person. With friends he gave off a pleasing hum deep from his throat and, if the conversation touched on something hilarious, he would erupt into a staccato of pinched-throat sounds. These were strange noises to a listener, but Pop had no problem letting go when Sal was around. Sal conversed with my father without descending into caricature or silly pantomime, as even well-intentioned hearing people do.

In no time, I had a privileged view from his second-floor apartment. In the same way that Butchy's family had taken me in, Sal's household became another home for me. And like Butchy, he became an unofficial brother. Sal had a sister, Nilsa, who became another reason to visit Sal's home.

6 Observing and Learning

ONE OF MY DUTIES, as the only hearing person in apartment 43, was to be the official sign-language interpreter. I was dispatched by my father to deal with interlopers from the hearing world who came knocking on our door, such as Mr. Bil the landlord, or Mr. Covello the Prudential Insurance agent, or anyone else wanting to separate our money from us. Pop knew perfectly well why they came and how much was owed them, but he had me as the buffer who could occasionally delay the inevitable. With Mr. Bil, I was Pop's advocate and negotiator, registering complaints about the leaky ceiling and bargaining for more time to pay the rent. I really came in handy, though, when it came to translating the TV.

With Pop, it was baseball. In the early 1960s the New York Mets came on the scene. My father, orphaned by the exodus of the New York Giants, quickly adopted the Mets as his favorite team; he couldn't stomach the arrogant and powerful Yankees. I followed suit and rooted for the newcomers too. In their early years the "Amazins," as they were nicknamed, were amazingly terrible, the doormat of the National League. They proved this by losing more games than any team since the 1800s.

Bill Gallo, sports cartoonist of the *Daily News*, created "Basement Bertha," a lovable caricature of the bumbling Mets. On summer mornings, Pop flipped straight to the sports pages to see Bertha's commentary on the previous day's loss. Laughing, he beckoned me to this side at breakfast, displaying the dumpy lady with the frazzled hair.

"Ahtay," he called out. Then signing, "Look; look at Basement Bertha today!"

We watched the Mets religiously on WOR-TV, Channel 9. At first it was glorious. They fielded a team that included familiar faces like Richie Ashburn, and later, the aging Willie Mays. Casey Stengel was recruited to manage them, the same Casey Stengel who, in his heyday, had commanded the Yankees to so many championships. Now in his seventies and way past his prime, he was a comic figure, arguing heatedly with umpires and boisterously spinning out folk wisdom to the press. After one particularly bad stretch of losses the exasperated Casey wailed, "Can anybody here play this game?" Who in New York City wasn't cheering on these underdogs?

Seated next to me on the sofa, a gray haze lifting from his Lucky Strikes, Pop diligently recorded each game's history. He explained how to keep a personal scorecard, showing me how to register outs, hits, runs batted in, and every conceivable outcome of an at-bat. I watched him update the batting average of his favorite players, working out the long division on the note pad he carried in his shirt pocket. He would check the accuracy of his math in the next day's *Daily News*.

But he needed me to confirm the game's proceedings, since there were no closed captions in those days. There were no on-screen box scores conveniently reminding you of the outs and score. There were no cute miniature diamonds in the corner depicting the runners on base. You had to pay close attention to the savvy analysis of the sportscasters, Ralph

Kiner, Bob Murphy, and Lindsey Nelson, if you wanted to know what was really going on. That was my job.

"How many balls; how many strikes?" "What are they arguing about?" "Why did they call that a hit?" he'd sign, his fingers moving quickly.

Pop needed me to fill in the gaps created by deafness. The true history of that game was not being faithfully transmitted to him by the technology of the day. There were missing pieces that had to be filled in, confusion that had to be dispelled. That's where I came in.

I was similarly helpful in Mom's enjoyment of television. In her case it was the "Million Dollar Movie." Starting at 4:30 PM on weekdays Mom and I watched this program, which showed the same film each day. There were constant interruptions—for her, preparing dinner and for me, doing my homework—so that we rarely saw the whole movie in one sitting. But we knew that, by Friday, we would cover the whole movie. It was in this fashion, movie-viewing on the installment plan, that we got to see old favorites like *The Adventures of Robin Hood*, *Ivanhoe*, and *Mighty Joe Young*.

As vivid as these classics were, inevitably there was a lapse in Mom's grasp of what was going on. So she relied on me to clarify character roles: "Is he a bad man or a good man?" She signed for me to explain plot twists: "Why is she kissing him, if she's supposed to marry the other man?" She wanted me to summarize drawn-out scenes with extended dialogue: "What are they talking about?"

Every so often there were crucial events in the plot that were revealed in the dialogue but not visually represented. For example, if a major character was killed offscreen, Mom wouldn't know unless I was there to explain. Otherwise she was left wondering: "What happened to the woman with the yellow hair?" It was a roundabout method. Nevertheless, by Friday she got the full story down, thanks to my patchwork and the repeats of the "Million Dollar Movie."

The demands on my translating reached a fever pitch in late November of 1963 when I was sixteen years old. I was in school one Friday

morning when the announcement came over the intercom: President
Kennedy was dead in Texas, shot by an assassin. We were stunned. The
Cathedral students were released early and I remember taking the IRT
#1 subway home from 86th Street, scared. When I reached home I told
Mom about the tragedy. She put her hands to her opened mouth and
shook her head noiselessly, tears streaming down her cheeks. We put
on the news to find out what was going on. Soon after, Pop arrived,
and the three of us were glued to the TV.

Like the rest of the country, we stayed riveted to the screen the entire weekend and for weeks after. A stream of images played with our
emotions: the arrest and mysterious murder of the suspected assassin,
the stoic widow, the young boy saluting his father's casket, the people
weeping in the streets. Each new turn of events heightened our anguish,
frustration, and feeling of impotence.

Pop quizzed me during each news broadcast, wanting me to explain
the various conspiracy theories being floated. "Why are they showing the pictures of Fidel Castro? And Khrushchev?" Before long he
was asking for *my* opinion. This was taking me a step beyond my
usual role as a passive and objective interpreter of televised entertainment. Now he was urging me to venture some of my own views of
important matters.

What did I know? All I could tell him was what was being said
on TV, at school, and on the Block. It wasn't a very sophisticated
understanding of current events, but what this teenager was picking up, was certainly more reliable than what Pop had access to in
the Deaf world.

After JFK's assassination, I became even more the conduit of facts
and analysis between the hearing world and my parents. From then
on, during the unrelenting barrage of crises and conflict that was the
sixties—the Civil Rights movement, the Vietnam War protests, the
urban rebellions, the assassinations of Martin Luther King Jr. and
Robert F. Kennedy, the Democratic Convention in Chicago—I kept
Mom and Pop informed.

My sign language repertoire, given me by Pop and consisting of only a few hundred symbols, was quickly outpaced by daily accretions of English words from the media and school. In translating TV I kept having to approximate the meanings of these new terms with the fixed set of symbols Pop had given me. It did no good to resort to fingerspelling, because letters strung together were meaningless if there wasn't already some symbol in sign language to which I could refer as a related concept.

If I translated "Jim Crow" literally, using the signs for "Jim" and "Black Bird," it meant nothing to Pop. Finger spelling "Jim Crow" was more absurd. I had learned what it referred to in my readings, and simply figured out a way to describe it to Pop using a combination of signs that conveyed the idea of ongoing discrimination practiced against blacks and condoned by the government. At the time, I didn't know the origin of the term, so I couldn't answer Pop's logical question, "Where does the word Jim Crow come from? Is Jim Crow a man?"

Pop often followed up these questions of fact by asking what I believed about the big issues of the day. Here I was on even shakier grounds. One thing was translating strange new words into sign language; it was another to take a stand on controversies that were dividing the country. It was through many long conversations with Pop and other family members that my social and political views evolved.

Then there was Mom's reaction to all of this. First she would nod her head in supposed acknowledgment of everything I was saying. Then ask me to repeat it. Then verify with Pop that what I said was true. Not until Pop confirmed the veracity of my explanation was she satisfied. Occasionally, though, it was Mom who asked the most probing question, while we were perched in front of our black-and-white Zenith with its V-shaped antennas on top. For example, at the time of JFK's killing, Mom tread where Pop would not. Why, she asked, did God allow them to kill a Catholic President?

My family's social life was centered on the Puerto Rican Society for the Catholic Deaf (PRSCD). For years after coming to New York, my father maintained a long-distance membership in an organization for the deaf based in San Juan, which he had co-founded with his boyhood friend Félix de Jesús. By the late 1950s he decided it was time for the Puerto Ricans in New York to form their own group. Along with his sisters Isaura (Tata) and Olga, and Olga's husband Seymour, they promoted the idea among their friends. In 1959 they approached the Archdiocese of New York for recognition as an autonomous group within the National Catholic Deaf Association.

At the time the Catholic Church in New York City had a few priests who ministered to the deaf. Among them were Monsignor Walter D'Arcy and Father James Lynch, who were well known to the Puerto Ricans. Fluent communicators both, they gave Mass in sign language and performed the sacraments for all the deaf Hispanics throughout the city. Fr. Lynch presided over all the weddings in my family, including my parents'. He baptized me and most of my cousins. Msgr. D'Arcy agreed to serve as chaplain to the PRSCD.

My father was elected president, and my Uncle Seymour was selected as treasurer. Isaura Quiñones became the first secretary. The vice president was William Fischbach, who was born on the Puerto Rican island of Vieques and was a friend of my father. Other early members were Celia Izaguirre, Rhadamés Torruellas, Juana Falú Shannon, and Oliverio Polanco.

Some fifty individuals joined the association in the first year. For their meetings the Archdiocese lent them the use of an office space on 29½ East 50th Street, in Rockefeller Center. Many times did we take the A train downtown, switching over at 59th Street to the D for one stop.

A Constitution was adopted defining the objectives of the group, which were to promote "the voluntary moral, physical, industrial, and philanthropic benefits and progress of the Catholic deaf; the spread of literature having special reference to the deaf; to be of assistance to its members in time of sickness, disability and death, and to provide a place or places for the carrying on and furtherance of such objectives." Every other Friday evening, the PRSCD met at 50th Street. There they shared news about their friends and acquaintances, planned social activities, collected dues and held raffles for the Benefit Fund, and offered refreshments and entertainment. Since quite a few of deaf Puerto Ricans lived in isolation and none of them had telephones, the meetings became the only way to keep in touch with each other.

These Fridays were a rare occasion to be their normal selves, without the gawking eyes from the hearing world. Often my cousins Jimmy and Mary would be present along with the children of other deaf families. Besides the kids, the only hearing persons were Msgr. Darcy or Father Lynch, who would sometimes stop by. We kids had our own reasons for enjoying the meetings. We ran up and down the back stairway escaping to other floors that had been abandoned for the evening. Our only witness was the old Irishman who operated the elevator. He was a kindly man who monitored our harmless adventures without betraying us to the unsuspecting elders. Our parents were free and had no need of the hearing here, so we were relieved of translation duty. Given the choice of conversing among themselves and being dependent on us to communicate with others, they always preferred the former.

Once the business portion of the meeting ended, the adults turned to socializing and entertainment. Bingo was ideal because it didn't rely on voices. Standing in front of the crowd, someone signed the letter-number combinations in succession until a winner was determined. As in the non-Deaf world, there were always participants who didn't catch the correct "pronunciation" and insisted, sometimes belligerently, on having the combination repeated. At the Puerto Rican Society for the Catholic Deaf, this happened not once, but *every* time a combination was read. This irritated the others to no end, having to slow down the action for the benefit of the usual stragglers.

Quite often the Society arranged to have a projector brought in for a film showing. Even though the movies were captioned, the adults preferred action-packed Westerns and comedies to dramas. The latter were difficult to follow for the less literate deaf and for those who were more fluent in Spanish than English. There was nothing too risqué, though, since the films were provided by the Church. Unlike the others, Pop didn't care for slapstick. He said the "dummy" roles played by the likes of the Three Stooges reminded him of hearing people making fun of the deaf. He disliked the films of Laurel and Hardy, Abbott and Costello, and Red Skelton. His tastes weren't shared by the others, though; they loved the physical comedy of these performers.

We learned the sign names of famous people. Kirk Douglas was the index finger to the chin, representing his famous dimple. There was no confusion when someone finger-spelled "M-M," the blonde bombshell, or "J-F-K," the young president.

When Msgr. D'Arcy or Fr. Lynch came by they were available to "see" confessions. Unlike for hearing Catholics there was no anonymity for deaf sinners. The priest knew the penitent's identity. He was privy to the failures and foibles of every deaf person. That was too much of a privilege for Mom to concede to the clergy. By the time I was in my mid-teens she had stopped sharing her most private thoughts and errors with those men in black.

The meetings served as my window into the wider Deaf world, outside the immediate family. I watched intently as they went about their activities, carefully noting new signs. At home I interrogated Pop on unfamiliar words and added them to my sign vocabulary.

With the permanent silences in my home, Satan had virtual free reign. I could never be at rest, so preoccupied was I with the constant struggles of flesh. No teenager should have to go through that. "An idle mind is the devil's workshop." So what? I wasn't doing anyone harm. You're standing there innocently and a woman casually brushes against you as she leaves the subway car. You remember a suggestive scene in the film *Splendor in the Grass*. You come across an erotic passage, like a seduction in Kathleen Winsor's novel *Forever Amber*. And that incredibly fine girl that just moved around the Block: you wonder how it would be slow dancing "You Really Got a Hold on Me" with her. Was I supposed to repress my imagination as it raced along?

So solemnly did I absorb the strictures of Church theology that each foray into impure thought and self-abuse submerged me into a state of depression; moreover, each violation disqualified me from continuing on the path to the priesthood. I flashed back to a younger me, when sweet Titi Mariamelia prepared me for Confirmation. We reviewed the Catechism and she quizzed me on the theological tenets that an eight-year-old boy should know. The book catalogued the various sins using drawings of milk bottles. We come into the world with original sin (black milk in the bottle). Baptism into the Church cleanses us and we enter a state of purity (white milk). Venial infractions such as lying and envy throw us off the path of morality (black speckles). Mortal sins such as violence and blasphemy put us in jeopardy of eternal damnation (black milk). The sacrament of Confession is the means by which we purify ourselves again (white milk).

Now, years later, a minor seminarian and well past puberty, I was subjected to constant tests of worthiness. The days and months were absorbed in a conflict of the flesh between prolonged tension and glorious relief. The moral conscious became a battlefield involving frequent cycles of sinfulness-forgiveness-penance-purification. Forgiveness and penance were doled out in the confession booth. Purification was ratified at the Communion rail. Impure thoughts, we were told, counted as venial sins; self-abuse was a mortal sin.

Sunday mornings at Incarnation became a public square in which the moral status of parishioners was on display for all. If you didn't rise to take the Host, I reasoned, you were walking around with mortal sin on your soul. So literally did I buy into the theology that I was driven to bouts of shame and paranoia. If something happened to me, the sinner incapable of abstinence, before I made it to the confession booth next Saturday—if I were killed by an onrushing car—would I go straight to hell? I never asked this question of my religious advisers. But neither did any of my confessors, who must have recognized the voice of a nervous young boy, ever console me with a few words: don't worry young man, you can lighten up; you're okay.

We validated the theory of attracting opposites: Nilsa, the dark-haired, dark-eyed cutie with brown skin and a longish face and thin nose; me the light-skinned stocky guy with an oval face and a broad nose. Her elongated body placed her as the tallest of the girls in our crowd. As our group proceeded along the teen years, the pairing-off process intensified. As if following the laws of evolution—urban youth subjected to the forces of competition, trial and error, and survival of the fittest—most individuals were sorted out into couples.

Nilsa was Sal's sister, the same Sal who was one of my best friends and whose family had the best real estate on the Block. Theirs was the apartment with the great second-floor view of 177th Street and which served as "party central" to our crowd. Nilsa's father, Salvador, was quite elderly and had been a musician in his younger days. He played the clarinet with Latin and swing bands, including the Joe Valle Orchestra, and was an official in the Puerto Rican musicians' union. Her mother, Carmen, worked as a pantry girl at Roosevelt Hospital. In the earlier years, as Sal and I prepared the line-ups for the baseball games and game plans for football, I often went to his apartment. Then, Nilsa was the baby sister and nuisance who interrupted our deep thought and strategizing. Gradually the two years in age that differentiated us seemed less and less substantial. By the time I hit seventeen, in my senior year at Cathedral, the two years' gap was meaningless.

Like other girls around the Block, Nilsa attended Cathedral High School. (This was a Catholic girls' school, unrelated to the preparatory seminary I attended that was also called Cathedral.) The Cathedral girls wore a blue-and-gray uniform over a white blouse, along with black patent leather shoes. They were supposed to follow strict guidelines regarding the length of the skirt: no higher than half the distance between knee and shoe. But to compete successfully against the public school girls, they would roll up the skirts several inches before getting on the subway home. Neither did they concede on the foul-language front: those prim and proper Catholic school girls could curse with the best of them.

In retrospect, my family was being awfully polite. Or were they just too busy to notice? When I started going steady with Nilsa, no one exposed the glaring contradiction in my life: why was Andy Torres, a minor seminarian at Cathedral College High, holding hands and going out on dates with Nilsa Coch Caballero? Nilsa and I had heard somewhere that a particularly scorching corner of Hell was reserved for women who enticed young men away from the priesthood. I promised her I would defend her on Judgment Day. I would assume responsibility for withdrawing from the path to the priesthood, a decision I made in my senior year of high school. When all was said and done, I wanted to have a normal life.

The decision to leave Cathedral, thereby foregoing a life in the priesthood, returned me to the same challenge I faced in the eighth grade: how to pursue the next level of education? I once again threw myself into the hunt for an appropriate place to land. Unfortunately, by my junior year, when I began doubting the viability of continuing in Cathedral beyond high school, I had run out of steam academically, and my grades showed it. Beginning my senior year I was a struggling B student, and my scores on the tests for college admission didn't uncover any special qualities. Andy Torres was basically in the middle of the college-going pack.

Obviously I didn't know what I was doing, because my next step was to go for the elites. I applied to Columbia, NYU, City College, and Syracuse—to the *engineering* schools. This brilliant maneuver was my way of following in Bobby Webster's footsteps. He too was leaving Cathedral and had applied to several engineering schools. The difference was that Bobby was a legitimate braniac, the winner of a New York State Regents scholarship. His smarts won Bobby an early admission ticket to Manhattan College Engineering School, one of the best in the region.

Needless to say the elites didn't think that I, with my B average, could succeed within their hallowed halls. I received polite rejection letters from all four schools; the only place to accept me was Bronx Community College. I thought I could do better. But what school would offer me a spot? Enter Monsignor Edward J. Waterson, pastor of Incarnation Parish. Monsignor was a big, bulky man with a face that seemed carved out of granite, so tough and craggy was his look. His rimless glasses offset the chiseled features. In his sixties and overseeing Incarnation as a final assignment before retiring, he had once served as rector of Cathedral College High. Occasionally I assisted as his altar boy at Sunday Mass, but we didn't talk much. The red trimmings on his collar and buttons, his rather serious demeanor, and official bearing made him unapproachable to me.

My last semester at Cathedral found me in limbo. There was no formal system for counseling graduating seniors who were leaving the seminary. Somehow Waterson learned that one of his flock was without academic guidance and he made it known I should call upon him. Soon I was in his office in the Incarnation Rectory, on St. Nicholas Avenue and 175th Street, describing my last-resort plan to enroll at Bronx Community College. He picked up his phone, placed a few calls, and told me to return the next week. "Let's see what we can do, Andrew. You should be going to a better school. You received an excellent education at Cathedral."

Back in his office, I received the good news.

"Manhattan College will take you, Andrew. I would have preferred they admit you into Liberal Arts, but it's too late. They'll enroll you in the Business School, which I recommend you try."

Manhattan College, located in the Riverdale section of the Bronx, was operated by the Christian Brothers, the order that taught the boys of Incarnation. It was where Bobby Webster would be studying mechanical engineering. Waterson had pulled some strings to find me a new academic home, perhaps even fearing that otherwise I would be a lost soul as a denizen of public higher education. A final meeting a month later became the occasion for a discussion about career plans.

"Do you know what you want to do after college, Andrew?"

"No, not really."

"Well, you're a bright young man. You might think about going into law, or government, even. The Spanish people are growing in the city and will need young men like you in the future. Keep that in mind."

Then, something I was uncomfortable mentioning but couldn't ignore.

"Monsignor, about the money I owe the Church. I promise I will pay it back."

"What do you mean? What money?"

"Well, the Church paid for my years at Cathedral High School."

"Oh, no, Andrew. Don't worry. You don't owe anybody anything."

I was glad be released from any pecuniary obligation to the Church. But there was another concern making the rounds within my conscience. Would my decision no longer to consecrate my life in service to God revive my parents' hopes that I would stay with them for the long haul? Would Pop be emboldened to propose a new plan for us to stay together forever? I don't think I was reading too much into his face after describing my luck in getting admitted to Manhattan College.

"So, Ahtay, what do you think? Since you are not going to be a priest, maybe we can still move to a house in Queens, like I used to say. Maybe after a few years in college we can try to buy a home."

He didn't put together the signs to say it in so many way words, but his eyes said as much. Indeed if he had asked me, I would have had to deflect his idea somehow.

"I don't know, Pop, I don't know."

Since adolescence I had been privately grappling with the big, multi-part question: Is it okay to break away from Mom and Pop; and if it's okay, when is the right time to make my move; and how do I pull it off?

After a semester, I knew I wanted to be like her. Dr. Emily Sun was a native of China, and she arrived at Manhattan College in 1964, the same year I did. She was a freshly minted PhD from the University of Michigan. Like Mom, she was short, a sub-five-footer. But the similarities ended there, for although Professor Sun was petite, she was supremely self-confident. Though the students—all male—towered above her and occasionally complained about her accent, she never ceded control of the classroom.

How did this thirty-ish woman of slight physique and outsider status succeed in quelling the potential uprising in her brood? By the awesome power of her intellect and artful pedagogy. Dr. Sun was a master of economics and astonished us with her grasp of the subject. At the blackboard the perfectly lettered formulas and neatly drawn graphs flowed easily from her chalk, supplemented with clear explanations and examples drawn from the real world. None of our questions stumped her.

From the beginning she won our begrudging respect; we realized there was no point in disrupting her performance. You either paid attention or zoned yourself out, though daydreaming would cost you at the next weekly quiz. Silly behavior would only embarrass you before your fellow classmates.

It wasn't just Dr. Sun's delivery that made economics appealing to me. In her lectures, Professor Sun showed how each element of the economy is dependent on each other for the overall benefit of society. Firms and consumers interact to produce the appropriate level of goods and services for society. The forces of supply and demand—inherent in all societies throughout history—guarantee that the best possible results are achieved: lowest prices for consumer products, jobs for everyone, and businesses that operate efficiently. The drives for profit and individual material gain ensure that societies can make the best use of their human and natural resources. She made it all sound so scientific and orderly. (Years later I would become adept at critiquing this unreal vision of the world.)

By the end of Economics 101, I was a convert to the Queen of the Social Sciences, believing it to contain the secret to the ways of the world, at least in the material dimension. I also hoped it would serve as a manual for making lots of money. But my studies in economics were too abstract to be of practical help in dealing with my first challenge as a freshman: how the hell to pay for tuition. Msgr. Waterson had been kind enough to press some levers for me with Manhattan's admissions office. But from there on, I was on my own. Bobby Webster came to the rescue, lending me fifteen hundred dollars with no interest. He was again a financial lifeline when a year later he got me a job working where he worked, at the Daitch Shopwell supermarket in his neighborhood. Piecing together these modest revenue streams, later receiving governmental support for work-study jobs on campus, and all the time benefiting from free room and board at apartment 43, I was able to finance my college education.

My Spanish instructor at Manhattan College was Professor Dominick Pucino, a charming Italian-American who fitted my image of the Renaissance man. Besides Spanish, he taught Italian and Portuguese. In general he was jovial and pleasant, interspersing his lectures with comic asides and lively anecdotes. But there was a nasty streak in him too.

This I discovered as soon as he realized my Spanish didn't meet his standards. He saw my name, asked about my background, and decided he could spice up his lectures at my expense.

"Now, class," he exhorted one day, "please don't discriminate against the *s, la letra ese.* Attach it to your plurals and, for God's sake, respect it enough to enunciate clearly when it appears in the middle of a word, as in the verb *estar.* For "we are": *estamos.* Say *est-a-mos,* and say it proudly! Not like Señor Torres, when he says, *eh-ta-mo.* With a name like that, he should know better, no?" On several prior occasions he had made me the butt of his caustic humor.

Often people had misconstrued the real reason behind my not speaking Spanish fluently. How often I had to explain: ". . . well yes, I come from a Puerto Rican family, but my parents are deaf and don't speak at all, and my first language is sign language; and so when we get together with my extended family, I'm exposed to Spanish, but out in the streets when I'm with my friends, we speak English because that's what most people speak; and not only that, but lots of Puerto Rican kids I know don't speak too much Spanish anyway, because they want to just fit into their schools, and . . ." Etc., etc., etc.

Once, I had applied for a job at a supermarket in East Harlem. The manager, who was looking for a bilingual cashier, chided me for not knowing Spanish. Another time, the mother of a Puerto Rican girl I had taken out on a date, queried me in broken English about my language deficiency. As I described my situation, their faces changed. There was no standard reaction. So I would never know what kind of response my explanation would lead to. Inevitably, the conversation took a drastically different turn and tone.

"Oh, I see; I'm sorry for you." (I think: I'm not asking for pity.)

"I'm sorry if I offended you." (I think: Apology accepted.)

"I feel so embarrassed." (I think: Now *I'm* feeling sorry.)

"So, why would that stop you from learning Spanish?" (I think: Don't you know anything about languages, idiot?)

"Whoa! You're lucky *you* didn't turn out deaf." (I think: Yeah, thanks for reminding me.)

"Can you show me some signs?" (I think: Well, maybe later; if it turns out I like you.)

"Does that mean *your* children might come out deaf?" (I think: Do I really have to say, for the umpteenth time, "I don't know"?)

"Don't be offended, but that's almost funny; I can't believe your parents are deaf." (I think: Do you see something about me that I don't? What is it about my having deaf parents that seems comical to you?)

By my late teen years, I was exhausted from having to account for my poor fluency in Spanish. I developed a stock reply: a slight acknowledging grin and a nodding of the head.

Then there was Professor Pucino, whose job was to enthrall us with the elegant beauty of Spanish literature, taking cheap shots at me. The day of his *eh-ta-mo* remark I smoldered with repressed anger, and struggled for a response. But quick repartee has never been my strength, having conditioned myself from early years to weigh responses carefully before blurting out. How I envy those who can retaliate with the sharply delivered response!

I ignored him and sat as if nothing had happened. This was a defining moment for me, for I decided from then on to conceal my native identity as a child of Deaf culture. Was it smart to shut down this aspect of my being? And shouldn't I have used the moment to educate him about the world of the non-hearing?

7

Family Truths

DURING MY FRESHMAN year at Manhattan College, in the winter of 1965, my grandmother Ita became gravely ill. Her last week was spent at Columbia Presbyterian Hospital. A short time later, my father's sister Titi Blanca asked me if I could babysit her daughter Edna on Wednesday evenings. Blanca's husband Carlos worked nights at Metropolitan Hospital, and she needed someone to watch over the four-year-old girl while she attended meetings of the *Cursillistas* (Spanish-language prayer groups) at Incarnation Church. Before long I regularly frequented the familiar second-story apartment at 2372 Amsterdam. Now, as I walked through the door, there was no Ita to seek *bendición* from.

Almost as if to fill the vacuum left by her, I became possessed by a need to learn every detail of my family's history. At the time I was a sophomore at Manhattan College, where I was receiving a business education, majoring in economics. Nowhere was Puerto Rican or Latin

American culture being discussed. I decided to supplement my college curriculum with tutorials from Titi Blanca.

I described to Titi Blanca my recollections of Ita: the obligatory petitioning of *bendición* each time I entered the apartment; the sadness on her face; how she greeted me always with a firm grasp of the wrist and a plaintive sigh, complaining how skinny I was, *"muchacho, que flaco tu estás"*; the Sunday afternoons alone with her at the kitchen table, watching her peel the orange for me; her exhortations that I be the dutiful and respectful son.

Each visit I rained questions on my aunt. How did my grandparents meet? What did Abuelo do for a living? What was it like growing up in Puerto Rico? What was it like having a deaf brother and deaf sisters? How did we become such a religious family, so tied to the Catholic Church? Why the move to New York? Those first years in Washington Heights, back in the 1940s, what were they like?

The storyteller in my aunt was unleashed. She transported me to turn-of-the-century rural San Germán, on the western coast of Puerto Rico, describing the farm on which the Quiñones family lived. Andrés Quiñones was Ita's father, married to Isabel Ramos. Widowed, he married Isabel's sister, Ramona. From both, he fathered seven children, all girls. Ita, the second born, was the natural leader of the children of Andrés Quiñones. She was only seventeen when she married my grandfather, Ramón "Moncho" Torres, who had worked on the Quiñones farm.

Abuelo was almost twice Ita's age, and had a reputation for being *mujeriego*, a ladies' man. But as soon as my grandfather settled down with Ita, Blanca said, he became a family man. Then came the problems: one after another, their children were born deaf; four of the first five. And there were the financial difficulties. Abuelo had no special skills to speak of; he hired himself out as a field laborer, and worked in central San Germán at various odd jobs and selling *piraguas,* fruit-flavored ice cones. Making matters worse, by the time he was in his mid-forties Ramón was suffering from a weak heart and declining vision.

Blanca said that the money problems started even earlier when the Quiñones family savings—a *tesoro* containing cash, gold, and jewelry and that had been buried by Andrés the patriarch—was inadvertently passed to a neighbor who had purchased the land. The neighbor knew somehow that Andrés had hidden the *tesoro* without telling his daughters of its whereabouts. Andrés died suddenly before revealing to his girls the secret burial ground's location. Ita and her sisters suspected that the neighbor had in effect swindled them but could never prove this. There just seemed to be no escaping from the constant worrying and fear. Every day was a struggle.

Ita took things into her own hands at this point. She heard of a special school for deaf children in Santurce and got her children enrolled. St. Gabriel's was run by the Sisters of Mercy, an American order of nuns, and was the only place in all of Puerto Rico where deaf children could get an education. She made sure the four deaf kids got as much schooling as possible. The nuns taught in sign language and also oral Spanish. Ita even convinced the nuns to send her son Andrés on a scholarship to the United States for high school. This is how my father ended up at St. Rita School for the Deaf in Cincinnati, Ohio, of all places, as the first one in the family to touch North American soil.

The next big step was the move to New York City. This was something I really wanted to know about. All through my school years, even into college, I learned that America was the land of immigrants, Germans, Irish, Jews, Italians, and Greeks. Yet never was there mention of my people, the Puerto Ricans. Tita Blanca described those first years of the Torres immigrants, back in the 1940s. How the family came in successive waves, and reunited in Washington Heights, on Amsterdam Avenue. The jobs in the garment industry, the first visits to Incarnation church, attending classes at JHS 115 and George Washington High School, family gatherings at Highbridge Park near the Water Tower.

It didn't help that Ita herself never learned sign language, and that ignorant attitudes toward deaf people were so prevalent. But Blanca herself didn't care about the stares and comments in the street. I knew she wasn't exaggerating to impress me. Often I would see Pop signing with his sister after Sunday Mass at Incarnation. He loved it, drawing the attention of the churchgoers, because everybody at Incarnation knew my aunt Blanca, who was also the school secretary. There was always a little crowd observing them as they talked.

As I listened to her stories, I marveled with pride at how united my family was. How my grandmother was able to keep everyone together; how Mariamelia and Blanca, the hearing sisters, had carried the burden of interpreting for their older siblings.

Compared to Puerto Rico, life was easier in New York. It wasn't such a struggle just getting by every day, worrying about having enough to feed everyone and take care of my grandfather Ramón's health and being fearful about the deaf kids' future. But it was also more complicated: learning a new language, dealing with different kinds of people, figuring out how to fit in the new culture.

The stories convinced me of two things: that Ita was an incredible woman who had willed her family out of poverty into a better situation; and that *I* was a Puerto Rican, and had plenty of reasons to be proud of it.

By no means was it Blanca's intention to foment cultural nationalism in her adoring nephew. Her loyalty to family and homeland was secondary to her religious faith. She was not a follower of Puerto Rican history or American politics. She liked John F. Kennedy for his Catholicism, not his Liberalism. However, the unintended effect of Titi Blanca's tales was to induce pride of origin in me.

I lacked a similar grasp of the story of my Ayala ancestors, of their origins in Las Piedras, Puerto Rico, and the events that led them to settle in New York City. Until later in life, I didn't have close personal ties with any of my Ayala elders who could tell me about my family origins. Mom's account of her adventures with the cows, cats, and horses on the farm were a joy to little Andy, but they weren't enough. I had to wait until adulthood, conversing with Mom and her siblings, to begin assembling the full Ayala story, and to compare the two lineages that produced me.

My grandparents Catalino and Eufrasia, like many rural families, must have believed in the strength-in-numbers path to social betterment. The Ayalas of Las Piedras were a veritable *campesino* army of fifteen offspring, not including the three that didn't survive infancy.

The piece of earth occupied by the Ayala family covered seventeen *cuerdas* of hilly terrain in Puerto Rico's southeastern region. This rocky landscape gave the area its name: *Las Piedras* (The Stones). In the first decades of the twentieth century you didn't have easy entry or exit from the *campo* of Las Piedras, which lacked gravel paths and paved roads, much less a highway.

A wooden farmhouse was home to Don Catalino's family. A thatched roof, made from palm leaves, protected them from the blazing sun and the occasional heavy winds during the storm season. Inside, the rectangular structure was partitioned off into two areas, a kitchen and an open area that served as family room and bedroom. Hanging in the middle of the open area was a hammock, a resting nook for the patriarch.

The Ayalas scratched out a subsistence living from the earth. They grew bananas, plantains, and other vegetables for themselves and cultivated tobacco for the market. They had a few chickens and a cow.

Mom, born in 1922, was the last of the girls. Already several waves of the fifteen children had lived on the family farm and gone off to start families nearby. Growing up my mother thought there were only three people in the world like her: her older sisters, Pancha, Diosa, and Carmela. The four sisters comprised the Ayala *mudas*, the girls born deaf.

Mom envied the others who could talk to each other so easily with their voices. The *mudas* "listened" by lipreading the mouth movements of their hearing brothers and sisters. They "talked" with their hands. If a stranger addressed them they pointed to their throat and mimicked the yelp of the cow, "mooo." That was supposed to mean *mudo*, mute.

Worse still, Mom couldn't get educated those early years in Las Piedras because there were no public schools for the deaf in Puerto Rico. (The Ayalas didn't know about St. Gabriel's School in Santurce where the Torres *mudos* went, and they were Protestants, anyway.) Every day she noticed her brothers going off for a few hours, returning in the afternoon. They must be doing something important, Mom thought, and it wasn't fair that she couldn't go too. Once when she was about nine she insisted that she accompany her younger brother Chelo to school. Entering the place she was amazed to see so many children sitting attentively in wooden chairs. She had never seen anything like this: A lady in front of the classroom and the respectful children penciling entries onto sheets of paper. One student was called up front by the lady and vocalized something to everyone, and the audience recited something back in unison. It was a blur of sights and sounds to her, but Mom found this exciting and, more than anything, it seemed important! She realized at this moment that she had been left out of something big. Like her older deaf sisters, she never attended school in Puerto Rico.

By the early 1930s Puerto Rico was catching the brunt of the Great Depression that was ravaging the United States. They hung on as long as they could but after years of faltering fortunes, the Ayalas decided to uproot themselves and try their chances *"en el Norte,"* where some of the older children had already moved.

Mom had a vivid recollection of those final days in Las Piedras. For the children, the excitement was overlaid with mystery. Having spent all of their young lives in the fields of Las Piedras they had no idea what the move meant for them. Yet they quickly sensed from the animated talk of the visitors who came to bid farewell that something important was happening.

As the day of exodus neared Mom asked about Peligro, her dog, whom she assumed would voyage with them. My grandmother Eufrasia explained, to her daughter's dismay, that it was not practical to bring him along on the seven-day boat ride. And besides, he wouldn't survive the cold of the North. Peligro would have to stay behind. The news drove Mom into bitter weeping as she realized she would lose her favorite companion.

Leading up to the big day, according to Mom, Peligro seemed to sense the drama unfolding. He must have picked up something from the air, dense with agitation and gloom, excitement and fear. The *jíbaros* (peasants) were on the move, but their fearless protector, (whose name in English was "Danger," as if a warning to strangers) was not to be part of the plan. The canine trailed the group of eight as they trekked the hills toward the main road. There they would rendezvous with the bus taking them to San Juan, capital and port city. As the bus pulled away Mom could see Peligro's diminishing figure through the window until he finally vanished from view. Ayala family lore (later recounted to me by various *tíos* and *tías*) relates that Peligro died just weeks after their departure.

In 1937 Catalino and Eufrasia left by boat for New York City, with their children in tow. Among the six Ayala children who settled in El Barrio, in a five-story walk-up on Madison Avenue and 104th Street, were the four *mudas*.

Mom held a special memory of one occasion shortly after the family arrived. Carmela had returned from the bodega and described seeing several young people in the store who were talking with their hands. She noticed that the signs were much more elaborate than the ones she used. Carmela approached the group and introduced herself to the deaf kids. After a few awkward moments of trying to understand each other, she deciphered that they wanted to know why she didn't talk the way they did.

Carmela explained that she had just come from Puerto Rico where she did not attend school. That's strange, they countered, because that's where they were from and that's where they learned to sign, in a school in Santurce run by nuns.

The *mudas* were in shock when Carmela described the encounter. Soon after, Pancha confirmed the discovery when she later met the same girls. Of the four *mudas* Pancha was the oldest and most upset, realizing that others had learned to speak "pretty" words while she was confined to loud vocalizing, lipreading, and a few hand movements.

Mom was there that day in the Ayala living room when Pancha exploded at her parents. It was an outburst releasing years of frustration, a violent moment of anger and weeping. To see her lashing out at the elders like that—arms flying, fist crashing down on the sofa, unintelligible wailing—was an unforgettable scene. Never had Mom seen anyone challenge the *viejos* like that. And she wondered quietly, why didn't her parents send the *mudas* to the school run by the nuns?

Don Catalino was astonished at Pancha's outburst. His still, somber face recognized the daughter's deep resentment, but there was nothing he could say or do to change what had happened those years back in Las Piedras. As for Pancha, in her early twenties, it was too late for her to make up for lost time, to attain the schooling her new friends had.

Over the years, these and other recollections passed on to me by Mom and her siblings helped me understand how the Ayalas coped with disability in their midst.

The many hours of conversation with Titi Blanca filled in gaps. I had always encouraged my parents' storytelling, and observed the chatter of my relatives, deaf and hearing. Gradually, what was but a hazy vision came into focus as I acquired new information and new perspective.

Within my father's family, there were two reasons for the extraordinary level of interaction between the deaf and hearing members. First was the fact that four of the first five children were born deaf. As the next group of Torres children came along, all of whom were hearing, the elder deaf siblings were already in a position of authority. Titi Olga, who was born fifth and who was the third deaf child born, took on the role of the family teacher, educating everyone in signed English, which she was learning at St. Gabriel's.

What made this transmission of language possible was Titi Olga's seniority vis-à-vis the hearing siblings, and the authority vested in her by my grandparents, who instructed the hearing children to accept Olga as their teacher. Moncho and Ita needed their hearing children to serve as interpreters within the household. In my experience with deaf families, I have never come across a case where hearing persons learned sign language from a deaf sibling who was *younger.* In the family, a hearing person who learns signs is implicitly accepting the role of interpreter and advocate. It's unusual to observe an older brother or sister readily accepting this responsibility for a younger sibling.

Once the family was settled in New York, Titi Olga's role as teacher extended to the *children* of her hearing sisters as well. My cousins Edwin, Nereida, Shirley, and Edna all learned sign from their Titi Olga. My cousins Aidita, Blanca, and Miguel Jr.—the children of Miguel, who was the only Torres to remain in Puerto Rico—were all born and raised in Puerto Rico and never had access to sign language.

Another reason why the Torres deaf and hearing kin achieved a remarkable level of integration had to do with the dominance of women. Of the eight surviving children only two were male. The six sisters, hearing and deaf, were an extremely tight unit, differences in age and personality notwithstanding. They spent a lot of time together at home, in Puerto Rico and New York. And since the deaf girls were older, they were not subordinated to the hearing ones, which in some families can lead to semi-servitude and resentment.

The two brothers, Andrés Ismael and Miguel, were separated by more than a decade and experienced childhood very differently. They were thoroughly part of the Torres household but not as involved in the inner dynamics of family communication and relationships. The men were expected to make their mark in the outside world. Most of the women left the world of paid work once they had their first child. It was the Torres women who ensured the integration of hearing and deaf members into a whole, transmitting the language even to the children of hearing siblings. My cousins, all of whom are hearing, were each expected to learn sign language, whether their parents were deaf or not.

Compared to most deaf people I knew, the Torres deaf were Ivy Leaguers; and none of my deaf relatives even received a high school diploma. Beyond the Puerto Rican enclave in New York, most deaf children in America could get a decent education, if their families could afford a private school or if they attended a state residential school. But even then, you couldn't say that these students were getting the same schooling as hearing children. Studies conducted during the 1970s revealed, for example, that the average deaf high school graduate was reading only at a fourth-grade level.

Unlike the Torres deaf, the Ayala *mudas* never attended schools for the deaf in their childhood. Not until they arrived in New York did Mom and her sisters learn sign language or even the ABCs of the manual alphabet. Even then, for the older ones, like Pancha and Diosa, it was too late and they never really acquired functional literacy in the official sign language. They spoke a version of home signs in English and Spanish.

Interacting with my deaf relatives and the many deaf friends who visited our home I noticed other fascinating aspects of Deaf life. Among the deaf I grew up with, I noticed a subtle difference in status depending on the *cause* of hearing loss. The ones who became deaf through an accident (a mishap during infancy, for example) or illness (meningitis) were perceived as "superior" because they, at least, were *born* hearing. If deafness came later in childhood, they already had experience in the hearing world. They could enunciate more clearly and probably lipread well. This allowed them to dominate conversation among the deaf, and enabled more fluid interaction with the hearing world, advantages that enhanced their social status within the Deaf community.

Hereditary deafness, on the other hand, carried the stigma of birth defect and was perceived—even among the deaf themselves—as an added deficiency. It could even affect perceptions of their hearing children. Prospective in-laws fear marrying their child to someone thought to carry a hereditary flaw. I recall several instances of being interrogated by a date's mother, chagrined by her pointed interest in the origins of my parents' disability.

Among those born deaf, it was not uncommon to deny the congenital origins of their condition, both because of the status factor and because of the fear of discrimination in the hearing world. To outsiders, my father claimed he was born hearing but became deaf at four. He pointed to a nasty protrusion of scar tissue on his forehead as collateral damage from the fall, a small, permanent mound on the surface, like a mosquito bite that never went away.

"Tell him I fell from a tall palm tree I was climbing back in Puerto Rico."

That was the answer he told me to give the Prudential salesman when he applied for life insurance. And when examined by medical people he instructed me, his interpreter, to give the same account of his handicap. Otherwise, he feared his request for help would be treated with less respect. I was amused by this explanation, and would be tempted to tease him afterwards:

"Hey, Pop, you got deaf going after the coconuts? Was that the same tree your three deaf sisters fell from?"

Then there was the flip side of this relationship between stigma and status. Since the non-hereditary deaf had a taste of the hearing world, was it more difficult for them to cope emotionally with their handicap? Were they like a rich man plunged into poverty overnight, still retaining memories of his previous wealth? Were they more embittered over their condition, compared to those who were born deaf? I can only speak from personal observation, but it seemed that way to me.

Somehow it entered Torres family lore that deafness arose from sexually transmitted disease. Although Ita never explicitly confirmed this with her children, it became the explanation that our aunts transmitted to us. Ita told stories that Abuelo, who was fourteen years older than Ita when they married, had many women when he was young. Once he settled down and married her, he was a model of loyalty and sobriety. She instructed her daughters to be very careful when it came time to select a husband.

After arriving in New York, my aunt Mariamelia read an Ann Landers column that said that deafness results from sexual promiscuity of a parent. A woman infected with syphilis during pregnancy can end up with a deaf baby. In conversations with me, Titi Mariamelia could not recall whether it was Ann Landers or the inquiring letter-writer who made this connection. However, she did remember Ita saying something about being "sick" during the time she gave birth to her deaf children and receiving vaccinations of some kind in each instance. My other cousins were also given variations of this story. Out of this jumble of innuendo, home-grown medical theory, and half-forgotten recollections was fashioned the belief that my grandfather Don Ramón "Moncho" Torres had caused four of his eight children to be born deaf.

I grew up wondering if the Torres family had been punished by the Almighty for the sins of my grandfather. Among the devout deaf people that I knew, it was commonly believed that they, like Jesus, were the bearers of a cross, sent to redeem the transgressions of their ancestors. Their presence was a reminder that God's judgment is implacable. In return, the deaf are showered with God's special affection. He knows they are not to blame for their condition and promises easier entry into heaven if they bear the burden with patience and dignity.

I often wondered if they blamed God for their disability, for separating them from humanity. Reading Biblical stories, I thought: here I am surrounded by people who can ask their Creator, along with Job, "What crime have I committed, How have I sinned against you?"

In my moments of anger and cynicism I put words in their minds. I imagined them saying, as they watched hearing people talk, "There, but for the so-called grace of God, go I."

If the unfairness of their condition pained them to the point of doubting their faith, I was never made aware of this. Pop never wavered in his religious devotion, never directed his anger at God. At his most

despairing moments he would simply say to me, "It doesn't matter . . .
it doesn't help to be angry at God." I understood Pop's stance; he was
anchored in a deep faith and sustained by a hope for redress in a future life.

At Mass you would never know he wasn't a full participant in the
rituals. Throughout he seemed in intimate dialogue with God, medi-
tating and signing prayers discreetly to himself, only his wrists and fingers moving. Concluding the Sign of the Cross, he brought the thumb
to his lips and kissed it. Under his shirt hung a gold chain and cross,
every day of the year. Pop held no grudges against God.

Later in life, in my thirties, I began to question the family's religious
view of why we had so many deaf members. During routine medical
examinations, when the physician asked about my family history, I
mentioned the prevalence of deafness. I inquired about the scientific
explanations of the disability, and invariably I was asked the question:
among your relatives, is there marriage among first or second cousins?

On another occasion I participated in a medical research project
conducted at Columbia Presbyterian that involved a genealogical study.
I watched in fascination as the researcher diagrammed my family tree,
tracing it back to the late 1800s. The young scientist interviewed me
rigorously about the medical history of each of my ancestors. She
pointed that there was a fair amount of intermarriage of first and second cousins among both the Torres and Ayala branches and guessed
this might have something to do with the deafness. She explained that
the condition usually has to do with the recurrence of a gene that is
linked to deafness. A lack of diversity within the gene pool—caused,
for example, by intermarriage among kin—raises the probability of the
occurrence of deafness.

So this was the explanation. Somewhere along the ancestral lineage
of both the Torres and Ayala families, intermarriage of cousins had created a precarious level of recessive genes, leading to hearing loss. My
grandparents on the Ayala side, Catalino and Eufrasia, were first cousins. With fifteen offspring—the Ayalas constituted a small army—it was

practically inevitable that they would give birth to children with some handicap. As to my father's side, no one could ever tell me if there was a blood relationship between Ita and Ramón, but there were other instances of cousins marrying cousins within Ita's paternal line, the Quiñoneses. When recounting family history, Titi Blanca had said that her maternal grandfather Andrés Quiñones had married Ramona Ramos after his first wife Isabel Ramos had died. Ramona and Isabel, as Titi Blanca had told me, were sisters. Several of their *grandchildren* had intermarried: Nereida, Mariamelia, Charlie, and Saturno. These were my *tías* and *tíos*. They shared the same grandfather and their grandmothers were sisters. And I knew of at least one other distant cousin among the Quiñoneses who was deaf. In the hinterlands of San Germán and Las Piedras, families were close-knit to a fault, forming clustered and self-contained societies.

Over the years, my Ayala relatives have come to accept the scientific explanation. Not so with the Torreses. And long after her passing, Ita's account of why there were so many deaf Torres children still held sway.

In the spring of 1967, I was at my desk hunched over a textbook when I heard the escalating sound of agitated language. The words would have been unintelligible to an outsider, but I deciphered the meaning behind the telltale noises making their way down the hallway into my room. Pop was on the defensive, his throat-clearing noises betraying the calm perseverance that was his nature. He sounded exasperated, incapable of containing Mom's release of anger. From her: accelerated sniffling, frenzied clapping of hands, and whimpering, gradually intensifying, then the crescendo toward a primal scream, an extended squeal I had never heard before.

"*Meeee! Meeee! Meeee!*"

I shivered, not knowing what was going on. I rushed to the living room to find Mom pounding her fists, repeatedly, one after the other, into Pop's chest. He retreated slightly, but she pursued him, continuing her assault.

"*Meeee! Meeee! Meeee!*"

She stopped when I entered.

"What's the matter," I pleaded. "Why are you fighting?"

Through the tears she detailed her complaints; they had become familiar to me, but never this emphatically.

"Your father. He never has money! We still live in this stinky apartment! We'll never get out of here! My sisters, they live in houses in Queens. Seymour and Olga, Romeo and Tata, they have houses too, in New Jersey. We are still here; we will always be here. Your father spends all his money on cigarettes, on playing numbers, on the horses. Look at the window curtains, all yellow from his smoking. I have no dresses for myself. He never takes me out to the movies. We never go on vacation; we never travel. We don't even have a car to visit our friends. Always riding the subway. In a few years, you will see, even you will leave us and I have nothing. Same, same, same; it never changes. I am tired. I am tired. I want to die. It is better for me to die."

I half expected her to come at me next. But she didn't. She just fell back into the couch, pulled out a handkerchief and covered her face, weeping uncontrollably, her body a shaking mass. I glanced at Pop but he was just standing there, saying nothing. His head drooped over one shoulder, like Christ on the Cross, he gazed down through half-closed watered eyes. A face of despair and defeat. In all the years leading up to this clash, my mother had never gone this far, actually hitting Pop. The terrifying shriek from her mouth, the sounds that scared me out of my room, now I understood them: "What about me? What about me? What about me?"

I don't recall the event that triggered Mom's raging outburst. Maybe she asked for a new television, to replace the old black-and-white Zenith that was falling apart. Maybe a paint job for the apartment, or something for her wardrobe. It could have been anything. The fact is Mom's frustration had been building up for years, since the beginning. Now I was twenty.

As far as Mom was concerned, my father had failed her. He cared more about the New York Mets, the *bolitas*, and hitting Yonkers Raceway than about the family's well-being. Twice he had abandoned plans for living in New Jersey. In 1960, he entered a pact with his brothers-in-law, Seymour and Romeo, to build their own houses. Together they had purchased land in Stanhope, New Jersey, and spent their weekends laboring on their dream houses. The idea was to work as a team putting up each house, one at a time, like immigrants pooling their resources in a mutual assistance organization. My cousins Jimmy and Mary would move to New Jersey and I would move after them.

But before long my father's enthusiasm fizzled. He missed weekends, until he had to drop out of the plan. He was approaching fifty, and he realized he didn't have the stomach for seven-day work weeks, even in pursuit of a suburban home. Mom was humiliated by this setback.

For a while, in a concession to Mom's pressures, Pop tried his hand as a door-to-door salesman for the Mason Shoe Company. He figured he could temper her frustration by raising spending money from part-time work. Mason was one of the first businesses in the United States to bring shoes to the home, like Avon did for women's beauty items and Fuller Brush for home cleaning products. Being deaf, though, Pop couldn't go knocking on just any doors and make a sales pitch. Instead he focused on cornering the "deaf market." The problem was, this niche was ridiculously limited. I think 90 percent of his business was confined to the Torres family and the Puerto Rican Society for the Catholic Deaf. Even a man as gregarious and charming as he could get only so far as a purveyor of footwear to the deaf.

Making matters worse was something that took me time to realize: there was no physical intimacy between my parents. They had no privacy, not even a bedroom of their own. I never saw them kiss on the lips, and only rarely did I observe a brushing of the cheeks or a hug. My cousin Mary once accompanied Mom to an appointment with a gynecologist and was told that Mom appeared not to have been sexually active. Another time, I noticed a box of condoms in the medicine cabinet I shared with Pop. I figured that was Pop's method of family planning, but it was unopened for several months. Then it dawned on me: the condoms were meant for me.

And now Mom was only in her mid-forties as she took stock of her life, saw that Pop would not answer her dreams, and sensed that the best times were over. What could she expect from the son who had his own plans, and, anyway, loved Pop more than her? At least that's how she was seeing things, I'm sure.

Mom knew that after I finished college I planned to get my own apartment. The only good thing about my moving out was that she would finally have her own privacy. She would take over my bedroom, as she had told me several times. No more pulling out the living room sofa every night, no more putting the bed back in the morning. Without me around she would let Pop worry about the damn convertible day in, day out. Yes, and without me around there would be one less person competing for the bathroom. Another thing Mom could look forward to. But she must have been horribly depressed thinking it would be just her and Pop left, to face the rest of their lives together in apartment 43.

Mom (second from left) with classmates at the Lexington School for the Deaf, 1941.

My parents' wedding, 1946, posing with my paternal grandmother, Ita, and Pop's sisters.

A gathering of my family's deaf friends, early 1950s.

Me and cousins with my maternal grandparents. From left: Victor, John, me, Frank, and Anthony, 1951.

Me and cousins with Ita, 1958.
From left: me, Mary, Nereida, Jimmy, Edwin.

My twelfth birthday, at Apartment 43, 1959.

The first Executive Committee of the Puerto Rican Society for the Catholic Deaf, 1959. Front row: Seymour Joseph, Olga Joseph (Torres), Isaura Quiñones. Back row: Juana Falú Shannon, Pop, Félix de Jesús, unknown, William Fischback.

Pop selling raffle tickets at the Society, early 1960s.

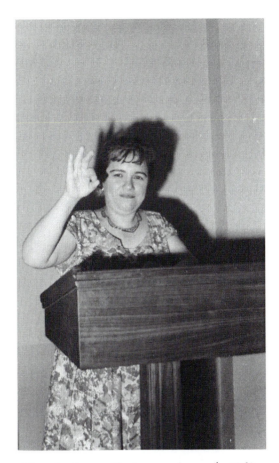

Mom signing at a Society meeting, early 1960s.

8 The Whole World Watching

ONE NIGHT IN my junior year of college, over dinner, I dropped a bombshell on Mom and Pop:

"I signed up for the U.S. Marine Corps. A man in a military uniform came to the college last month. He was recruiting students for a program called the Officers Candidate School, the OCS. This program is very tough. It prepares young men to be officers in the Marines. I have to go to training camp next summer. If I complete the training, then, when I graduate from college, I will become a Second Lieutenant in the Marines. From there I will serve three years. With my college degree and military record, I will have an excellent future. I think this is a great idea for me, so I joined the OCS. Next summer, I will be in training camp for two and a half months, so I won't be here."

The signed interrogation began:

"Where is the training camp?"

"Will they pay you a salary?"

"When you graduate and go into the army, will they send you away? Does that mean you will no longer live with us?"

"The Marines . . . aren't they in Vietnam? Isn't it dangerous there, where many boys are dying?"

I patiently answered their questions. Military service was a given in our family. Several of my Ayala uncles had served, Tomás, Estéban, and César in World War II, Chelo in Korea. Pop's only brother Miguel also served in the Army. Pop's deafness kept him out of uniform, but he proudly said that a lot of deaf people helped during World War II.

"We were in the Defense work," which he signed by clasping his hands into fists, and crossing his arms in front of his chest. He vocalized "defense" loudly and firmly. The gesture reminded me of those railroad-crossing signs you saw in TV programs like *Lassie* and *The Andy Griffith Show.*

By the time I was finishing college most of my Ayala and Torres cousins had enlisted or had been drafted. So as I described my plans to Mom and Pop, they mostly kept their reserve and nodded their acceptance. Years earlier when I was just an eighth grader they were surprised when I announced my intention to be a Christian Brother; then soon after they were perplexed as I switched to try out the priesthood. Now in the middle of college, I was alerting them to my post-collegiate life. Motionlessly, they stared at me.

"We don't know what you're up to this time, but let's hope you know what you're doing."

That's what their faces said to me.

I spent the summer of 1967 in the ninety-five-degree heat of Quantico, Virginia, as "Candidate Torres of A Company, Third Platoon, Officer Candidates School, U.S. Marine Corps." From the first day we were subjected to a test of will. The job of our platoon sergeants was to determine our physical and psychological readiness for war and to detect if we had the "intestinal fortitude," as they constantly repeated, to lead men into battle.

We were led on forced marches and other tests of stamina, with full gear. (Hey, who did they think they were dealing with, a punk? This was Andy Torres, veteran of years of Ring-a-Leevio and handball on the Block! Having ascended the four stories of "Mount 514" thousands of times, I could handle these tests with no problem!)

We learned martial arts and practiced hand-to-hand combat. We marched and marched and marched all day long: "Left face," "Right face," "Right Column . . . March" (Damn, those I remembered from Boy Scout days!).

For endless time we stood at silent, lifeless attention in the baking sun, flies buzzing our noses and ears. Breaking discipline, just once, to flick away an insect or to scratch oneself invited rebuke and threats. At attention, you could be overtaken by pure boredom if you hadn't devised mental stratagems. (Thank God I had memorized scores of doo-wop and Motown songs. Singing to myself kept my heart pumping and alert, and I never dozed off.)

On occasion, a candidate weakened under the onslaught of sun rays and drudgery, and, out of curiosity, sneaked a sideways glance at the Sergeant. This violated the cardinal rule of standing at attention, which was to stare *straight ahead* at all times. This miscue invited holy terror and rebuke. "Are you looking at ME, Candidate; do you LIKE ME, Candidate?" What followed was a perfectly delivered, emotionally pitched diatribe in which the Sergeant fixated on whatever flaw he had detected in the candidate: too tall? too short? too slim? too bulky? too pretty? too smart? too nice? too "salty"?

It was a customized riot report on your unsuitability for wearing the Globe and Anchor. If you couldn't do something as simple as stand at attention, how could you even *think* you could be an officer in the Corps? You might even end up giving *him* orders down the line. Are you kidding? All this was designed to cut you down, and make you ask yourself: "Is this really worth it? I could be at Rockaway Beach with my buddies instead of sweating in these khakis and helmet." After the Sergeant finished with the candidate verbally, he ordered him to "hit the deck" and do push-ups until his biceps gave out and he collapsed on the sun-drenched ground.

Day after day, week after week, they intimidated us. They questioned our manhood and they prodded us into self-doubt. They reminded us during our final combat training sessions that we would have to run the cold steel of our bayonets into the "Gook's" stomach, before he did it to us.

The Third Platoon, A Company, began with fifty-one candidates. By the end of the summer, thirty-four had completed the program. I was one of them. And damn proud of it. I showed Mom and Pop the letter that the Company Commander sent home with us: "The challenge is over, the goal has been reached . . . You have proven, after ten weeks of physical and mental stress, that you deserve to serve with the finest . . . I respect and salute each of you." My self-confidence was in the stratosphere, as was my patriotic zeal.

We who were at OCS, college students from around the country, knew this was only a dry run. We were fitted with M1 carbine training rifles, remnants of World War II. We had no bullets and our bayonets were blunted. The Corps didn't trust us *that* much. Nevertheless, bones were broken and bodies bloodied. And some minds were crushed under the pressure (these were the first candidates to be sent home).

The Marine Corps Officer Candidates School was a modified boot camp. It was the first of two tests I would have to pass in order to prepare myself for leadership in the Corps. The summer in Quantico was designed to weed out the softies from the pool of young men aspiring to leadership. The second test, immediately upon graduation from college, would involve three months of *real* basic training. Completion of this phase anointed us as "90-Day Wonders," as our drill sergeants referred to them, hopefully qualified to lead combat units. After this, we would be assigned to permanent duty as an Infantry Lieutenant in Vietnam, or so we assumed.

While I was contemplating that my future lay in the Marines, I was still working to get through college and come of age in an incredibly turbulent time. It now strikes me that 1968 was a year when a decade's worth of history was compressed into a single 365-day cycle. It was the year "the whole world was watching" as America veered out of control.

The year began with 486,000 U.S. troops mired in the jungles of Vietnam. Few of these soldiers had even heard of the place before being sent there. In March, President Lyndon B. Johnson declared, "with a heavy heart," that he would not run for re-election. It was an admission that he could not lead the country out of its internal strife. Since the mid-1960s antiwar protestors had declared this an immoral and unwinnable war. LBJ's decision gave hope that their voices had finally been heard.

But the country was far from a peaceful resolution of its ills. Out of nowhere, like a blast of lightning on a calm day, word arrived from Memphis: Martin Luther King Jr. had been killed. Everyone recoiled before the immensity of the crime, and worried about black America's reaction. The assassination of the greatest African American leader, by a white man, promised only rage and rebellion.

That evening of April fourth, when the killing happened, I was at work standing before a tall file cabinet, processing the contents of a manila folder. I was in the gigantic file room of the New York Life Insurance Company, located on the Avenue of the Americas. A few months earlier Rose Medina, whose father was the superintendent of my grandmother Ita's building on Amsterdam Avenue, had gotten me a job at New York Life, where she herself worked full-time. The Medina family was as numerous as the Chin family and most of the eight Medina kids bore a remarkable facial similarity to each other. By this time Rose was married to Sal, one of my best friends from around the Block. And by this time I had been going steady again with Nilsa, Sal's sister. In high school everyone around the Block had joked that Nilsa was the cause of my abandonment of the priesthood. We had parted ways during my early years in college, and now had reunited, this time as more serious partners.

Each weekday night, along with a few other part-timers, I had the mind-numbing chore of inspecting, arranging, and updating each of the client folders that were maintained by the mammoth corporation. Entering the brightly lit file room, situated in the upper reaches of corporate headquarters, you were assaulted by the overwhelming sight of file cabinets—cold, gleaming metal columns in every shade of gray, in every hue of green.

We were left on our own. As long as we satisfied a daily quota of files that had to be "processed," New York Life was happy. After we got the knack of it, it was easy going, and we engaged in long conversations or debates. Some shouted over and in between the file cabinets, passionately discussing the issues of the day. Others, uninterested in these things, flirted behind the cabinets. And for those who kept to themselves, there was the radio, set to the rock 'n' roll station. Whatever the diversions, we always met our quotas.

Trevor was my companion in the political chatter. He attended a public college in the city, where he was involved in black student activism. He had a trim, athletic build, a short-cropped Afro, and he was slightly taller than me. Trevor patterned himself after the late Malcom X, down to the unpretentious dress, the dark-rimmed glasses, and serious manner.

I was the liberal to Trevor's militant. He said he had given up on any hopes for racial integration. U.S. society would never accept black people as full members. Malcom's assassination, in 1965, had proved that. "Look at Vietnam. Look at all the ghettoes in this country. And already they're backing off on the so-called War on Poverty."

Night after night, standing before the file cabinets as we compared index cards and computer sheets, Trevor laid out his version of America to me. The young black militant delivered his riot report. It was familiar to me, from the media. But until then I had not had a continuous, political one-on-one dialogue with anyone. No one had emoted America's racial problems to me as clearly and perceptively as Trevor.

Yes, I had some acquaintances and friends who were black, like Ray Jones from around the Block, but we didn't get into the nitty-gritty of race in America. The Joneses were superintendents of one of the buildings on 177th, and Ray had an intellectual cast about him, able to talk about literature, unlike most of the crowd. In later years, reading the works of the writer James Baldwin, I was reminded much of Ray. Yes, there were black *Puerto Ricans* among my circle of friends, and among Pop's deaf friends, but I had still not worked out, in my mind, the meaning of my ethnic identity, let alone the equally complicated and more sensitive issue of my racial identity. And the race issue was not a topic among the Puerto Ricans I dealt with, either family or friends. We referred to black Americans as *morenos* (colored), even if they happened to be lighter-skinned than some of our own dark-skinned Boricuas. (*Boricua* is another term for Puerto Rican; it comes from *Boríken,* the name given the island by the native Tainos who inhabited it before Columbus.) Within my own family, I felt singled out for my broad nose and unruly hair, as when Titi Tata persuaded Mom to make me wear a hairnet cut from her stockings to bed, and when my aunt would hail me with a nose-clinching greeting.

When the news from Memphis came over the airwaves, we could not believe our ears. Like a flash storm extinguishing a campfire in the woods, it halted the joking around and the flirting and the political chatter in the big file room. Trevor turned sullen, and glared at everyone, including me. His eyes said, "You see? You see how racist this country is?" I wanted to call him aside and share his grief, to let him know that we all suffered from this loss. But he gathered his things and left.

By April of 1968, my last semester in college and only eight months after completing the Quantico summer, I submitted my resignation from OCS and declared I would not accept a commission as a 2nd Lieutenant in the U.S. Marine Corps. The nationwide student protests, the assassination of Dr. King in Memphis, and Lyndon Johnson's withdrawal from the presidential campaign unmoored me from a belief in America's moral superiority.

The first public expression of doubt came in the form of the annual elocution contest held during Manhattan's Spring Homecoming. I was one of five contestants, each of whom had to deliver an original speech on a current issue. I chose as my topic "Personal Freedom and the Draft." It was a calmly reasoned plea for tolerance, asking the American people to respect the right of youths who opposed the military draft on moral grounds. Another student took a pro-war position, making the familiar argument that worldwide communism had to be stopped in Southeast Asia, and that Americans had to show loyalty to their president.

Campuses across the country were already inflamed in diatribe and confrontation, with student takeovers of buildings and repressive police actions. At Manhattan College we were still dueling with intellect and oratory. Standing on the podium addressing the auditorium I made my case:

"As the draft law stands today, exemption is granted to conscientious objectors. To qualify for this status, an individual must object to all war. But when it comes to the question of whether this or that war is moral, the individual is not given a prerogative. This privilege is reserved for the Pentagon. Considering the changing nature of international conflicts, is it not possible that I may recognize the necessity of one war but object to another war? Is it not unfair that we are forced to an all-or-nothing position? Either we object to all wars or support all wars! And any position in between is to be determined by the government!"

I threw a lot more into the argument, drawing upon the Christian humanist tradition of personal freedom and a defense of the antiwar movement. I received respectful applause from the audience, and Mom, Pop, and Nilsa were there to cheer me on, but my speech didn't win the day. That honor went to the pro-war guy. Yet I did have the satisfaction of organizing my thoughts and having my say. It was a step further in defining myself morally and politically. A middle-aged woman pulled me aside later to say she thought the judges should have declared me the winner. That was enough for me.

In June, only two months after the shooting of Martin Luther King, yet another devastating blow was delivered with the assassination of Robert F. Kennedy. The younger brother of the fallen John F. Kennedy, "Bobby" had earlier declared his candidacy for president. The inexpressible horror of those back-to-back slayings brought the country to the border of chaos. A once-proud and secure America waited desperately for clear answers to heart-wrenching questions: How is this happening? Isn't anyone in control of things? Is it just a coincidence that King and Kennedy were men of peace, who had called for racial unity and an end to the war?

A month earlier, and after King's death, I had signed up to work in Kennedy's primary campaign after an organizer visited Manhattan College. The charismatic organizer spoke eloquently about Kennedy's vision for America. Like his politician-hero, the young man rolled up the sleeves of his white shirt and gestured emphatically, pointing his right finger, when making his points. I was struck by the passion and earnestness in his voice. He made a big impression on me, even though I never saw him again.

The following week I found myself in the campaign's New York City headquarters, a huge storefront on 5th Avenue. Along with plenty of other young people, I stuck mailing labels on envelopes, telephoned people for donations, and cut out press clippings for a media album that we compiled.

At dinnertime I described my activities to Mom and Pop, who were fascinated by my reports from the front line. As we watched the campaign coverage on TV, I filled in a lot of details: how the primary system worked; what were the differences between Kennedy and Johnson; and the significance of Eugene McCarthy, the early antiwar candidate who was the first to challenge Johnson. It was a rare thing for some-one within the same political party to challenge an incumbent president, as Kennedy and McCarthy were doing, I explained. But these were times of national crisis.

My parents were immediately drawn to Bobby Kennedy. He seemed more personable and down-to-earth than Johnson and McCarthy. And they shared a sentimental attachment to him, for being the younger Kennedy brother, and for his Catholicism.

Around midnight of an early June day, my attention was riveted to the TV screen as Kennedy delivered a victory speech after winning the California primary. With its huge block of electoral votes, the country's largest state had delivered a breakthrough for the campaign. Not many minutes after stepping off the stage and walking out of view, as reporters were analyzing the significance of the win, Kennedy was shot and mortally wounded.

It was as if I had been right there in Los Angeles' Ambassador Hotel, and not in a New York City living room. At the time, Mom and I had been watching the celebrations on the TV, excited but tired. She was lying down, her back propped up on the headboard of the sofa convertible. Pop was asleep next to her, curled up and facing away from the screen. I sat in the chair next to them. We had the floor lamp on a low light, so as not to disturb the snoring breadwinner. When the announcement came, I signed to Mom what they were saying: that Kennedy had been attacked by someone just as he was exiting the hotel through a rear passageway.

"But where? I don't see anything."

"No, it all happened behind the stage. We can't see it from here. It happened behind the stage, inside the hotel."

"But how could that happen? Wasn't anyone protecting him? Who killed him?"

"I don't know; I don't know. They haven't said anything."

Each time some reporter came on, I relayed the information to Mom, who was quietly weeping by now. Her crumpled flesh was wet with tears and she swayed her head, her lips pressed together in resignation. Then she put her hand out as if rubbing Ethel Kennedy's back to console her, and signed,

"The wife . . . and so many children." I cried too. We decided not to wake up Pop. What good would it do to deprive him of a night's sleep? Soon enough he would know.

That first week of June coincided with my last days as a Manhattan College student. Nilsa and I, joined by Bobby Webster and his girlfriend Cathy, went to Prom Night at the Grand Ballroom of the Waldorf Astoria. Later that week, Titi Blanca and Tío Carlos joined us, along with Mom and Pop, for Graduation Day at the New York Hilton. It should have been a time of jubilation, a time to rest on my laurels, as a graduate *cum laude* and recipient of academic awards, including the Economics Award. But only the self-deluded could be festive in these circumstances.

Nilsa and her mother Carmen had previously planned a graduation party for me for the following week, and it was decided to go ahead with it, despite the period of national mourning. In their Valentine Avenue apartment, my family gathered, along with Sal and Rose and other friends, including Trevor, my co-worker at New York Life. It was a party with a split personality. In the living room we Monkey-timed to Smokey Robinson and the Miracles, swiveled to The Four Tops and the Temptations, and hopped to boogaloo. In the adjacent bedroom, where the TV was stationed, people watched scenes from a national memorial for Kennedy that was taking place at the same time. Passing through the open doorway was to subject oneself to completely different sensations, from celebratory music and dancing to somber and dark silence, and back again.

The slaying of Bobby Kennedy, so soon a sequel to the assassination of Martin Luther King, was a turning point for me. From then on I refused to believe in the existence of real democracy in America. I accepted the conspiracy theories of the day, which said there was a sophisticated network of powerful (white) men who were in de facto control of the U.S. government. (As for Sirhan Sirhan, the Arab American who was convicted of killing Robert Kennedy, I could never fit him neatly into these theories.) These men had ultimate power over the military-industrial complex and feared that withdrawing from Vietnam would be a lasting defeat in the cold war.

I saw not a Promised Land in which anyone could succeed if they tried hard enough, but a rigged economic system dominated by the elites. I saw in America not a model for social harmony, but a hierarchy of privilege and power, historically founded on the genocide of Native Americans and the enslavement of Africans, and then, expanded and perpetuated into the present by an ideology of racism. Soon I would see America the colonizer, in its treatment of Puerto Rico. I foreswore naiveté, abandoned my liberal sensibilities, and hardened myself.

Later that summer, another crisis unfolded right before our eyes, at the Democratic Convention in Chicago. Thousands of dissenters were assembling in the city to protest the party's compliance with the war. Their goal was to embarrass Mayor Richard Daley, the pro-war host, and cause the collapse of the convention. Over several days, we watched the Chicago police overwhelm the young protesters, kicking and beating them in front of the cameras. It was hardly different from scenes during the Civil Rights struggle, when police were televised clubbing and shooting at blacks. But America reacted with greater moral indignation and outrage this time. These were white youth, and this was a convention of the supposedly liberal Democratic Party. Race makes all the difference in America.

As with the double tragedy of King and Kennedy, Mom, Pop, and I were riveted to the news coverage. With their constant questioning, they unwittingly helped shape my thoughts about what was going on in the country. They were less interested in the "whos," "whats," and "whens," and flooded me with "*whys*." They wanted more elaborate explanations, more detailed rationales, from their twenty-one-year-old son. They rarely challenged me, as I offered snippets of my evolving views. Were they deferring to me, the one with privileged access to the hearing world? Or, happy to see me excitedly talking about these things, were they just pleased to have the "face time" with me? I think it was a little of both.

As 1968 drew to a close, I saw an America spent with conflict and violence. That was not all. Richard Nixon was the new president, and more troops were fighting and dying in Vietnam than when the year began.

In the midst of defining myself politically and in relation to the world around me, those years found me growing up in other ways as well. Nilsa and I had one of those on-again, off-again relationships since high school and we were among the many steady pairs that got started on the Block. Now I was twenty-one and she nineteen and we had resumed our relationship. And just as we were when we started out in high school, we were an example of opposites attracting.

Now the contrasts took other forms, beyond our contrasting physical appearance. Although a practicing Catholic she was attracted to the ideas of reincarnation as described in the writings of Edgar Cayce—a modern take, perhaps, on her mother's *espiritismo*. A favorite book was *Rosemary's Baby*. I was the rationalist gradually abandoning notions of heaven, hell, and the afterlife. Her affectionate, romantic side was a counter to my cool, stoic demeanor. These contrasts sparked long walks, endless conversation, and increasing intimacy.

Through the tumultuous time that was the late sixties we became closer and got more serious. She listened with curiosity as I described the gradual politicization I was undergoing. She cheered me on at Manhattan College when I spoke on behalf of the antiwar activists and in defense of civil disobedience. For me, our relationship seemed to offer a safe haven from the madness of the real world—just being together and sharing dreams and anxieties. In the summer of 1968, right after I graduated from college, we were engaged, and before the year ended we married. Sal was my best man and my cousin Mary the maid of honor. Msgr. Lynch, the priest who had married my parents and most of my relatives, and who had baptized me, officiated at the wedding ceremony. The day after, Bobby and Cathy were wed. Since high school, Bobby and I seemed to do a lot of things in tandem. But a week later, he was off to Vietnam, having already been commissioned an officer in the U.S. Navy.

During the second half of 1968 I had graduated from Manhattan, gotten engaged, and then married Nilsa. Mom and Pop were certainly surprised by the rush to marriage but didn't say anything. Neither did they raise the questions that had always been in the back of their minds and to which they alluded from time to time during my college years: "Ahtay, what are your plans? How long will you stay with us here in the apartment? Where will you live when you get older? Do you think we will be together?" It wasn't necessary to pose these questions now, because they were in the back of my mind too. But I didn't want to answer them to their face.

Getting married meant abandoning the Block for good. It meant bidding farewell to my home-in-the-streets of the past twelve years and leaving behind the time of passage into hearing-world adulthood. The Block was to have a riveting hold on me for decades after, the source of countless memories, stories, and dreams.

By early January 1969, having left Mom and Pop, I settled into my first home with Nilsa, located on Valentine Avenue in the West Bronx. I was happy to be living in a first-floor apartment (ah, no more four-story walk-ups!) and to have more space for my books and music. Nilsa bought a gorgeous teak dresser topped by a revolving vanity mirror, which she had eyed several times during our strolls through Greenwich Village. On top of our record player, a beautiful credenza-like piece in a light brown veneer, sat a brass bull, a wedding gift from Ray Jones. The finishing touch to the newly painted apartment was a huge green and yellow daisy that Nilsa tastefully painted onto the living-room wall.

My contribution to the hippie flair of our home was a portrait of Jesus, which I posted in the bathroom. "Wanted Dead or Alive, for Revolutionary Activities" said the lettering under his bearded, slightly smiling image. It was a simple black-and-white print; his hair was scraggly down to the shoulders and the dark shadows beneath his eyes gave the impression of a busy, worried man. The poster was wildly popular at the time and captured exactly how I envisioned the man: an incorruptible rebel who sided with the poor and outcasts, ran the greedy merchants out of the temple, and was executed for fostering social revolution. My kind of hero.

That previous September I had begun graduate studies in economics at New York University. Since my first years at Manhattan College I had become a passionate student of economics, thanks to Dr. Emily Sun who had inspired my love for the "dismal science." I became interested in the subfields of economic development and labor and became the department's top student, winning a medal for my grades. That track record earned me a part-time job as a graduate assistant at Manhattan, as I began my studies at NYU. So after marrying Nilsa, my routine consisted of bus and train rides to the Riverdale section of the Bronx, where Manhattan was located, then to the NYU campus at Greenwich Village, and back home to Valentine Avenue (near 180th Street) in the West Bronx. My stipend from the assistantship at Manhattan was a modest supplement to Nilsa's salary as a clerical worker in a downtown corporation.

The next months after we settled in our home, I found the political situation of 1969 unbearable as President Nixon took us deeper into war and began rolling back the social agenda of the sixties. Up to now my political activities had been minimal. I was an observer. The only direct involvement was a short-lived participation in Bobby Kennedy's campaign and my anti-draft speech on

Homecoming Day at Manhattan College. In the early spring I met undergraduate Puerto Rican students at NYU who were organizing a new group, which they called LUCHA (Struggle). I immediately joined and became involved in their activities, including a demand for more courses and programs dealing with Puerto Rican and Latino issues. Then our focus turned outward to the general strife of the time: the war, civil rights, affirmative action, and the colonial situation in Puerto Rico. We were following the path of other student groups throughout the country.

Soon, during that same spring, a new issue drew our attention. At City College, African American and Puerto Rican students took over and barricaded the campus in a bold move to institute a policy of open admissions. I joined with others at NYU in getting community support for the struggle. We organized evening marches through Harlem to bring people, food, and morale to the students holed up on campus. At Manhattan College I teamed up with Puerto Rican undergraduate students and formed a LUCHA chapter, the first Puerto Rican/Latino student advocacy group. Here I met Alfredo López, an English major from the Bronx with a bent for fiery rhetoric. Like me he was delving into Karl Marx's writings, an oeuvre clearly inferior to the works of St. Augustine and St. Thomas Aquinas in the eyes of the Christian Brothers who ran Manhattan College. In the first years after graduating Alfredo would lead a movement in the defense of political prisoners and write a book, *The Puerto Rican Papers*. Then we would find ourselves reunited in our political efforts.

LUCHA's first campaign at Manhattan was a protest of the low wages being paid the cafeteria workers, who were mostly Latino. We published a newsletter and organized forums. Following the example of African Americans on campus, LUCHA called attention to Manhattan's need to admit more Puerto Rican and Latino students. We selected as our motto the resonant phrase *"Educación es Poder."* If this incursion into political activity, this gradual transformation of Andy

Torres from observer to participant, was straining my marriage with
Nilsa, who labored diligently in her daily nine-to-five routine, I did not
notice. Or perhaps I did not want to notice.

During this same time, the last of my surviving grandparents died.
At age eighty-six, my maternal grandmother Eufrasia passed away. I
accompanied Mom and Pop to the Ortiz Funeral parlor in the Bronx
where the entire Ayala clan gathered to grieve. The place was packed
with faces that I dimly recalled from my Bronx childhood and from
family visits over the years. Strangers were introduced to me as distant
blood relatives, whose connections to the Ayalas dated to Las Piedras
times. They were names that Mom had shown me on her scribblings
of family history: Piñero, Pérez, Soto, Carrasquillo, García. All somehow related to me.

No one could deny that Eufrasia and Catalino, who had died in
1961 also at the age of eighty-six, had led full lives. Theirs were hard
lives, but in the end their struggles became easier, as their children provided for them with care and love. They had extricated themselves from
the Depression and had spawned such a vast tree of descendants. Now
their offspring were spread throughout New York City and Puerto Rico,
and their children's' children were poised to spread further beyond.
They had long ago abandoned the farm that had given them their start.

One of the Ayala elders I spoke with—I don't recall which one—
described a conversation he had had with Don Catalino before he died,
and which Doña Eufrasia repeated among her last words. It was among
their last requests that the hearing Ayala children would always keep
an eye out for *las mudas*.

9 God and Marriage

DURING THAT SAME SPRING, on a visit to building 514 and now as an outsider, Pop told me of a request he had received. It was a sensitive matter and he wasn't sure how to handle it. He wanted my advice.

"Your cousin Mary; she asked me for a favor. She wants me to give her away at the wedding in May."

Uh oh, I thought, the shit had hit the fan. The incident had been brewing for a year. My cousin Mary, daughter of Seymour and Titi Olga, had decided to wed her boyfriend Bob, a non-Catholic. I was already aware that she had been in the process of converting to Bob's church. For the family this was anathema. Mary had been groomed to be the next matriarch; and now she was charting her own course in open defiance of family expectations.

Several related events in family history had added fuel to the fire. First was the fact that Mary's father, Seymour Joseph, came from a Jewish background. He was welcomed with open arms when he declared his intentions to marry Titi Olga in the mid-1940s. But my grandparents Moncho and Ita insisted that he accept Catholicism. It was never clear to us what constituted the greater discomfort in Seymour's family, that Olga was Puerto Rican or that she was Catholic. Suffice it to say that he was ostracized by his parents and that his relatives—all hearing—never participated in our family gatherings. If the perceived violation was religious you could hardly blame them. After all my family, like many Catholics of the time harbored an anti-Semitic streak. And among the deaf Catholics I knew, the sign for "Jewish" (the hand pulling at the chin to signify a goatee) was often accompanied by a disapproving facial expression.

Seymour became as devout a Catholic as any of us. For years he worked actively, along my father's side, to build the Puerto Rican Society for the Catholic Deaf. For a while he even presided over the organization. If there was some impropriety in a Russian Jew leading a Puerto Rican organization, no one ever remarked on it publicly. Two decades later Seymour Joseph, the Jew turned Catholic, could not accept that his only daughter was herself switching religions to unite with her love. He opposed the wedding as vehemently as his Puerto Rican in-laws did and said he would not attend the ceremony.

No one was more wounded by Mary's rebellion than Titi Blanca. The youngest of the Torres siblings, and fifteen years older than me, Blanca became the central family figure when Ita died a few years before. Proficient in Spanish, English, and Sign, it was no wonder that family members turned to her for help and advice in all affairs.

After completing high school in suburban New Jersey, Mary decided to enroll in business school where she could specialize in bilingual secretarial skills. Cousin Jimmy had already graduated and enrolled in the Air Force, and he was now stationed in Europe. So she returned to New York City, staying with Titi Blanca who accepted stewardship of her favorite niece. Once again the second floor apartment at 2372 Amsterdam served as a waystation for a Torres family member, much as it had since the mid-forties.

Before Mary moved in with Blanca and Carlos, I myself was half-way through Manhattan College and already in the middle of a philosophical and political transformation. I was at Titi Blanca's weekly to babysit her daughter Edna, taking advantage of these visits to have my aunt regale me with stories of family life in Puerto Rico. But as the Civil Rights movement pressed on and the war in Vietnam persisted, our conversations took on a more serious turn.

I was disappointed that Blanca dismissed my liberal views. I sensed that her religious loyalties were hamstringing her views on current events. The Church was notoriously slow to support the struggle for equal rights and to end the U.S. war in Indochina. And it became clear to me that my family had a bias against racial intermarriage.

The conversations became heated but they never breached the bond of love and respect that existed between Titi Blanca and me. We even poked fun at each other across the generational divide: she playfully mocking my idealistic youthfulness, I accusing her of being a "fuddy-duddy."

When Mary moved back she took over the role of babysitting Edna, but the conversations continued. Now when I visited they were a three-way dialogue. It soon became clear that my cousin was undergoing a change of her own, and she increasingly steered the topic to religion. I recognized that she was adopting a deadly serious critique of the Church, especially its material wealth and controlling hierarchy. As far as she was concerned, the Church had lost its legitimacy a few centuries after Christ's death. Catholicism had become a rigid institution that interfered with Man's relation to God and the Bible. She accepted a version of Christian Fundamentalism that did away with Catholic theology (rejecting the Holy Trinity, for example) and ritual. From here on, she said, she would observe the Sabbath on Saturdays and would not celebrate Christmas or Easter.

So when Mary and Bob announced their wedding plans and when family asked what I thought, I said that Mary should have the right to choose her beliefs, and that no one should boycott her wedding. In the

debates that took place, I questioned how any religion could claim to
have a monopoly on the truth. I described myself as closer to agnosti-
cism than any religious faith, saying that each individual has to decide
upon a philosophy of life.

Para qué fue eso? Whatever leverage I had as a mediator disappeared
immediately. It was okay for Andy to ramble on about the crisis in
American society, headlined in the daily newspapers, but to counte-
nance a world without God—that was ridiculous! Even Mary had to
feel uncomfortable having me as an ally. I became irrelevant to the
growing crisis, but out of loyalty and sympathy I accepted her invitation to be an usher in the wedding party.

As Mary's spiritual conversion became irrevocable, my aunts and
uncles could barely contain their disappointment and anger. Blanca,
during whose watch Mary had rejected the Catholic faith, took the whole
affair very personally. She announced that she would not attend the wedding and everyone else followed suit. Everyone, that is, except Pop.

It made sense that Mary would appeal to Pop for help. He was a
favorite uncle to my cousins. He was free with a smile and hug, ever ready
for some teasing and willing to overlook a youthful indiscretion. Like the
time my cousin Edwin, son of Titi Nereida and Tío Saturno and brother
to Ney, got into a jam thanks to Pop. One time, when Edwin was about
six, my father was engaging him in conversation. He became impatient
trying to answer Pop's questions. His limited repertoire of signs was
of little help and he was having trouble making himself understood.
Straight-jacketed by the tedious method of finger-spelling, he yelled at
Pop and stomped out of the living room.

Edwin's father Saturno was a husky man, orphaned in Puerto Rico
at the age of two, and not a light-hearted man. He ran Edwin down,
gave him a few swift ones across his legs, and yanked him back into
Pop's presence, demanding an apology. The last thing Pop wanted was
to have his poor nephew crying because he didn't know enough signs.
He left the apartment and returned a few minutes later with an ice
cream cone, a peace offering to the young boy.

"I do not think it is right to leave Mary alone," he told me, the day I visited him at 514. "Someone from the family should take her down the aisle. I know Seymour and Olga are very angry with Mary, but they are very stubborn. I will go to the wedding and take Seymour's place. What do you think?"

"I'm glad you will do this. We should be there for Mary. Besides, she was Nilsa's maid of honor at our wedding."

Privately, and in a relative calm that belied the charged bickering that was going on elsewhere in the family, Pop and I had been arguing the previous months about Mary's decision. He was upset over her plans to marry a non-Catholic. But purging Mary from the family didn't make sense to him. Unlike the others, he put family unity before religious conviction.

The wedding ceremony was a simple affair, opening a view into my cousin's new life. A one-story wooden structure in Brooklyn, devoid of Incarnation's architectural splendor, served as the site for the exchanging of vows. Most of those in attendance were acquaintances from Mary's new religious community; only a handful of the Torres family, including Mom and Nilsa, was present. On an otherwise somber day, my heart filled with pride watching Pop escort his niece down the aisle.

My father was able to rise above the unreasonable strictures of faith and allegiance to family. From whence or how he received this independence of mind is a mystery to me. Was there a hidden reservoir of common sense that he drew upon in such situations? Did he have other sources of wisdom or inspiration? I have only his actions to go by, but they have been ever sufficient guideposts for me.

A few months after Mary's wedding, the whirlwind pace of events came to a screeching halt when Nilsa announced she was pregnant. Now the big issues facing the country, the family tensions surrounding Mary's wedding, my growing involvement in political activities, and thoughts about a career in economics—all these were pushed aside by the announcement that a baby would be joining our Valentine Avenue household in late November. I was terribly conflicted over the news. On the one hand I glowed with prideful excitement over the idea that a new generation of Torreses was on the way (the new child would inaugurate the fourth generation descending from Ramón and Amelia Torres). On the other hand, I was anguished over the increased obligations that fatherhood would bring. Not only that, already I had been gradually signaling to Nilsa that our marriage may have been a premature decision. At one point we had even briefly separated and I found an apartment of my own in the Bronx, near Yankee Stadium, but then we reunited. Inside, I had the sinking feeling that, at twenty-two, I simply wasn't ready for married life.

For the moment, though, the impending birth meant that I had to make some changes. As far as my economics studies were concerned, I would switch to part-time studies at NYU next fall. For now it was time for Andrew Torres to get a real job, a nine-to-fiver, making real money. After a few weeks searching for work—during which I was cautioned by one personnel director that I would need to buy some suits, trim my sideburns, and shave off my mustache—I found success.

My new workplace was on Madison Avenue, at the headquarters of the Riegel Paper Corporation. I was hired as a credit analyst, responsible for tracking account receivables of our customers, such as Frito-Lay Potato Chips, to whom Riegel supplied vast quantities of paper bags. I was fairly good at making sure clients kept their accounts current and at assessing the credit-worthiness of potential buyers. But it wasn't the most exciting work. Not a few times did I wonder if this was the best use of my economics training.

The best part of my new job was the happy hour at McCann's Bar and Grill. My co-workers were Bill Bell and Bill Woodworth, a pair of young Irish guys whose humor and light-heartedness were a refreshing antidote to the serious demeanor I had assumed for myself. McCann's was a hangout for dozens of young professional men, and a few women, who worked in midtown offices. After a day of inspecting accounting sheets or auditing financial records, we barged into the place, bleary-eyed and thirsty. The bar was dimly lit and the air was flush with an aroma of beer and hard liquor. It was a comforting alternative to the stale office environment.

Over chicken wings, beer nuts, and stiff drinks, we debated the week's headlines. My friends too had graduated from Catholic colleges but unlike the conservative-leaning students that dominated at my alma mater, Manhattan College, the two Bills were guys I could talk with. Walking the hallways of Riegel, they reminded me of Laurel and Hardy, with Woodworth representing the thin Laurel and Bell the portly Hardy. We had mild disagreements over Vietnam, capitalism, civil rights, the hippies, and religion, but we all agreed that marital bliss was hard to come by. They made it impossible for me to lambaste all white people for America's troubles, as some people I knew did, or equate the business world with everything evil, as the Marxists were doing at the time.

Despite the friendship extended me by my co-workers, I sensed this initial foray of mine into the corporate scene would not be a lasting commitment. Throughout the summer and into the fall, I kept in touch with my growing network of Puerto Rican connections.

In early October Pop, Mom, and I celebrated the Mets' first World Series victory. From the *Daily News* Pop had clipped his favorite cartoon character, "Basement Bertha," and put it on the refrigerator for my next visit. There was Bertha on Mom's Frigidaire, resuscitating her historic scream when the Brooklyn Dodgers won their first World Series in the 1950s, gleefully wailing, "Who's a Bum!?!?"

A few weeks later I hopped on a slow-moving school bus and rode to Washington, D.C., to be at the Vietnam Moratorium, the largest antiwar demonstration of the time. I went with Louie Shapiro, my fellow ex-seminarian from Cathedral. He had pretty much grown out of his obsessions with raw hamburger meat and horror movies by the time he graduated from Seton Hall University, which he enrolled in after leaving Cathedral the same time I did. By now it was photography and writing that claimed the Venezuelan's enthusiasm. He was also trying to understand the quagmire of America's conflicts.

The October 15th journey was an eight-hour trip in a long yellow convoy of buses to the nation's capital, near the Lincoln Memorial. When we arrived we saw that people had been coming from many other points. I was stunned by the size and energy of that protest—the speeches, street theater, music, chants, and raw anger. Louie had a field day with his camera.

Toward the end of the main program, a large detachment of young people in semi-military outfits and gas masks, about a thousand or so, broke off from the assembled mass and marched directly at the Department of Justice building. They were bent on direct confrontation with authority. As they marched by right in front of us, their eyes barely visible behind the gas masks, my heart pounded with anticipation. Shortly later, we heard the clash of bodies, the sounds of clubbing and striking and kicking, the voices screaming and cursing. Our view was blocked by buildings but in the distance we could see rising columns of fumes. After a long ride back, Louie and I returned to the dark night of New York City, the buses depositing us at Times Square. In our dungarees and knapsacks we embraced each other in farewell. He knew I was unhappy living the straight life as a credit analyst and father-to-be. And I knew he was nervous about his next steps. The following month he began boot camp in the Air Force, at a time when even these inductees were being farmed to the Far East.

Later that fall the newspapers released photos of the My Lai massacre. The killings had occurred more than a year before, but not until these photos appeared did the awesome terror of that day impact the American people. An excruciating impotence overtook me. That my government allowed this to happen, then covered up the scandal, and

I was incapable of doing anything about this. My only outlet was to write a poem (a rant, really), adopting the voice of the perpetrator. I cast a pox on all houses, even My Lai's peasants. I was a soldier rebuking the phony expressions of Americans horrified by the slaughter. This was war, after all, and no one had a moral claim on shock or shame, not at this late date. The words exploded from a dark place of my soul. I composed a four-page pamphlet, with the bloody cadavers on the cover page. It was a personally designed and privately published work. It went into a drawer and permanent obscurity.

In late November, Nilsa gave birth to a girl. Like me, Rachel was born within a year of her parents' marriage. And like me hers was a difficult delivery, involving many hours of labor. Two bumps on her head, thanks to the forceps that were required to bring her into the world, were the most immediately recognizable features. Did she somehow, while waiting in the womb, catch wind of our troubled marriage? Otherwise, everyone said she was a clone of me.

Saturday mornings, to cuddle a tiny mass of flesh and bone was a delight. To behold her, as the weeks passed, gathering strength in the limbs and neck. To wonder how she would ultimately look, absorbing which traits of her parents, in what combination. She took on a deeper creamy tone to her skin, settling into a compromise between Nilsa and me. The roundness of her face and breadth of her nose were concessions to her father. I wrote an ode to her, in rhyming lines, that is now long lost. Mom and Pop visited frequently to be with their first grandchild, reawakening in me a worry I had long harbored: would my children be deaf? Rachel was the first child born to my generation. All of my cousins were hearing, including those from the Torreses and *las mudas* Ayalas. But there was always talk—where it originated we could never determine—that deafness skipped a generation. We would have to have Rachel's hearing tested as soon as possible.

We moved to a larger apartment on Valentine Avenue, and Nilsa's mother Carmen joined us. Rachel's birth must have triggered a long-suppressed desire in me to have a pet. We brought in a gorgeous blonde cocker spaniel and named him Jag. On weekends we picnicked in Van Cortlandt Park. While Rachel crawled on the grass, Jag raced through the reeds; the only visible sign were his floppy brown and white ears bouncing above the green stems.

I felt some discomfort when Mom and Pop visited. I could see a concern in their faces and in their signed asides to me. They weren't explicit, but did they want to say something like, "Ahtay, are you planning to stay in the Bronx a long time in this new apartment? Is your mother-in-law going to live with you from now on? Now that you have a daughter, we can help out too, you know. Maybe we could all live together in a house of our own, now that you have a good job, and Nilsa is working too?" Was I reading too much between the lines of their faces? I didn't think so.

A month after Rachel was born a group of Puerto Rican radicals did the unthinkable: they stormed a Manhattan church and barricaded themselves inside, demanding that the church make the underused space available for community programs. It was an audacious tactic organized by the Young Lords, the most active and exciting Puerto Rican group to emerge from the political ferment of the time. The peaceful takeover lasted several weeks, through the snowy Christmas holidays, and brought media attention to the Puerto Rican community, the likes of which had never been seen. The only other time Puerto Ricans would appear on television or print, it seemed, was to display violent behavior, whether political or criminal. This time a creative act of civil disobedience in a house of worship, however contrary to the sensitivities of people like me, won the sympathies of New York's public, or at least the liberal segment. The amazing thing about the Young Lords' takeover of the First Spanish Methodist Church in El Barrio, or East Harlem, which I watched intently on the evening news, was that it was successful!

The young Boricuas who were born and raised in New York City—like me—were able to win most of their demands through negotiation and public pressure. And they envisioned a larger agenda that addressed the need for an end to the war in Vietnam, an end to racism, and an end to the inequities in U.S. society. And true to their heritage, they called for the independence of Puerto Rico. I was filled with pride and a yearning to get more involved.

I had been at Riegel Paper Corporation less than a year when I was recruited to a new job. I left Riegel, taking a drop in pay from my $8,500 salary, to work at ASPIRA of New York, Inc., a nonprofit agency led by Puerto Ricans that provided educational counseling and leadership development. In exchange for the lower salary, I grew back my mustache and sideburns, let my wavy brown hair flourish, and assumed my original name and the accented *e* that came with it—after having been Andrew since the sixth grade at Incarnation School, I was Andrés again. These changes were of much greater value to me than the decline in pay grade. My new role was as an educational counselor for Puerto Rican and Latino students, most of whom were like me, the first in their family to attend college. It was challenging but rewarding work helping these Boricuas, many of whom were my age or older. They were pioneers in that first wave of New York City students who took advantage of the open admissions policy recently instituted by the City University of New York. Many private colleges were also creating special programs for minority youth, and ASPIRA was also assisting these students.

They faced numerous obstacles: financial obligations that exceeded the funds provided them, family pressures to help out with responsibilities at home, and often a lack of academic preparation for the rigors of the university classroom. As if these weren't enough to hinder their dreams, our students were also being swept up in the political struggles of the time. Many of them were involved in the student militancy on campuses throughout the city. My job was to advocate for their interests at school and help them design strategies for managing the competing demands on their time and emotions.

My work had that special quality that appealed to young professionals of my generation: it was "relevant." I had the sense of performing a good deed, of being useful to the larger society. My graduate studies in economics were even less useful to my new job than they were at Riegel, but I continued to pursue them anyway. In leaving Riegel Paper Corporation, I was leaving my first and last job in the private sector.

Eight months after Rachel was born, and shortly after starting work at ASPIRA, I left my home in Valentine, leaving a long goodbye letter to Nilsa. Our time living together was a fraction of the years we knew each other, going all the way back to high school, all the way back to the early years on the Block. The world had changed so dramatically since the time of our innocence. Or was it I who had changed drastically, as to be almost indistinguishable from young Andy of Washington Heights? Our interests and passions diverged sharply just as our life together was getting underway. Making a household seemed incompatible with the other passions I wanted to pursue: to become more involved in the political struggle, to explore more thoroughly the meaning of my growing Puerto Rican identity. Whereas our differing sensibilities initially struck me as complementing each other early in our marriage, now our differences seemed to overwhelmingly work against us. Nilsa felt betrayed and let me know it.

Once we attended the Broadway production of *Hair* with Sal and Rose. The musical performances were fabulous and the countercultural themes were powerful. What most stayed in my mind was being disturbed by one scene in particular that resonated with my emotional unrest. In "Easy to Be Hard," a woman sings plaintively of her lover who had a passion for social justice, but who disregarded her needs and hopes. Even in the Age of Aquarius, when love and peace are supposed to reign, there were no easy answers.

Part of the anguish of my failed marriage was the accounting I had to provide to loved ones. Pop gave out a loud groan, his face contorted, and Mom quietly cried when I explained that our marriage was over. They had suspected we were going through much difficulty, but had held on to some hope. They worried about Rachel, concerned they might not see her again.

The split also meant I would lose my connection to Sal. He wasn't the political animal I was, and now it was impossible for us to hang out and for me to be part of his family. The ties were loosened for good. It was always us, with Butchy, preparing the baseball line-up for the Block and drafting plays for our football team. Sal was like a second son to Mom and Pop, so fun-loving and demonstrative in his ways toward them. When we were younger we had even fantasized of going into business together. We talked of opening up a joint savings account, putting aside five dollars weekly to build enough capital eventually to open up a furniture store. The plan never got off the ground—I never was the entrepreneurial type—but it was a necessary dream for two young kids looking to break out of Washington Heights.

The most difficult accounting had to be delayed a long time, for Rachel was barely a toddler when the divorce happened. All I could do was silently promise her that I would never leave her really, that I would always love her and ever be a force in her life. If she had miraculously spoken out: *where* are you going? *why* are you going? No answer would have made sense to her. The one consolation I had was that her hearing was intact, thanks to negative results on her test for deafness.

In early 1971 my marriage officially ended in divorce. The next few years I migrated throughout the Bronx and Manhattan. When I didn't have my own apartment I roomed with friends, declining my parents' offers to return to 514. To accept their shelter would only revive the hope of a joint future with Ahtay.

On a fall day in 1970, the newspapers trumpeted the results of the draft lottery held the day before. Parallel columns of data—lottery numbers paired with birthdates—told the story of who was likely to be sent to Southeast Asia, and who was not. I was still taking economics courses at NYU and I joined a large group of students gathered in the Loeb Student Center on Washington Square South. Some fifty thousand soldiers had already been sacrificed in an insane, unjust war; it was obvious that we were never going to "win" in Vietnam, and nobody wanted to be part of the endgame. Nervously, students took turns perusing the list. Several of them were finishing their undergraduate studies and their future was to be determined by the luck of the draw.

As for me there was curiosity but not drama because I had been assured by a draft counselor that I was not likely to be drafted. Since graduating from Manhattan College I had appealed using every argument I could amass. Over the previous year I had filed several appeals, the first one on the basis of the emotional hardship it would cause my parents to be deprived of my presence. I supplied a letter from Pop's aging physician, Dr. Samuel Stein, who certified that "Mr. and Mrs. Torres have been my patients since April 4, 1947, and they are deaf mutes" and that I was their son. For good measure, I stated in a following letter my conscientious objection to the war in Vietnam and that I could not "place myself in a situation wherein I may have to kill a man without just cause." A third letter, after Rachel's birth in late 1969, added a new argument: economic hardship since I was the sole support for wife and child. The advisor I had been consulting said that the first appeal was the only one I really needed. The Army would not take away the only child from his deaf parents. A voice inside me laughed: How do you like that, finally some benefit from my special condition!

So the day I opened up the *New York Times* at the Loeb Student Center I wasn't burdened with the anxiety and fear others had to deal with. I searched for my birth date on the right hand column. Further and further down the list I scanned, wondering where on the list my name was, what the probability of my going off to war would be if I was a "normal." But my number failed to appear as I continued reading. Halfway down the long columns I stopped and doubled back up the list to make sure I hadn't skipped over my birth date. I resumed scanning. Finally, I reached the end. February 26—the date Mom delivered me—came in dead last! My "random sequence number," the euphemism concocted by the Draft Board to indicate each person's position in the queue, was 365. There was nothing to celebrate when, in the back of your mind, you knew some other guy would be filling your combat boots in a war that made no sense. A few months later I received a letter from the Draft Board saying the "chance of your being inducted is quite remote for the foreseeable future."

10 Despierta Boricua

WHEN I BEGAN WORKING at ASPIRA I quickly realized that there was a heavy political air among the employees, from clericals to professionals. Just about everyone was Puerto Rican, and therefore just about everyone had an opinion about the state of affairs on the island and in the U.S. Puerto Rican community. It was an exhilarating time and place.

Like me, Digna Sánchez and José Navarro were educational counselors. I was amazed by and envious of their knowledge of Puerto Rican history and culture, as well as of their mastery of both Spanish and English. They easily switched from one to the other, in mid-sentence, without a semblance of the tortured "Spanglish" that I struggled with. Both were raised in the U.S.—José in Philadelphia, Digna in New York City—and their families strongly encouraged maintenance of their Puerto Rican heritage. Digna, like Mom, was short with wavy brown hair, but unlike her was a livewire and had strong, passionate views on everything. She translated Puerto Rican poetry into English and had excelled at school. I had never known anyone, let alone a Puerto Rican, who had studied Chinese. For Digna, a product of the Lower East Side, adjacent to Chinatown, it must have seemed a natural course of study.

José was even more animated than Digna. He was taller than me by a head and had a wiry frame, just minimally sufficient to carry his slight, sinewy body. He ate plenty but his body never showed it. He believed my broad nose was a residual indicator of an African root; and I was one of many who believed he must have descended directly from the indigenous Indians (Tainos) of Puerto Rico. His coloring, straight black hair, long nose and flaring nostrils could mean nothing else. José's cubicle was next to mine and we often discussed our counseling "cases," comparing notes and ideas on how to help our "clients."

Digna and José, like me, were the first of their generation to go to college, and both came from working-class backgrounds. I learned they were followers of the Movimiento Pro Independencia (MPI; Movement for Independence in English), one of the most active and militant of the radical groups in Puerto Rico. The MPI, they said, was planning to expand their reach with an organizing initiative among Puerto Ricans in the U.S.

Not long after meeting Digna and José, Philip Rivera joined the ASPIRA staff. I dubbed Philip the "Tallest Puerto Rican in Captivity." His six-and-a-quarter-foot body towered over everyone. You could almost pile two Dignas on top of each other and still not surpass Philip's auburn, wavy hair. Incredibly, I discovered that Philip had lived around the Block. He was five years older than me, so he didn't remember me. But he remembered my family because his father owned a candy store on 178th Street, just around the corner from my grandmother Ita's on Amsterdam Avenue. When he was a teenager, he used to set aside a folded *Daily News* for my aunts and uncles, who he remembered signing in the store. And, of course, he remembered the Chins. Philip had just graduated from Pace College, after a four year stint in the Navy, and was recruited as another counselor. Like all of us at ASPIRA, Philip was a political animal.

Before long, a group of us who were based in ASPIRA, such as José, Philip, and me, but also other friends and political acquaintances, decided to form our own "collective." This was in the manner of the times, for Puerto Rican collectives were blossoming all over the city in colleges, community groups, and workplaces. Many were inspired by the successes of groups like the Young Lords and the Puerto Rican Student Union (PRSU), and by groups in Puerto Rico such as MPI and the Puerto Rican Independence Party (PIP; Partido Independentista Puertorriqueño in Spanish). Most were either nationalist or socialist, or some melding of the two. There were never more than ten or fifteen active members in these groupings, though a small group of committed, creative people could get an awful lot done. We called our own collective Puerto Ricans for Self-Determination (PRSD).

The first issue of our newsletter *El Atrevido* ("The Bold One") announced our policy: "To struggle for the Independence of Puerto Rico and for the Self-Determination of Puerto Ricans in this country. Neither struggle can exist in isolation to the other." In the fall and winter we engaged in several activities and campaigns: a national student conference held at Columbia University, sponsored by the Young Lords and PRSU, followed by a spirited march through Manhattan and into the South Bronx; a week-long "takeover" of Benjamin Franklin High School in East Harlem, to support community demands for relevant curricula and counseling; a forum at NYU to expose the horrible treatment and working conditions of Puerto Ricans in the migrant worker camps of New Jersey and Connecticut; and testimony at a White House Conference on Youth decrying the lack of attention to educational needs of young Puerto Ricans.

Each month *El Atrevido* appeared with satirical commentary on politicians, poverty programs, the drug crisis, economic exploitation, and racist media coverage of Puerto Ricans. Other writings informed our small readership about Puerto Rican history and culture and the contemporary independence struggle. We delighted in the power of words and in our ability to influence with our ideas. Our long "political education" sessions inevitably led us to the big question. Where are we going from here? Do we continue as we are, an interesting, but small collective with our own voice? Or do we aspire for more strength in numbers, by joining up with one of the larger groups? The Young Lords? The MPI or PIP? A radical group within the U.S. Left?

By June of 1971 PRSD was dissolved and most of the members of our collective joined the MPI. The overriding factor was a desire to have an organic connection with the island-based revolutionary movement. Since the early 1960s the MPI had maintained an official presence in New York City, a sort of satellite group in exile that was affiliated to the national organization based in Puerto Rico. Composed of a few score of dedicated activists, it had worked on getting public support on behalf of Puerto Rican independence. A main effort was an international campaign to obtain United Nations recognition that Puerto Rico was a colony of the United States, something that irritated the U.S. government to no end. During the 1940s and 1950s, the United States had succeeded in stifling international discussion about Puerto Rico, the colony in its own backyard.

The Cuban Revolution of 1959 changed this by providing Puerto Rican *independentistas* with a fervent and effective ally. To be associated with Fidel Castro, a thorn in the side of American presidents from Eisenhower to Nixon, was no easy proposition during the cold war. But to the MPI and other Puerto Rican nationalists, Fidel was a hero, someone unafraid of sticking up for the tiny island. In fact, Castro was proud of saying that one of the first times he ever got beat up by the Cuban police was back in the 1930s, in a student demonstration at the University of Havana in support of Puerto Rican independence.

Another appealing aspect of the MPI was its plans to become a full-fledged revolutionary party, the Partido Socialista Puertorriqueño (PSP; Puerto Rican Socialist Party in English) by the end of the year. For all intents and purposes, the MPI was already the PSP.

The Young Lords were an attractive alternative but we felt they were literally too young and inexperienced and lacked roots in the island's political scene. There was inconsistency in my own thinking: I felt strongly about the need for radical organizing among Puerto Ricans in the U.S. for our social uplift here, a goal the Young Lords postulated, but saw the island-based PSP as the best vehicle for achieving this. This inverted logic would underlie my political energies for a good time to come.

Digna Sánchez, who was a supporter of our collective but who had already joined the MPI-PSP, facilitated our entry into the organization. It was agreed that for a while we would continue to publish *El Atrevido* as an insert into the PSP's weekly newspaper, *Claridad*. Besides José, Philip, and me, other PRSD participants joined, including Mariana, José's wife, who was quiet and mellow and spoke Spanish better than I. We naturally assumed she was Puerto Rican but later learned she was African American. Philip's youngest sister, Vivian, had also been active in PRSD. She was a student at City College and had friends active in PRSU and the Young Lords. She shared a measure of her brother's height, making her taller than me, and had sparkling sea-green eyes. Where did those eyes come from?

We weren't the only ones gravitating toward the PSP. Boricuas from all over were gathering at Casa Puerto Rico, the group's headquarters and cultural center, located in a second-story loft of an old building at 106 East Fourteenth Street near Union Square. With its creaking, wooden floors, open space and ancient-looking bathroom it could have been a factory in an earlier life. Once upon a time, someone said, there were rows of sewing machines arrayed on that floor. But now it was a loft decorated with the symbols of Puerto Rican culture and pride: *La Bandera* (the flag), scenes of the island's beauty, and portraits of the great figures of Puerto Rican history: Ramón Emeterio Betances, Eugenio María de Hostos, and Don Pedro Albizu Campos. Betances had registered his historic lament during the mid-1800s, referring to Spanish colonialism: "What is the matter with Puerto Ricans that they don't rebel?" The MPI's response now a century later was a defiant call to action: "*¡Despierta Boricua, Defiende Lo Tuyo!*" Wake up, Puerto Rican, defend what is yours!

Friday nights at Casa Puerto Rico were a cornucopia of politics and art, offering speakers from revolutionary movements such as the Nation of Islam, the Palestinian Liberation Organization, the Black Panthers, the Irish

Republican Army, the Dominican Left, the U.S. Left, and all manner of antiwar organizations. The great political movies of the time were presented: *The Battle of Algiers*, *La Hora de los Hornos*, *Burn*. And of course, poets and singers: Pedro Pietri, Suni Paz, Pépe y Flora. Casa Puerto Rico became an enclave of our own countercultural and revolutionary artistic and political scene.

Entering the PSP opened me up to a world of names and characters unlike anything I had experienced since the days of the Block. But unlike Washington Heights, and my piece of it based in Highbridge, the new political world I had chosen was a nearly undiluted Puerto Rican-ness. Few non-Spanish names were to be heard. This was no United Nations of diversity. Accents abounded, as did *z*'s and rolling *r*'s. In the years to come my interactions were circumscribed within a homogenous but expanding universe of names: Aguiar, Alicéa, Alvarez, Arbona, Arrastía, Baérga, Barreto, Bomexí, Cabézas, Carrión, Cintrón, Colón, Cruz, Díaz, Domenech, Escobar, Inclán, La Lúz, López, Malavet, Mátos, Mercéd, Miranda, Morales, Nadal, Pérez, Quiñones, Quintana, Reyes, Ríos, Rivera, Rodríguez, Sánchez, Sanabria, Santiago, Serrano, Sorrentini, Torres, Vargas, Vázquez, Velázquez, Vélez, Vera. Of course, there were the occasional exceptions that proved the rule: Berger, Bergman, Blaught, Hamberg, Karliner, Perry.

It seemed the way was clear for my full involvement in political struggle. I was even considering the idea of eventually leaving my position at ASPIRA to become a full-time organizer when the MPI officially became the Puerto Rican Socialist Party. Such a move meant getting the meager pay of a political cadre, but I was willing to trade in the steady income for the life of personal heroes such as Che Guevara and Malcom X.

My principal concern was my parents. In a few years Pop would be retiring, and then how would they get by? Mom had long since been out of the workforce, having devoted her years to the unpaid labors of homemaking.

What employer would hire a deaf woman at her age, unskilled and virtually illiterate? Pop's Social Security would barely suffice to keep a roof over their heads. But would they stay forever at 514?

In the early 1970s the Highbridge section of Washington Heights was deteriorating rapidly. Once, bringing three-year-old Rachel to see her grandparents, we were greeted by a huge pothole in the middle of 176th Street. It extended from building 514 down to the next building, 512, at least ten feet in diameter. I joked to Rachel, who was sitting on my shoulders, that it looked like a meteor had crashed into my old neighborhood. The hole was cordoned off by police barriers and passing cars carefully edged by. Apparently no one among local officialdom had a vested interest in patching up the eyesore; it grew steadily in the months that followed. And unlike in other parts of the city, where residents protested on behalf of their needs, Highbridge was a political hinterland where apathy seemed to reign. With each subsequent visit the pothole spread like a cancer, exposing a brown and gray underground world of dirt, stones, and sewage pipes. By the time the city got around to repairing the damage, which had attained moon-crater proportions, 176th Street had been closed off completely to traffic.

With the passing months, the apartment buildings were taking on the look of run-down tenements. It appeared my beloved Highbridge would degrade into the classic urban ghetto. At each visit to 514 Mom hit me with a barrage of complaints about the apartment: no heat, leaking pipes and ceilings, peeling wall paint. The roaches were more bothersome than ever. The building didn't even have a super anymore. Couldn't I get a lawyer to sue the landlord? Didn't I have political friends who could get them a better place to live?

As far as I could tell, Pop had no plan for the future. He had always dreamed that he and Mom would live with me. A double-decker in Queens or Brooklyn would be ideal, with easy access into Manhattan. Anywhere that wouldn't isolate him from his deaf friends. I cautioned him that these were not my plans, that he couldn't rely on me to be with him and Mom. After the breakup of my marriage and seeing that I was getting further involved in the political realm, Pop didn't openly raise the idea of combining forces. In the meantime, though, I couldn't determine exactly what his post-retirement plans were.

It was in this context that he mentioned to me one day that I didn't need to worry about Mom, because he had a life insurance plan that would take care of her should anything happen to him. He had purchased the policy from the Prudential Insurance Co. in 1959 and had faithfully kept up the monthly payments. This came as a huge relief to me. I recalled translating for him when he lied to the Prudential man, saying he became deaf by falling from a palm tree when a little boy in Puerto Rico. And I remembered when the curly red-haired insurance agent Mr. Covello came every few months to apartment 43 to collect the premium.

Pop said the plan was worth "thousands of dollars" and that it would cover Mom's needs. I anxiously asked to see the policy, in my mind valued in the five-figure range. Pop said it was buried among a messy pile of papers in one of his desk draws. As soon as he located it, he would mail it to me and we could talk about it the next time. After dining on Mom's delicious *carne guisada* I left, comforted that Mom would have financial security.

Alas, that peace of mind lasted but a week, abruptly ending when the paperwork arrived in the mail. In reviewing the insurance policy, which I had never seen before, I realized Pop was grossly confused about its contents. As I carefully read and re-read the terms of the policy, my heart sank. What Pop had signed onto was not a life insurance plan, which would provide for Mom's security after his death, but something called an "Endowment at Age 65 Intermediate Ordinary Policy." This was gobbledygook for a benefit should Pop die or become disabled before the age of sixty-five. All this time Pop thought he had ensured Mom's stability, but this was far from true.

The legalistic prose typed on the Prudential policy was Greek to my father. There was no mention of the thousands of dollars for Mom. The monthly amount he had to pay was all of three dollars and sixty-five cents. In the section specifying the payoff for his payments—where the words

"Face Amount of Insurance" appeared—was a grand total of $750. This was the total value of the policy! Dying before sixty-five would leave Mom barely enough to cover one year's rent in apartment 43. That was also the payoff assuming Pop survived his sixty-fifth birthday. This would be the tiny bounty for retirement, enough for a two-week vacation in Florida.

Pop had confused the concept of life insurance with a simple death benefit. As I poured over the pages again, it brought back painful memories of how the deaf were regularly misinformed, if not swindled, in consumer transactions. But I was angry too, at Pop, for having been so badly off the mark. I called Mr. Covello to verify my reading of the policy. He confirmed what I suspected. I was too embarrassed even to explain my father's erroneous assumption. I retreated back to square one in the obsessive desire to free myself of filial responsibilities. How was I going to handle this at my next visit to 514?

It was about a week later when I returned to 514 to report my findings. I arrived in the late afternoon before Pop had finished his workday. I pressed the round, white button that ignited the flashing light in the apartment. From outside I could hear Mom's slippers dragging along the floor as she waddled down the hallway toward the door. With a hug and kiss she greeted me, throwing her short arms up over my shoulders. Seated on the vinyl-covered sofa, we talked about the events of the past week. I didn't mention anything about the insurance policy. It was too complicated a matter to bring up with her; I would wait for Pop to come home.

Since leaving home to get married three years earlier, visits to 514 were more often than not a somber occasion for me, even with Rachel along. The place seemed so empty and lifeless. Mom spent the day all by herself, waiting for Pop to come home. Dinner was not the same, I imagined, without me there. Those first weeks after I left must have been especially difficult for them, having to somehow fill the void created by my departure. No one to interpret the TV news, no one for Pop to discuss sports with, no one to liven up Mom's monotonous routine. Now it was just the two of them. They treasured my visits, but my sporadic appearances could not alter the loneliness that permeated their lives. Things might have been different, I thought, if only they had had more children.

After the initial exchange of greetings I asked Mom how she was feeling. Not surprisingly, she launched into a catalogue of the maladies brought on by advancing age: back pains, high blood pressure, tightness of breath, migraines. This day, though, I wasn't in the mood to patiently absorb her complaints.

"You know, you don't have to just sit there and let these problems take over your life," I counseled her. "Think for yourself. You see how heavy you are? That's not good. From the heavy weight come many of the problems you have, especially the back pains and the blood pressure."

Mom signed her retort. "I take medicines, but the pills do not help me. I follow the instructions. The doctor stinks; he gives me pills but they do not help me." She nodded sullenly to affirm her innocence.

"The pills are not going to do any good, if you don't reduce your weight and do more exercise. You have to go on a diet. You have to be more active. You eat too much cake and sweets. I told you this before but you never listen to me."

She didn't appreciate my advice and raised the tension level another notch. "What do you mean? I *am* busy. Every day I clean the house, the clothing; I walk down and up four floors to do shopping, and carrying big bags with heavy cans. I *am* active! Oh yes, I *am* active! Your father; *he* is not active. We never go out. He never takes me to the movies or nothing. We never go to visit anyone. We just stay here watching TV."

"Pop has nothing to do with this. This is separate." I signed back heatedly, vigorously shaking my head in disagreement. "Look, come with me."

Taking her hand, I escorted her into the kitchen, and opened the beige-colored tin cabinet that was lodged below the sink. Alongside the boxes of Tide and Brillo soap pads was Mom's makeshift medicine chest. Arrayed like toy soldiers in the Tupperware tray were more than thirty plastic medicine bottles, of varying sizes, colors, and vintage. Some had never been opened. I seized the tray and placed it on the floor in front of the kitchen sink. I knelt on the linoleum with the pills in front of me, and looked up at Mom, standing beside me.

"Look, see how many bottles you have? Diet pills, blood pressure pills, Aspirin, vitamin pills. You have too many pills. This is not good for you. Medicine will not make you feel better if you don't change your habits. You have to stop eating snacks all day long. This is why you feel bad!"

Then, I grabbed each plastic container from the tray and slammed it to the floor. One by one, I denounced the contents to Mom. "This, this is no good! This, this is no good! This, this is no good!"

She watched, unsure of how to react. Never had I unleashed my emotions like this to Mom. She nodded nervously, not in agreement, but in anxiety. She had come to assume that I would always accept her complaints with understanding, that I was a willing target of the anger she felt toward Pop and the world. She didn't expect me to solve her problems, just to receive the fusillade. But I had enough of being the punching bag.

I gathered the pill cases that were strewn about, returned them to the tray that I placed back inside the cabinet. I got up off my knees, walked past Mom into the living room where I put on the TV, and waited for Pop. Mom busied herself in the kitchen.

When Pop finally arrived and settled himself, he embraced me with a smile. He was ready for breezy conversation. But I didn't reciprocate, opting to salute him solemnly. He immediately picked up that something was awry. Mom had joined us in the living room, seating herself on the sofa, not letting on about the incident with the pills. Before Pop had a chance to sit down, I addressed him, myself standing too. I cut to the chase, my arms stiffening as I signed.

"I have bad news about the insurance. There is no life insurance for Mom. There is only a small amount, seven hundred and fifty dollars, when you reach sixty-five. If something happens to you before that age, Mom gets the money. That's it."

His jaw dropped in disbelief. "What? That can't be. When I bought the insurance in 1959, the man said it was like life insurance, that it would take care of your mother when I die. I don't understand. How can that be?"

I launched into a tirade, signing and vocalizing at the same time.

"If you had paid attention to what the insurance man was saying you wouldn't have been so confused. How could you think that sending in three dollars and sixty-five cents a month was going to help Mom with what she needs? Instead of wasting money on the numbers and the horses, if you had sacrificed wisely and put it away in savings or a real life insurance plan, we wouldn't be here worried about the future. In a few years you will retire, and then what? How are you two going to survive? You have nothing. You're still stuck in this apartment. Now, I have to find a way to set you up. This is not what I wanted to be dealing with at the age of twenty-five, with my own child. Why can't I be free to think about my own future? Every time I come here Mom complains. Her headaches and back pains; she's lonely and bored. You never spend time with her, you never take her out. All you two do is work, watch TV, and sleep. Is this what you're going to do for the rest of your life?"

He looked at me glumly and said nothing. Mom's eyes twitched agitatedly. I told them I was too upset to stay for dinner and would be back next week. Surely, I was entitled to a rare blow-up. But I felt small.

The following week I returned to 514. I had left them with several days to ponder my outburst. There were no phone conversations, obviously, in the intervening period. No opportunities to talk calmly about that day and defuse the tension. Mom received me with a straight face when she opened the door. Then, as I passed her to enter the apartment, she jolted the door shut. From behind, she shuffled me down the hallway into the living room, her fingers pressed against my shoulders.

In the living room, she broke into a tantrum, tossing a table lamp and scattering a pile of Pop's *Daily News*. Now it was her turn. She glared at me with her bulldog face and began.

"You can't talk to your father like that! He cried when you left; tears came down his face like I have never seen. He suffered all week, with cramps in his stomach. After all these years this is how you behave toward him? Aren't you ashamed? Don't you think he feels bad about how we live? What, now you're a big shot, because you have college and a big job? Who took care of you when you were small, cleaned and fed you? You think that's easy? You'll see, you'll see how hard life is. Everybody shits on deaf people; they make fun of us, think we're stupid. Being deaf is not funny. You'll see. Then you'll be sorry for us. God will punish you. You will see."

Mom's attack struck violently at the façade of self-assurance I had adopted. Unlike Pop, dignified Pop, Mom was capable of doing physical damage, to others and herself. I was poised to protect myself from her, expecting a slap or a punch, even. But I was bowed down in shame too. Didn't I go overboard in condemning Pop last week? How could I wound him like that?

There was no point in a rejoinder. She had her say and I left it at that. I thought of leaving, but Mom demanded I wait for Pop. She began preparing dinner. When my father came home he was glad to see me. I apologized for my harshness the previous week, and hugged him close to me. He grabbed me too.

"Do not worry; forget about it," he said. "Now we eat."

There couldn't have been more than fifty of us that cold Sunday afternoon in late 1971. This surprised me since the meeting had been called as a national gathering of the most active and trusted members of the PSP in the United States. I was honored to be included in the session. But was this all we were, just fifty people? Nevertheless there we were in our folding chairs, waiting for the meeting to start and hoping that the steam would soon warm up Casa Puerto Rico.

Years earlier, barely a teenager, I sat in the meeting room of the Archdiocese of New York in Rockefeller Plaza. There I observed Pop presiding over meetings of the Puerto Rican Society for the Catholic Deaf. How long ago that seemed. Today I was a full participant in very different proceedings. The words "Puerto Rican" were common to the two settings, but little else. The two groups didn't even speak the same language.

The purpose of the meeting was to work out a vision that would make the PSP relevant to the many young Puerto Ricans who had become radicalized during the late 1960s. The success of the Young Lords and other U.S.-based groups caused a significant sector of the island-oriented, older members of the PSP to rethink their mission in the U.S. For several months leading up to the meeting at Casa Puerto Rico, discussion groups had hashed out the outline for a new political formula that would expand the group's scope and reach in cities where Puerto Rican communities were growing fast.

Members started to realize that more attention had to be directed toward the day-to-day concerns of Boricuas on the mainland. Having already decided to transform itself into a socialist organization, with a greater focus on class exploitation in Puerto Rico, it stood to reason that the same blueprint should be applied to the Puerto Ricans in the U.S.

It made no sense to ask Puerto Ricans in the Diaspora, most of who were here for good, to denounce colonialism, poverty, and social injustice on the island without addressing the same problems in their own neighborhoods. In dealing with immediate problems like unemployment, discrimination, and lack of housing, people could be educated on the ills of capitalist society and imperialism. Many members, especially younger ones like me, believed we could easily make the connections to the colonial situation of Puerto Rico. After all, the United States government was behind the mass migration that literally exiled so many native sons and daughters from their homeland during the 1940s.

That December afternoon the political debate that had absorbed our attention during the previous months was to culminate in a vote. There were two basic views put on the table. The first, voiced mostly by island-based "veterans," favored a focused conception of the new Seccional as a vehicle for solidarity work, including such issues as the fight to liberate the Nationalist Prisoners. The second view, supported most actively by second-generation Boricuas, argued for an additional role, that of organizing in our communities and workplaces around a program of democratic rights and contributing to a socialist transformation in the United States. In retrospect, to pose this grandiose double agenda was the height of ambition, to say the least. Yet such was the historical moment and such was our self-confidence that we believed ourselves capable of monumental achievements.

Along with others favoring a double agenda, I argued for an aggressive organizing strategy in Puerto Rican communities, one that would show the link between the oppression of Boricuas in the U.S. with colonialism on the Island.

The more veteran members, those deeply attached to the homeland, feared this new proposal would dilute the organization's mission. They worried that it was simply too much for the organization to take on the struggle in both the mainland and the colony. Others said that we would get drawn into the contentious debates and rivalries with the U.S. Left. To accentuate their point, they reminded us of an incident that happened a year earlier when the PSP was still the MPI.

A group called the Progressive Labor Party, notorious for provoking clashes within the Left, attempted an "invasion" of Casa Puerto Rico. They had previously condemned us in their newspaper for "bourgeois national-ism," saying Puerto Ricans should organize directly for proletarian revo-lution in the United States. One Friday night about twenty of them entered the street level doorway of the building where "Casa" was located at 106 East Fourteenth Street. Then they came charging up to the second floor, bent on disrupting our weekly public program. Big mistake. They got as far as the front door where members were stationed. The second-floor land-ing filled up with tensed bodies, then raised voices, then a bilingual bar-rage of political sloganeering from both sides. About a half dozen *MPIistas* stood outside the entrance to Casa blocking the leftist extremists from entering the main hall. As tensions escalated, suddenly louder screams of pain were heard and the intruders abruptly backpedaled. Several of them had received knife wounds and they retreated hurriedly down the narrow stairway and disappeared onto Fourteenth Street.

The following day's *New York Times* reported the melee, saying this was evidence of the violent nature of the Puerto Rican independence move-ment. Incidents such as these were cited by the veterans as reasons for the

PSP to have a narrowly focused mission in the United States. Others distrusted those of the younger breed. In their eyes, we were ambitious new recruits trying to take over the organization. We had little knowledge of Puerto Rico and were more comfortable speaking the language of the colonizer. The veterans were reserved in their enthusiasm for the "Nuyoricans" (a term often used by island Puerto Ricans to refer to Puerto Ricans in the U.S.).

After hours of ideological debate, the question of what role the new PSP would play in the U.S. was called to a vote. Despite resistance from some of the old guard the outcome was positive: two thirds of those present raised their hands to affirm a new direction. Though the organization was still dominated by "islanders" most of them were savvy enough to realize that the future of the organization lay in its potential to bring in second-generation Boricuas.

The Party was quick to remedy my lack of familiarity with the island. Not many weeks after the meeting at Casa Puerto Rico I was sent to a labor seminar at national headquarters in Rio Piedras. Little did my *camaradas* realize just how unfamiliar I was with *La Isla del Encanto*, for that was the first time I had ever touched that soil.

Even before joining the MPI, during the late sixties as I began affirming my Puerto Rican identity, I had always let people assume that I had been born in Puerto Rico. And if directly asked, I fibbed about my origins. My parents had met and married in Puerto Rico, I said. There they had me, and shortly after, they migrated to New York. Mom and Pop had never gone back since leaving in the 1940s, and neither did they ever have the wherewithal to send me on a trip.

I had become practiced in compartmentalizing my private history through the habit of obscuring my parents' deafness. Concealing my true birthplace, the South Bronx, was another embellishment to the image. I fell victim to a self-imposed need to present myself as a "real" Puerto Rican, that is, one who was born on the island. Such was the nationalist spirit of the time that a toddler's brief initial residency in the homeland carried greater status than birth in the hated Metropolis. This was never anything officially declared to me by *compañeros* in the struggle, but patriotic zeal swayed me into revising my autobiography.

In my defense, I should point out that there were others who fell victim to the preference for a native birth. Some took extraordinary measures to achieve the dream. I recall one *compañera militante,* an expectant mother, who relocated to the Island months prior to the due date, just so that her baby would be delivered *"en el país nativo."* Shortly thereafter, she and her husband resumed life back in New York City, the newborn infant in tow.

That first trip to the ancestral soil was nothing more than a fleeting weekend jaunt, spent indoors in a cement block without air conditioning. Our objective was to discuss the state of the union movement and the Party's labor organizing strategy. Even with the metal blinders drawn open to welcome the breeze, the place was a sweat box. The space was so small that, when we broke up into discussion groups, some of us had to relocate to the roof, exposed to the midday sun.

I was among my colleagues in the struggle, members of the same organization, but I couldn't quite overcome the feeling of being a stranger. Just arrived from the winter climate, I was the target of much staring, and some people commented how *hincho* (pale) I looked. One referred to me teasingly as *el gringo de Nueva York.* Then there was the nemesis of language. My Spanish paled in comparison to that of my fellow *militantes.* I knew that the first words out of my mouth would point out my cultural limitations.

Shades of the Professor Pucino moments in my life, those moments when I was singled out for my lack of Spanish fluency! Should I justify my flawed diction and vocabulary? Should I bother to explain my personal history growing up in Deaf culture? Should I detail the intricate linguistic interactions between Spanish, English, and sign language in my very special family? Should I offer a sophisticated analysis of the effect of Deaf culture on my identity? As in high school and college, I kept my Deaf side closeted.

I didn't appreciate the kidding around of the few who took advantage of my newcomer status. When I didn't smile at their teasing comments, they knew I didn't find it funny. In general, though, I was received warmly and treated with fraternal hospitality. On this first trip I stayed with Benjamín Ortíz, a leader of the environmental movement, and his wife Carmen Noelia, also known as Joy. A pleasant woman of small stature and straight brown hair, Joy could deceive you with her blue-eyed smiling innocence. Like many *compañeras* I came to know in the movement, her outward appearance belied a fierce emotional commitment to her ideals.

Joy was famous for having smacked the president of the University of Puerto Rico in the face as she received her graduation diploma. This was in retaliation for Jaime Benítez's earlier decision to call in the military to suppress a student antiwar rally. In the ensuing conflict a young woman had been shot to death by the police, and many others were injured and arrested. Joy was a participant in the student protest and had apparently vowed to avenge the president's decision. She waited three months to vent her anger.

In no time, the labor seminar was over, and I was back in the New York cold. That first visit to Puerto Rico turned out to be the shortest I ever made. After that weekend, the flights multiplied. I traveled again and again, sometimes for politics, sometimes for pleasure. I continued working full-time at ASPIRA, now as director of a new Office of Information and Research, but my evenings and weekends were taken up by radical political organizing. With each sojourn the understanding of my family history deepened, the comprehension of my place in the world was clarified.

Until I had a visceral experience of Puerto Rico, I could not pigeonhole myself neatly along the spectrum of Boricua identities. Puerto Rico reminded me of what I was not: a bona fide, born and bred *puertorriqueño*. I was unlike my island-based *compañeros* in many ways. Growing up, Spanish came to me in fragmentary bursts of caress and command from my hearing relatives, then later in textbooks. Only gradually and in my twenties did I have the confidence of assembling paragraphs in conversation or discourse. My entrée into Latin culture was through salsa music, and I was surprised to see that so few of the political types danced the way we danced in New York. Puerto Rican literature and art were foreign to me.

Despite its striking beauty, *La Isla del Encanto* wielded no bewitching spell over me. Its rolling green hills and lush forests, its crystalline beaches, its skies that could transform instantly from a blanket of blue to a storm-ridden grey: these were worthy of martyrdom for the *independentistas* in my company. But the only turf I was ever attached to was the Block, the corner of 177th Street and Amsterdam Avenue. And in contrast to many of my fellow activists, I had no lineage within the nationalist or radical movements of Puerto Rico. Each trip solidified my political passions and my Puerto Rican-ness, but also differentiated me from the typical *militante* on the Island. Each trip reminded me of what I was not.

Meanwhile my upbringing in the U.S. had reinforced that I was not quite a red-blooded American. The four letter word, the deprecating comments about Zorro being the only famous Spanish person, being kicked off of basketball courts where "I didn't belong," the kids' stares from the other side of the Mason-Dixon line. The dominant culture reminded me of what I was not. Pop had accepted the traditional formula. I was born and bred in the U.S., and therefore *americano* (signed by clasping the hands together and circling them in front of your chest—where that sign came from, I haven't the slightest idea!). But Pop didn't know any of this, for I shielded him from my life in the hearing world.

Beyond the Block I could only be defined in negatives, what I was not. Eventually I worked out my own truth. I'm somewhere in between—for lack of a better word, a Nuyorican. And yet, even this label is but a half-truth, for my deepest roots were in Deaf culture, a side of me that remained private throughout my political activism.

In April of 1973, after a year and a half of intense organizing throughout the Northeast and Midwest, we harvested the fruits of our missionary zeal. At Casa Puerto Rico we were fifty. Now, at the old Manhattan Center, located on 34th Street off Eighth Avenue, we were three thousand. On a sunny spring day, we held the First Congress of the U.S. Branch of the

Puerto Rican Socialist Party (PSP). La Seccional, the Spanish term for the PSP's organization in the U.S. Puerto Rican communities, issued its landmark publication, *Desde las Entrañas*, and introduced its leadership. When my name was announced I nervously joined my fellow *compañeros* and *compañeras* on the stage, presented as a member of the Political Commission and Secretary of the PSP's New York Region.

From fifty individuals to three thousand: it seemed unreal. Yet there was no mystery to our success, which was borne of old-fashioned, painstaking organizing. Along with occasional dramatics and publicity. I couldn't begin to quantify the human effort that went into our organizational growth. The meetings. The marches, rallies, and pickets. The public forums and debates. The press conferences and interviews. The selling of our newspaper *Claridad* on the streets. More meetings. The home visits to our financial supporters. The cultural productions and fundraisers. The speeches on the street corners and appearances at colleges and conferences. And more meetings.

The jubilant enthusiasm and raucous chanting that filled that historic meeting hall confirmed our belief, first articulated on that cold Sunday afternoon in late 1971, that a new radical movement could be aroused. We could do this by uniting the issues affecting our community in the Diaspora with the demand for Puerto Rican independence. Looking out on the cheering audience, drawn from every walk of Puerto Rican life, I flashed back to the meeting at Casa Puerto Rico, bemused that a small group of dedicated activists could transform itself into such a force.

Every "look" in the Boricua constellation made its appearance: the black suit and tie, the loosely hanging dashiki, the tight-fitting thigh-high skirt, the bell-bottom dungarees, the pressed *guayabera*, the beret topping off a flourishing Afro, the field jacket of fading olive green. Every stratum of Boricua society was represented: factory worker, office secretary, student, intellectual, professional, housewife, street youth, and the migrant farm laborer who had come in from Connecticut and southern New Jersey. There was a proud and self-assured demeanor on all those Puerto Rican faces, black, brown, and white, and every hue in between.

The event at Manhattan Center was a perfect outcome to the fevered pace of the previous year and a half. It established the PSP as the dominant force in the Puerto Rican Left, as a visible entity within the Puerto Rican community at large, and as a rising influence within the U.S. Left. For those of us at the center of the maelstrom of activity it was confirmation that hard work applied to a clear vision could produce real results.

We were attempting to build a classic vanguard political organization, following the model of Marxist-Leninist groups throughout the world. These groups had spread like wildfire among Third World countries. Our goal was to effect revolutionary social change, in a direct challenge to imperialism and capitalism. In the case of Puerto Rico, the vanguard party had the immediate task of leading the struggle for national independence. This was a tall order, to say the least, but we were undaunted by the undertaking. We were young, full of raw energy, and convinced of the justice of our cause.

We knew our meetings were being taped, our phones bugged. We could see our demonstrations were photographed and filmed. Our homes were broken into and our possessions scoured for anything that might be incriminating. We were told by family and acquaintances of visits by police and FBI agents. There were confrontations with police and with courthouse security guards. There were grand jury hearings and arrests and time in jail. And there was worse. We never thought about the danger to our future, at least not in the beginning. There was no future outside the revolution.

The infant Seccional of the PSP was wildly successful in building a vibrant political organization. Our members took on numerous campaigns in the growing network of cities where we established chapters: Boston, Springfield, Hartford, Waterbury, New Haven, Hoboken, Newark, Jersey City, Trenton, Philadelphia. As far as Gary, Indiana, and Chicago and even in Los Angeles and the Bay Area, Puerto Ricans joined up to build the vanguard party. And of course in New York City, home to a million Boricuas, there was fertile terrain for a group like ours.

By the time we marshaled our forces at Manhattan Center our confidence had zoomed sky-high. It was no wonder that, during this time, my Puerto Rican "side" took over center stage and absorbed me totally. My politics and my identity were one. I had no time to attend to Mom and Pop. What little free time I permitted myself, I devoted to Rachel. And if few of my *compañeros* were aware of my family history, I didn't go out of my way to clue them in on it. One might have thought I didn't have any parents at all.

11 A Garden

L ITTLE DID MY PARENTS know, as they wondered how well my plans were aligned with their imagined future, that I was gradually remaking the personal side of my life. They were surprised when, in early 1974, I told them that I was going to remarry. My future wife was Vivian Rivera, the one with the sea-green eyes, whose brother Philip worked with me at ASPIRA. Mom and Pop had met Vivian only once before we announced our wedding but they approved of her. She was Puerto Rican, a lovely and serious young woman. In a reference to her almost nonexistent waist, Mom teased me about Vivian's tall, curvaceous lines. Behind her back she winked at me and, with outstretched palms, drew the outline of Vivian's hourglass shape in the air. I described their future daughter-in-law, as they interrogated me. Yes, she's very involved in the PSP (a worry), and gets along well with Rachel (a relief). Her family also lived in Washington Heights for a while. In fact, they had a candy store on 178th Street and remember our deaf family signing in the store, and her brothers hung out with some of the same kids I did. Yes, the Riveras remember Butchy's family and the Chins too.

Vivian's full name was Carmen Vivian and her world could be divided into three groups: those who knew her as Vivian (her siblings and several close friends), those who knew her as Carmen (fellow employees and several close friends), and those who knew her as Carmen Vivian (fellow political activists and several close friends). That she had a mischievous edge to her was evidenced by the fact that her most intimate friends were confused by her real name. She delighted in this. To establish my exclusivity in her orbit of relations, I eventually gave her another name: Viveroni.

In 1958 when she was nine and living in Washington Heights, her father Felípe died suddenly of a heart attack. The family came home one day to find him on the living room floor as the TV was tuned to *Gunsmoke*. This left Vivian's mother María alone to raise her and three teenage children. Besides Philip, the oldest of the children, Vivian had a sister, Vicky, and a brother, Rubén. Like his youngest sister, Rubén had very light eyes, whose source I eventually discovered: María's ancestors had come to Puerto Rico from Ireland. After their father's death the Riveras were a wandering band in the Bronx, with an occasional foray back to Washington Heights. Few landlords would rent to a single Puerto Rican woman raising four kids.

How badly they had misread María's character. She was a no-nonsense woman who trekked daily to a Brooklyn factory to keep the household afloat. She sacrificed her own chances for remarriage for her children, staying aloof from the men who approached her. The trauma of instant widowhood seemed to have removed any trace of sentimentality and romanticism from the attractive forty-year-old. It was no mean feat for a divorced man and father like me to have won her blessing to be Vivian's husband. "Las Riveritas," as my fellow brother-in-law Gilbert Carrillo would dub Vicky and Vivian, had descended from a strong Puerto Rican woman. María was the "Queen Bee" in our eyes.

By the time I ran into Philip at ASPIRA, in the early 1970s, the Riveras were settled in the West Bronx, and the three oldest children were married. They were a socializing brew and loved to host parties. It was a joy to observe the Riveras at a party. Over the years they had collectively rehearsed each new dance craze: chachacha, guaguancó, pachanga, boogaloo. They had developed their own choreography of stepping and twisting, switching and twirling.

Pairing off, they would take a song like Eddie Palmieri's "Vamonos Pa'l Monte" ("Let's Go to the Mountain") and turn it into an exaltation of salsa dancing. The piece opens with a throbbing conga then segues strangely into an organ riff (not common in a Latin song!). A vocal chorus breaks in with the song's theme of escaping urban restlessness, and this is followed by a rush of trumpets and timbales. In the second half of this seven-minute masterpiece the pace kicks up to a breathtaking speed, the percussion instruments, the horns and organ (always the organ weaving in and out) clashing and crosscutting, only to stop suddenly. Throughout the song, the four Riveras kept perfect pace with the changing rhythms and speeds, and switching partners— now Philip with Vivian and Ruben with Vicky, then Philip with Vicky and Ruben with Vivian. They even allowed for inventive solo performances, each showcasing favorite steps, smooth and gliding, avoiding grandiose acrobatics.

I considered myself a fairly competent *salsero*, but I didn't compare to anyone in that that quartet. I was intimidated at the idea of breaking into the foursome. To interrupt them seemed foolish. One should just watch.

In late March of 1974, Vivian and I were married by a justice of the peace in the Manhattan Municipal Building downtown. We were on an assembly line of couples who were transformed from sweethearts to newlyweds. As we filed in line toward the chapel behind several other pairs, Pop rushed to the men's room, saying he'd be "back fast." "Back fast" was too late. When he returned Vivian and I were already man and wife. After exchanging vows in City Hall, we all proceeded to a sumptuous lunch of dim sum in Chinatown just a few blocks away. No more than a dozen family members and friends were with us, including the Riveras, José Navarro, my best man, and Louie Shapiro, on military leave. My parents were accustomed to church weddings in full dress and pompous solemnity, in front of a fully ordained priest (preferably Fr. Lynch) and followed by an elaborate reception. They probably wondered how long this match would last.

In late 1973 the PSP leadership in Puerto Rico decided that the time was ripe for a major event, an Acto Nacional, that would rally people to denounce U.S. colonialism and capitalism. It should coincide with the U.N.'s discussion about Puerto Rico's colonial status, and it should involve the American Left. Puerto Rican independence should become the *cause célèbre* of the progressive forces in the United States, now that the war in Indochina was winding down. The world's oldest democracy was hanging onto the oldest colony, and we needed to end this tragic farce.

The activists in La Seccional were charged with organizing the solidarity event. The challenge was clear: the Acto Nacional had to involve as much of the Left as possible; it had to be held in New York City, where we could make an impact on the national and international media; and it had to deliver a hard-hitting message to the U.S. government. The big question was whether we could fill Madison Square Garden, New York City's famed arena. Could we mobilize twenty thousand people?

By now I had resigned my regular job at ASPIRA to become a full-time cadre of the PSP. I was the New York regional director, so there was a lot of pressure on me and my *compañeros*. The city was home to half of the one-and-a-half million Boricuas who lived in this country. From early 1974 the Acto Nacional became our main focus, and we threw all our efforts into ensuring a successful event. I got a few tickets for Pop, who promised he would come. He had never been in the Garden, and he got excited about the idea after I explained that it would be a historic day for Puerto Ricans. I even recruited Rachel, now a lithe and vibrant five-year-old with long brown hair, to help me paste posters and stickers on subway walls. Technically I was inducing a minor to deface public property, but her eyes widened with excitement as I explained she was doing important work.

Any reservations we had about our ability to organize the Acto were swept aside by the rhetoric of Juan Mari Bras, the general secretary of the PSP. He was a brilliant strategist, an internationally known figure, an inspiring speaker, and the single most important person to revive the Puerto Rican independence movement in the 1960s. He was also known for controversial statements that imperialist violence had to be countered with revolutionary violence, if necessary.

Mari Bras was one of the first Puerto Rican intellectuals I had personally known. But he was much more than that; he was a political leader engaged in making history, whose adversary was no less than the United States—the United States that I had been born in but which had betrayed its own, and my, ideals. I was ready for my marching orders. Mari Bras cajoled me and my *compañeros* beyond our doubts and limitations.

In late September, someone from Madison Square Garden notified us that they were cancelling our contract. Their pretext was a scheduling conflict with the hockey game set for that night. Alfredo López, our lead organizer, went into trouble-shooting mode. He called a press conference, our lawyers threatened to sue the Garden, and we mounted several protest pickets on 34th Street, right outside the building. A contract is a contract, we said, and there was no legitimate basis for reneging on the agreement. Within a week, Garden officials relented and permitted us to proceed with the event, but they insisted on beefed-up police security. In the few remaining weeks we pulled out all the stops to fill up the Garden.

In the early dark hours of Saturday, October 26, the day before the Acto, five New York City banks were firebombed. A group calling itself the Fuerzas Armadas de Liberación Nacional (FALN; Armed Forces of National Liberation in English) claimed responsibility for the action and demanded freedom for the Nationalist prisoners and immediate independence for Puerto Rico. The group also endorsed the Acto. We never expected that our efforts to attract a mass turnout would lead to this kind of "support."

Garden officials quickly responded, telling us to cancel the event. Alfredo López, with the lawyers by his side, answered equally firmly. There was no turning back now.

"There is no way we can stop people coming," López explained. "There are going to be twenty thousand people showing up at the front gates tomorrow. Are you going to send them away? Besides, this is the safest place to be."

They knew he was right, and the Acto was on once again. We disguised the mild state of panic that we were in. And we worried: Will people be scared away? Will we fill the Garden?

On October 27, 1974, we converged on Madison Square Garden. Many came marching through lower Manhattan, more could be seen pouring from the subway exits of 34th Street, and others arrived in caravans of cars and chartered buses. As we filed into the arena we knew we were making Puerto Rican history. Because of my assignment that Sunday, I would be one of the last to join the massive crowd. My role was to supervise the cadres, conspicuously identified with red armbands, who were stationed throughout the stadium. Officially our task was to escort people to their seats and to pass the collection box during the fundraising appeal. Unofficially we were on the lookout for troublemakers in the audience—discontents from other Left organizations, provocateurs at the service of New York City Police Department's secret "Red Squad" unit, or the FBI. We knew from past experience that disruption could come from the Left or the Right.

Since early morning a small team of us controlled the security entrance located in the basement of the Garden. The special guests and program participants—political speakers, celebrities, and musicians—had to pass through us to access the Garden's central court, from where they would address the crowd. That morning I literally rubbed elbows with well-known figures as they squeezed through my cramped entry area on their way to the Garden's main floor: Angela Davis, Jane Fonda, Geraldo Rivera, David Dellinger, Piri Thomas, Arthur Kinoy, and Chief Philip Deer of the American Indian Movement.

I could dimly sense the crowd noise when the program began at one o'clock. As the backstage manager, I was cut off from the main attraction. Mine was a crucial assignment, though—guaranteeing that our speakers, and no one else, had access to the main stage. Every ten minutes an assistant excitedly fed me an update from the inside. So far no problems, no incidents. With me in the basement were three cops, standing guard and eyeballing me and my team. October 27th was here, and even the NYPD didn't want Madison Square Garden to break out in violent confrontation.

After more than an hour of not being able to hear the speeches, I decided I had to see for myself how the program was going. Another cadre replaced me, and I made my way to the mezzanine section. Scoping the arena in a three-hundred-sixty-degree vista I could see no empty seats, just people everywhere. The place was jammed! We did it! ¡Llenamos el Garden! I sighed in exhilaration and relief.

Amid the deafening noise, I gazed in awe. I had been in plenty of marches and rallies, some larger than this and also full of emotion and militancy. But I had never experienced such compact intensity. In the outdoors, the roar dissolves into the open air. Here in the Garden, there was no outlet. The noise just swirled around the arena. I scanned the place for Pop but could not pick him out of the mass of bodies.

That afternoon the charismatic and brilliant speakers brought us to our feet. We cheered till our voices were hoarse and we clapped till our hands hurt. Like evangelical preachers at a Sunday revival, they beckoned us to manifest our credo. The congregation responded militantly with our favorite slogans: *"¡Despierta Boricua, Defiende lo Tuyo!"* "The People, United, Will Never Be Defeated!" *"Jíbaro Sí, Yanki No!"* "Free Puerto Rico—Right Now!" "Black, Brown, Red and White— All the People Must Unite!" *"¡Si los Yankis no se van, en Borínqen morirán!"*

Chief Philip Deer, dignified and serene in his traditional dress and feathered headpiece, brought down the house with a simple metaphor, showing how Puerto Rico could be a symbol of unity for all America. Reacting to the striking palette of colors in the audience, he said, "Take a good look at yourselves. If you blend the colors that make up the people—black, white, red, brown, and yellow—what do you get? You end up with the 'brown' of the Puerto Ricans."

The three-hour program was embellished with powerful musical performances from the likes of Ray Barreto and Frank Ferrer. It culminated in a rousing declaration by Mari Bras, who surpassed even our expectations. We had worried that his message—always delivered in an exquisite Spanish—would be lost upon the many English-speaking folks, including U.S.-born Puerto Ricans. It didn't matter. No one was sitting idly as he roared to the finale, both arms in the air and words booming skyward. And I didn't worry about Pop, since he was just there for the spectacle anyway. Then Puerto Rican protest singer Roy Brown closed the day, leading the throng with the haunting chant of *"¡Fuego, Fuego, Los Yankis quieren fuego!"* ("Fire, Fire, the Yankees want fire!") The audience, spread to the rafters, went wild.

The call-and-response between speakers and audience was an orchestrated exchange. We were practiced participants, having conducted this political ritual in so many rallies and demonstrations. We knew the language of slogans and *consignas*, the way parishioners memorize the mass's prayers and songs. What was different that glorious 27th of October, 1974, what most impressed me, was the spontaneous call for unity. It confirmed for me that average people had the capacity for sophisticated political analysis and for thinking on their feet. These were not the educated elite. Most were working-class people, the vast majority from first- and second- generation migrant families.

The audience's *sabiduría popular* (commonsense wisdom), I had seen time and time again among the supporters of our movement. Sometimes this wisdom was outweighed by our nationalist instinct and idealistic visions, leading us into exaggerated perceptions of our strength and capacity. I knew, but did not like to dwell on the fact that we faced long odds in our challenge to U.S. colonialism. That critical moment when the crowd raised its voice for *¡Unidad! ¡Unidad!* was a needed affirmation that we were on the right track.

It took us weeks to wind down from the Acto Nacional. The Party membership was thoroughly spent after a mighty effort. We could now afford the luxury of some respite before resuming our frenzied pace.

One day, as a group of us traded stories about the Acto, someone related a strange incident. She was one of our security people in the red armbands who were keeping an eye out for troublemakers. At one point during the program, she saw two short women rise and walk along a rear hallway, away from the crowded rows of seats. They held crumpled brown paper bags.

Discreetly she tailed them toward their apparent destination, the restroom. Standing by the entrance, peering in, she noticed half-understood voices and hand movements. They each took out sandwich remnants from their brown bags, inspected them, and threw everything into the garbage. This was followed by more hand movements, a visit by one of the ladies into a bathroom stall, and tidying up at the wash basin. Exiting the bathroom they smiled and waved at the *compañera*.

"They had to be my people," I said.

The next time I saw Pop he confirmed my guess. He had gone to the Acto Nacional with Titi Tata and Titi Olga. They'd had a great time.

Shortly thereafter, Mari Bras wrote that the Acto was one of the most important days in the history of the Puerto Rican revolution, and that it would be remembered for a long time. He credited our organization in the United States with being the decisive force in its success. He cited three momentous events in recent years that resonated forcefully with him as milestones in our progress: the founding Congress of the PSP in San Juan in 1971; the inauguration of Salvador Allende as President of Chile in 1973, where he was invited to address hundreds of thousands of celebrants; and the Acto Nacional in Madison Square Garden.

12 Puerto Rican and Deaf

IT MIGHT HAVE SEEMED odd to anyone familiar with my family background that I was so immersed in Puerto Rican politics of the time. After all, what did the Puerto Rican deaf care about Puerto Rican politics? I rarely dwelt on this question then but many years later I did think more systematically about the connections between hearing and deaf Puerto Ricans.

I refrain from defining my family's Deaf networks as a "community" in the way sociologists use the term. But certainly they had characteristics that qualify them as more than just a random grouping of individuals who shared a disability. They were united by language, special customs, attitudes toward the hearing world, and social networks, just like Deaf communities everywhere at the time. Ethnic and religious loyalties also played a part in their lives.

The principal coalescent was sign language. Sign bonded them and demarcated them from the hearing. They used various forms of sign language among themselves—Spanish home sign, English home sign, signed English, and eventually American Sign Language. And despite the potentially confusing forms they always preferred interacting with each other than with hearing people. Communication was punctuated with physical warmth and contact. In private company, away from hearing people, there was much pointing, fingering, poking, grabbing, laughing, and yelling. Over time they increasingly dared to be themselves in public and hearing people found these scenes less discomforting.

This change in public attitude was yet another legacy of the great Civil Rights movement that was later extended to people with disabilities. But not until after the 1970s did awareness and sensitivity among the hearing become more generalized. Until then, deaf people harbored much skepticism toward the hearing, coupled with a sense of amusement and chagrin at their patronizing attitudes. These feelings were still very evident to me when I was coming of age. (And only in 1990 did Congress pass the Americans with Disabilities Act, the most comprehensive anti-discrimination bill of the time.) One of Pop's favorite ways of making fun of hearing people was to mock their incessant chattering.

"Blah-blah-blah-blah!" His right hand flapping like a duck's bill, his mouth opening and closing in bloated fashion so I could see his tongue. When he accompanied his signs with that sort of theatrics you could feel the sarcasm edging into contempt.

I didn't remind him that there were quite a few blabberhands among our own deaf!

Among the special rites prevalent within our families was the giving of "name signs" to children. Parents invented names for the little ones. One basic technique was to construct a sign working with the first letter of the official birth name, which was then displayed in some relation to part of the body. My cousin Jimmy's name sign was the letter *J* swinging back and forth from the wrist. "Mary" was the *M* poking at the chin. As I mentioned earlier, my name sign was *A* (closed fist, outstretched thumb) tapping twice on the other fisted hand. Sometimes, if the person had a short name it was simply fingerspelled. If a newcomer joined a Deaf social network (and had a name sign that already duplicated someone else's name sign), he was given a new name by an authority figure in the network. That's how one of my father's friends acquired the name "Carlos Blue Eyes" (the letter *C* pounded lightly on the chest, followed by the sign for "blue," then pointing to the eyes).

As with the assigning of names, other unique behaviors had to do with parent-child relationships and roles, for example, teaching sign language, "translating" media, and communicating with doctors, teachers, policemen, salesmen, and other authority figures in the hearing world. Often, translation (we children never thought of ourselves as "interpreters") turned into arguing on behalf of our parents (neither were we familiar with the term "advocate," but that's what we were).

Among the scores of cousins my Torres and Ayala relatives gave me, there were a dozen of us who were children of the *mudos*. We sensed a tighter bond among ourselves—you might think that given the unique childhood we experienced we would have spent hours upon hours comparing notes and analyzing our special circumstances. But we didn't, not until adulthood offered us the perspective to review our childhood at a distance. We each had our difficulties coping with what we perceived was an unfair lot in life but while we were in the thick of it, it never occurred to us collectively to diagnose our situation. We knew we weren't living "normal" lives, but we also knew there was nothing we could do about it, except to live it.

Social networks were important too. In addition to the Puerto Rican Society for the Catholic Deaf, founded by Pop and his cohorts, another group of Puerto Rican and Caribbean deaf people was active in the Brooklyn Archdiocese. It included the families of Mom's three *mudita* sisters, Pancha, Diosa, and Carmela. Christmas parties were held, drawing deaf families from all over the city, including the ones based in Manhattan and the Bronx. It was a rare time for me to reunite with cousins on the Ayala side who also grew up in deaf households: Tony, Johnny, Liz, Victor, Willie, Frank, and Lindsey. In that large auditorium was an exciting scene of voices and hands in the air, a teeming multitude of adults moving about, and little ones rolling and crawling on the wood-paneled floor. Priests and nuns tried to keep us under control as we grabbed for clothing, toys, and dolls that were donated through Catholic Charities. I can't say it was an exclusively Puerto Rican crowd, but the Puerto Ricans seemed to predominate.

My deaf Puerto Rican world was doubly separated: from the hearing world and from the larger Puerto Rican community. The very features that bonded us—language, customs, rituals, organizational networks— separated us from my parents' ethnic community. My parents and deaf relatives took pride in the symbols and celebrities of their co-ethnics. The Feast of San Juan Bautista and Three Kings Day were important days on the religious calendar, and public figures such as José Ferrer, Rita Moreno, and Roberto Clemente gave them something to brag about. So did Muñoz Marín, governor of Puerto Rico, and Herman Badillo when he ran for mayor of New York City in1968.

But they were cut off from the Spanish-language media and from Hispanic institutions and culture in the city. They didn't listen to Radio WADO or read *El Diario–La Prensa*, as did my hearing relatives. They didn't watch Spanish TV programs (and I was glad because I would have had to translate those too!). During the 1960s when Puerto Rican community organizations and political clubs emerged as a serious force, Puerto Rican deaf people were invisible, as participants and as a group in need.

Closer ties would have required the existence of a corps of profes- sional sign language interpreters in the Puerto Rican community, but this did not exist. Not until the national movement for disability rights achieved some victories did some of these services trickle down to the Puerto Rican and Latino deaf. And even then, the Puerto Rican social agencies were stretched thin attending to the general population, one- third of which was mired in poverty, and unable to deliver specialized services to the deaf. As a consequence, the connection of the Puerto Rican deaf to its hearing population was quite tenuous. I was far more familiar with the history, personalities, and organizations within the New York Puerto Rican and Hispanic community than were my deaf relatives. At the Acto Nacional in Madison Square Garden, they were attending their first political event in the hearing community.

With loose roots in their ethnic origins, the Puerto Rican deaf people I was familiar with considered the Catholic Church as the most important social institution in their lives. The Archdioceses of New York and Brooklyn each had missions for the deaf. There were clergy, including brothers and nuns, who were proficient signers, and they offered Masses and sacraments for their deaf congregants, among which were Puerto Rican and Hispanic participants. Pop had told me he wanted his deaf organization to have a Puerto Rican name so they could have their own identity. But beyond the title there was no reference in the by-laws to the ethnic aspect. It lacked language calling on the members to promote Puerto Rican culture or other ethnic-specific activities. The by-laws read as a boilerplate document applicable to any collection of Church members. I was proud that Pop insisted on this identifier, but it was a symbolic, not substantive, statement. And yet symbols can be powerful statements, for the organization continued to retain its identifier long after Pop's time.

The Puerto Rican deaf population in New York City was small, perhaps no more than one or two thousand. This is my educated guess, developed in later years and based on studies of deaf populations in the United States. This would largely account for the invisibility of this subgroup vis-à-vis the larger hearing Puerto Rican community.

Furthermore, continuity from one generation of Deaf networks to the next was not bolstered by kinship networks. Ninety-five percent of deaf parents have hearing children. None of my Torres or Ayala cousins were deaf, and none of their children were born deaf. Bloodlines were interrupted so the Deaf community could reproduce itself only through social interaction and extra-familial contacts.

These were some of the special features of the Puerto Rican Deaf world, of which I was an insider-outsider.

Not long after the Acto Nacional I received a letter from Pop, with these few words:

"Dear Andy. Come next Saturday. I have something to discuss."

He signed off in his usual incorrect and formalistic manner:

"Your Loving Son, Andrés Torres."

His way of signing off letters made me laugh. I never bothered explaining to Pop that I could not be both the author and recipient of a letter. But like a lot of deaf people, his grammar and knowledge of writing rules left a lot to be desired. I always remembered reading somewhere that the literacy level of deaf high school students was really at the grade-school level. No matter; when Pop closed his letters with "Your Loving Son, Andrés Torres," I knew what he meant, and I knew he was signing off with affection.

The cryptic note, scribbled on a half-sheet of blue-lined paper, sent my mind into worried speculation. The first thing that occurred to me was that it had to do with his health. Pop had just reached his sixtieth year and was showing the signs of life's wear and tear. Decades of lifting boxes, in the garment center and in the book industry, did his back no favors. He was plagued by muscle spasms and chronic pain. Over the years I had filled out dozens of applications of various kinds—college admission, financial aid, loans, employment, and apartment rental—and there always appeared that blank space next to the question: occupation of father. My answer was clear and simple: stock clerk.

That term completely failed to capture the significance of his work. One third of his being was poured into that role. Yet I knew nothing of what went on during those eight hours: his relationships, how his co-workers handled his deafness. Did they take advantage of him? Or did he win them over with his charm and simplicity? He rarely brought home stories to us, except to say once in a while that he knew people in the car pool made jokes about him. And after all these years what did he have to show for his labors? A messed-up spine.

In the back of my mind I worried about Pop's petty vices. He was still chain-smoking his Lucky Strikes, deepening the yellow veneer on his remaining teeth. In the bathroom cabinet still sat the plastic cup holding his partial dentures. What a strange sight I beheld each night when I lived at 43, those enamel substitutes perched on the fake, pink gums. Seeing them strengthened my resolve never to smoke, never to lose my teeth. The Lucky Strikes were to blame for his hacking cough, which all his sisters were noticing, deaf and hearing. Health conscious, he was not.

We found a physician who had an office right in the Heights, on the first floor of an old apartment building on 178th Street between Audubon and St. Nicholas. Outside his window hung a metal shingle with his name, credentials, and hours. I remembered that I used to walk by his window each day on my way to classes at Manhattan College. On the day of the appointment we entered the office to encounter an aging man who apparently had no assistant, clerical or medical. And there were no other patients waiting to see him.

The doctor had a heavy European accent and peered at us through thick glasses. I assumed my usual role of interpreter between Pop and the hearing world. The bearded old man in the white smock seemed unimpressed by the patient and his translator son.

"Tell him to strip down to his underpants" he said to me matter-of-factly.

Pop stood in front of me, embarrassed, in his white briefs. During all those years of cramped quarters at apartment 43, I had never seen him this bare. The only image of his body I had was from photos of him in a bathing suit in his younger years. He didn't like exposing himself even just partially.

The doctor proceeded with the examination, instructing me to tell Pop what he had to do. Weight, blood circulation and pressure, eye and ear check. A few minutes later he motioned to Pop to remove his underpants and lie down on his side. Pop didn't follow so he asked me what the doctor was saying. I told him and he frowned back, the ends of his mouth dropping.

"What for?"

"I don't know. Just do what he says."

The sound of snapping plastic on the doctor's hands, then

"Aieeeee!"

Could it be that here I was in my twenties and I had never heard that sound from Pop? He cried out a screeching yelp rising from deep in the lungs, manifesting loss of dignity more than anything else.

Again,

"Aieeeee!"

After the rectal exam, probably Pop's first ever, things didn't get any better. The good doctor then proceeded to hook up the wires from his EKG to Pop, first plastering his chest with a sticky ointment. Apparently one of the few things that discomforted Pop more than appearing half-nude was being slathered with sticky substances. He threatened right there to dress himself and walk out of the office but I signed that he should stay put.

The doctor spent a lot of time with the EKG test, and Pop suspected that he didn't know what he was doing. But after it was all said and done, we could not ignore the doctor's advice. He said my father had high blood pressure and a weak heart. He had to stop smoking and cut down on fried food.

As we walked out of the office Pop's only comment was, "That machine is so old, so many wires and papers. I think he was using me as a guinea pig."

Did Pop's letter have something to do with his health? His heart? His diabetes? Since I visited every few weeks, he usually didn't write to me like this unless it was something urgent. It would be another few days before I knew. I just hoped it wasn't anything serious. I had other things on my mind, including that fact that the PSP was sending me on a political assignment to Cuba that would keep me there for several months.

"We will move to Puerto Rico next year."

Pop's announcement floored me. Like a lot of Pop's conversations with me, I couldn't tell if he was serious or just looking for a reaction. This was for real.

I had suspected he had been toying with the idea of returning to the Island. But now he confirmed his plans. The previous summer, Pop said, when he and Mom had visited, they discussed the idea with his brother Miguel and with the Ayalas. Everyone agreed: Pop should retire early and they should make plans to come back home to Puerto Rico. The family on both sides would help them relocate. In fact, they could move to a nice area in Caguas, called Bairoa Park, right where Mom's sister Carmela and her husband Victor had settled a few years before. A modest cement block home, with two bedrooms and tiny green patch of a backyard, just enough for Mom to grow her beans and *viandas* and *aguacátes*. The Ayalas would even make the down payment on the place. And Pop could buy a used car for himself. It would be perfect.

The feeling grew on me, as I recalled this day many times over the years, that Pop's decision to move was his way of throwing in the towel. Since childhood, we had been embroiled in an extended wrestling match. I had realized this only gradually with each passing year. It wasn't a physical confrontation; but a battle for position and control. The contest was to be concluded not by swift and physical submission, but by one outlasting the other in a test of stamina. The victor would determine the nature of the father-son relationship.

We grappled with each other delicately, obliquely. Pop was careful not to alienate me by abusing his physical strength or paternal authority—not only because it wasn't in his nature, but because he knew of deaf families in which the children were exploited and mistreated. Sometimes the hearing kids just disappeared . . . forever. I knew of cases myself. He was never going to let that happen with us. He used the nice-guy, sweet-talking approach, controlling me with kindness. And when that didn't work, he played on the *¡aye bendito!* sentiment inherent in my Puerto Rican genes.

With time I gradually gained the upper hand in our struggle. Perhaps emboldened by the realization that Pop wouldn't or couldn't *force* me to his will, I became more assertive and antagonistic. In retrospect, I would recall that devastating moment at apartment 43 when I bitterly attacked Pop for not providing for Mom's financial security, when I realized his Prudential insurance policy would provide only a meager pittance for Mom. He saw how angry I was over being left with the sole responsibility for taking care of Mom. By then I had wrestled free from his grip and stood alone on my two feet.

Then as I reflected again and again on these things, I would turn the table on myself: What's the matter with you, Andy Torres? Ain't you one self-indulgent asshole? Is this how you repay your parents? They centered their whole lives on you, placed you on a pedestal and kept you there. Unconditional love. They gave you the only bedroom, for God's sake!

Did you think you had the right to just walk out that door when you were good and ready to start a life of your own, without any obligations to them? Pop never opposed any of your career plans. He didn't expect you to make your whole life in the Deaf world. Maybe they just wanted to experience the hearing world *through you,* you idiot! Was that too much to ask? Was it too much for them to hope that you would always be close by? Was it such an outlandish fantasy for him to dream of the double-decker in Queens? Didn't you owe them anything?

By deciding to move to Puerto Rico Pop was throwing in the towel of surrender and releasing me. But my conscience refused to allow for a clean break. Not then, not now.

13

Bicentennial Moves

IN EARLY 1975 I found myself in Cuba. I was sent to work for a few months in the PSP Mission in Havana, specifically to help make preparations for the First International Conference of Solidarity with the Independence of Puerto Rico. An outcome of the Acto Nacional at Madison Square Garden was an agreement to assemble the international community for a similar event. The conference would publicize the Puerto Rican issue to Socialist and Third World leaders in anticipation of a new round of debates at the United Nations in the fall of 1975.

It was my first trip to *"La Hermana República,"* the staunch ally of Puerto Rican independence. Technically such trips were illegal, but there were ways of circumventing the U.S. blockade. We weren't the only ones. For years delegations of U.S. citizens were going on the Venceremos Brigades to cut sugar cane and work on other projects of solidarity with the Cuban Revolution. Other progressives had visited the island, to denounce the U.S. blockade, and show the world that not all Americans were myopic reactionaries on the Cuban question.

In no time I was transformed from tourist to citizen, another "Cuban" on the street. I soon picked up the local accent and merged into the general populace. Much of my time was spent in meetings with Cuban officials involved with international events and with foreign embassies securing cooperation for the Conference.

It was my first experience of daily life in another hearing culture. I found the average Cuban to be quite informed about Puerto Rico's history, certainly much more than the average American, and sympathetic to the cause of independence. They were familiar with José Martí's saying that Cuba and Puerto Rico were "two wings of the same bird." They talked fondly of artists like Daniel Santos, who often toured Cuba before the Blockade.

The Cubans were less familiar with Puerto Ricans living in the United States. The more political types seemed in awe that Puerto Ricans were defying the United States. Having survived fifteen years of counter-revolutionary incursions from *el imperialismo yanqui*, they knew we Puerto Rican *independentistas* had an uphill struggle on our hands. And they respected us all the more for it.

I also got to play the diplomat, at times with amusing results. One evening I was regaled by mid-level officials at the North Korean Embassy, where I was dined and then induced into a stupor with several rounds of *raíz de la vida*. My hosts poured generous amounts of this mysterious libation from a bottle containing stringy brown roots. Before long I slipped into a hazy semiconsciousness.

Then they peppered me with questions about the PSP and the U.S. Left. How many members did we have? What was our position on the Sino-Soviet split? Did we have any contacts with Puerto Ricans serving in the Armed Forces, and were they stationed on the 38th parallel (the demilitarized zone between North and South Korea)? The "conversation" lasted hours before they chauffeured me back to my apartment. Did I ever compromise my organization's integrity? Damned if

I know. I was so deep under the spell of *raíz de la vida*, I don't remember what I said.

Another time, I was asked to speak to the Venceremos Brigade, in an agricultural camp on the outskirts of Havana. There were three of us invited, myself and two other *compañeros* from the PSP in Puerto Rico. I looked forward to the evening because I knew there would be a few PSPers from New York in the group of mostly North American activists. They would bring news about my organization and update me on my family, from whom I had been separated for two months.

As we approached the camp, I noticed a crowd of mostly young white Americans outside the camp's main entrance, carrying banners and chanting, *"¡Que Viva Puerto Rico Libre y Socialista!—¡Que Viva!"* We moved through the group, the enthusiastic greeters shaking our hands and patting our backs. Then I saw two long columns of *brigadístas*, lined up like football players in a reception line for the starting team. It was then that I realized the whole commotion was in our honor. We were being accorded the traditional welcome to Third World Liberation fighters. Caught up in the excitement, we broke into a trot and jogged down the reception aisle, chanting along with the cheerleaders lined up on either side.

From the corner of my eyes I glimpsed some familiar faces, PSP members and other friends from New York who were participants in the Brigade that year. Two of them were fellow residents of the Chelsea neighborhood in Manhattan, and lived only a few blocks from where Vivian and I had settled shortly after we had married. They joined in the festive proceedings, smiling and singing, receiving me, the representative of a Third World Liberation movement.

One month later I was back at Chelsea with Vivian. Since our marriage in early 1974 my travels, foreign and domestic, had separated us too many months. As a full-time PSP organizer in the finance area she had clocked a lot of mileage as well. I relished the times I could bring Rachel to our apartment on the corner of Eighth Avenue and Seventeenth Street, so she could spend a nonpolitical weekend with us.

During those heady and heated times I didn't have the luxury to reflect on an interesting question: Did my upbringing in the Deaf world influence my political activism? In subsequent years, I revisited this issue in my mind and the answer became clearer. I could recall numerous incidents in which my parents had been subjected to injustice and discrimination at the hands of hearing society. Until I was in my late teens I was a mere observer. At best, I was a messenger of bad news, aching in my powerlessness to do anything. There was the infamous insurance plan that Pop had been talked into, which was supposed to secure Mom's future but turned out to be a worthless dream with a pitiful payoff. If the fine print and legalese on those documents are difficult for educated hearing people to figure out, imagine how impenetrable they are to deaf people without a high school education, much more so to those raised in a Spanish-language culture.

I bristled at Pop's description of his car pool riders, who were all hearing. He swore they cracked jokes at his expense on the commute to the New Jersey warehouse where he worked in his later years. And they never trusted him to take the driver's seat.

In those Stone Age days there was little awareness, much less sympathy, for the problems faced by the marginalized deaf population. Professional sign language interpreters were scarcely available in hospitals and courthouses. Teletype machines and video interpretation devices had not been invented. There were no social programs responding to their special needs. The principle of "rights" for the disabled hadn't been established.

Every foray into the hearing world—a trip into a department store, a ride on the subway—potentially exposed them to discomfort or ridicule. They confronted greater hazards at the workplace. There was the deaf guy killed by an onrushing car because he couldn't hear it honking. There was the deaf girl raped in Central Park, whose muffled cries for help went unheard. Mom described her mother's two-part warning about being in the street after dusk: never walk alone, and even if you're with the other *mudas*, don't sign in public. They should never draw attention at dark.

Why was it so hard for them to just live a decent, normal life? They worked hard and played by all the rules. Why should people with a physical disability have to carry a heavier burden in this world? I seethed with anger over these questions. Surely something should be done about this.

However, it wasn't until I became politically radicalized, during my late teens, that I saw how broad social change was necessary to right injustices in society. By the late sixties what drew my attention were the antiwar struggle and the struggles around Puerto Rican rights and Puerto Rican independence. The movement for the rights of the disabled had not yet emerged. My political passions centered on my ethnic identity, not on the Deaf culture in which I had been raised. I didn't want to be attached forever to my parents, as their interpreter and advocate. I feared it would distract me from my drive for achievement in the hearing world.

After almost twenty years, Mom and Pop moved out of apartment 43. With the apartment now emptied of all furnishings, Pop's deaf talk echoed in an eerie hollowness; Mom's whispered phrases pierced the quiet. They examined the rooms one last time, meticulously removing all remaining traces of their stewardship: a toothbrush, a tin garbage can, crumpled Con Edison bills. They seemed untouched by nostalgic feelings. Their thoughts were drawn excitedly to the future, and to the year-long sun that would replace perennial alternations of freezing Januaries and sticky, humid Augusts.

I, on the other hand, reeled under the onslaught of flashbacks. My emotions were overtaken by memory, not anticipation, by the past, not the future. Here was the safety and warmth of my adolescence, the incubator of my manhood. Here were the ghosts of hundreds of stories, beckoning me to one last reverie, pleading that I not forget them. Now the space was desolate and spare. Only a few naked light bulbs remained to light the way for the next family.

A few days before, I stopped by to help Mom and Pop pack for the move. True to form, Mom held onto most of the furniture and clothes and wanted them delivered. The only major item consigned to the dump was the sofa, that poor excuse for a master bed. How many nights did that four-legged beast open up for Mom and Pop? How did it possibly survive all these years, with only one repair job that I could recall?

They consulted me on everything. Did I want to hold onto the family photos? Should they keep the original copies of their baptismal and wedding certificates, or should they leave them with me? What about their Social Security records? I might need these documents here in New York if some problem came up that I'd have to follow up on for them. Pop offered me his mementos from St. Rita's, including his trophies and baseball glove. The glove, stiff as a board, had to be forty years old. It was half the size of modern baseball mitts. Inscribed in the palm was the name of Marty Marion, a player obscure to everyone around the Block but me. I felt a strange power, having the final say about these possessions. How convenient to be the only child. I was pleased with the neat and simple handling of this tiny estate. No bickering with siblings, no interference from lawyers. Nothing to hide from the tax man.

We hired Flor de Mayo, the moving company that had shuttled migrating Puerto Rican families for decades. (Clever, this company! From the Mayflower to *Flor de Mayo*, marketing themselves as movers of modern-day Boricua pilgrims.) And this morning they had come to clear out the apartment. Soon all my folks' worldly goods would be sailing down the Atlantic toward the "Rich Port." Tomorrow, Mom would be on the plane to San Juan, to be picked up by the Ayala brothers. Pop was going to stay with me and Vivian for a few weeks until after the Christmas holidays. He timed his retirement to begin on New Year's Day, 1976. *Borrón y cuenta nueva.* A clean slate.

The plans for the American Bicentennial prompted the PSP and our political allies—civil rights and labor groups, organizers involved in antiracist and environmental work, and international solidarity activists—to form a July 4th Coalition to stage a "Peoples' Bicentennial" (we also called it the "Bicentennial Without Colonies" or "Bicentenario" in Spanish) in Philadelphia. We didn't hope to compete on the same scale as the official festivities, but we could draw significant media attention by positioning ourselves close to the main event.

With a clear plan of action and an effective coalition, we believed we could mobilize tens of thousands of people from the East Coast. We would represent the voice of the neglected, the poor, the disenfranchised in American society. We would expose the official Bicentennial as a farce, controlled by a corporate America that was turning it into a giant commercial. While the elites celebrated in glamour, we would be in the streets, raining on their phony parade.

From early to mid-1976, the PSP immersed itself in the build-up to the Philadelphia demonstration. Everything we learned in the previous years, all the resources we had accumulated, all the structures we had established were put to the service of the mobilization. It was the greatest test yet of our skills. The ad hoc July 4th Coalition had been established throughout the East Coast and Midwest, and reports from local chapters predicted a major turnout. By early spring it was clear that we would pull off another successful action.

In May the FBI announced plans to investigate the July 4th Coalition, citing the leadership role of the PSP and other left groups. Exhibit A in their message of alarm was a Congressional Report on terrorist activity, entitled "The Cuban Connection in Puerto Rico." The pages contained organizational charts and names of many members, clearly designed to intimidate our supporters, and said the PSP was acting on orders of Fidel Castro himself. The government also insinuated that the PSP was linked to the FALN, the radical group responsible for bombings and other attacks directed at facilities seen as symbols of U.S. imperialism. The PSP and most of the Puerto Rican movement had condemned the bombings.

In addition to our counter-Bicentennial activities, the PSP had decided to mount an all-out campaign to elect Juan Mari Bras governor of Puerto Rico. It was to be a symbolic campaign to bring our message to a larger public. Our organization in the U.S. would raise funds for the Island-based effort and mobilize a large contingent of poll watchers who would go to Puerto Rico in November.

In March terrifying news hit the airwaves in Puerto Rico and reached us immediately. Santiago Mari, the twenty-three-year-old son of our candidate, was shot and killed under mysterious circumstances. Chagui, as he was known, had been a student and antiwar activist, one of many Puerto Ricans who had refused to serve in Vietnam. He was murdered by a young man who had connections to an ultra-right-wing group of Cuban exiles. We had no doubts that Chagui was the target of a political assassination. The killing was meant to provoke the independence movement, especially the PSP, into vengeful reaction. By associating us with a violent event we would lose the support of voters in the middle of an electoral contest. Was this a prelude to a major confrontation? Were our political enemies, including the FBI, drawing us into a violent confrontation designed to destroy us? In Puerto Rico and the U.S. selected cadres were quietly sent "underground" in anticipation of mass arrests. We were under party orders to cut off all communications with our loved ones. It felt as if the solitude and silence I had grown up with had once again become my daily companions.

A third round of tensions arose when Philadelphia Mayor Frank L. Rizzo accused the July 4th Coalition of planning to violently disrupt the official Bicentennial events being held at various historical landmarks. Rizzo, an arch-conservative and the city's former police chief asked President Gerald Ford for fifteen thousand federal troops to keep control over the Peoples' Bicentennial. We brought in our lawyers to forestall this move, and the federal authorities backed off.

Finally the big day arrived. In the early afternoon we disembarked from our assembly point in North Philadelphia to begin the two-hour march through primarily African American communities toward Fairmount Park. Long columns of protester-celebrants chanted political mantras and shouldered message-laden banners, accompanied by all sorts of percussive instruments. Young people joined the parade as we passed by their homes. Led by two parallel lines of Native American and African American militants, we weaved and switched-back through streets and avenues under overcast skies. The Boricua imprint was indelible. Dozens of contingents from the cities where we lived marched together, spearheaded by sound trucks and waves of Puerto Rican flags. Sprinkled throughout were flags containing a white star on a red field: the PSP's emblem.

At the park we listened to speakers from various organizations, including the Southern Christian Leadership Conference, the National Organization of Women, the American Indian Movement, the Black Panther Party, CASA (a Chicano civil rights group), several unions, and many more. The cloudy skies of early afternoon darkened and sprayed us with light showers throughout the three-hour program. As at the Madison Square Garden rally in October of 1974, Juan Mari Bras was the featured orator. Once again, he delivered a soaring message to the crowd. I was amazed at how he could sustain this level of energy and commitment just a few months after his son's death. Toward the end of the program the sporadic soft showers broke out into a full-fledged summer thunderstorm. By then we didn't care. Triumphantly slogging through Fairmount's muddy patches, our waterlogged backpacks weighing us down, we returned to the buses for the trip home.

According to the Leftist press, upwards of fifty thousand people participated in the Peoples' Bicentennial, counting both the Philadelphia and San Francisco rallies. The *New York Times* was less impressed, claiming a turnout of thirty thousand. In our eyes it was as a total success. We had reason to believe that the July 4th Coalition could emerge as a unifying force within the progressive wing of the U.S. political spectrum. We hoped the coalition would be converted into a permanent organization with the "decolonization" of Puerto Rican as one of its central tenets. I was among those who quietly assumed that the PSP would also finally dedicate itself to organizing for better living conditions within our own barrios and communities.

Events would soon prove these to be unreasonable expectations. Just a few months later, in November, the results of the Puerto Rican elections revealed how much we had misjudged the receptivity of the public to our message. Not only did the electorate choose the pro-statehood PNP (Partido Nuevo Progresista; New Progressive Party in English), our own party received less than 1 percent of the vote. The Puerto Rican Independence Party (PIP), our competitor for the independence vote, secured less than 5 percent. The results forced us all back to the drawing board. Within the PSP recriminations were unleashed, fingers were pointed. From then on, an intense debate permeated our meetings and filled the pages of *Claridad*. Informally, *militantes* began to cluster around shared views. Secretly, factions met and strategized. The first cracks in Party unity were revealed in Puerto Rico. Soon they migrated to the U.S. branch. We did not know, as 1976 came to a close, if we could heal the differences, if we could redefine our goals to make our movement more relevant to the common people. We retained our ideals and passionate beliefs in the need for social and political change, but we did not possess a clear roadmap to the future. We only knew that a way out of this dilemma wouldn't come quickly.

14   Border Crossings

I VISITED MY PARENTS a few times during 1976, their first year in Puerto Rico. Their two-bedroom cement home was in an area where houses lined up a few feet from each other—technically unattached, but so close as to render the space between irrelevant. Housing in Caguas, Puerto Rico's third largest city, was inexpensive compared to New York City, so with their modest savings and a lot of help from the Ayala brothers, Mom and Pop were able to buy their very first home. The Ayalas were delivering on Don Catalino and Doña Eufrasia's last request to keep an eye on *las mudas*. Between Social Security and the pension from Pop's last job with the Paulist Press, they covered their bills.

The permeability of their new living quarters would amuse anyone. The windows, to the extent you could call them such, consisted of adjustable tin slats that kept out the rain, but not heat, noise, or odors. Even shut tight, I was privy to the next-door family's every movement: the wailing pleas of their toddler, the plaintive ballads of the young mother and, at dinnertime, the crackling grease in a frying pan. These sounds, however, never disturbed Mom and Pop.

Looking around, I saw familiar props that reminded me of the past: our old TV, the two vinyl-covered living room chairs with the blue and red floral designs, the mahogany frame and headboard that had been my bed since 1960, which Mom took over when I left apartment 43. Mom, ever the frugal one, had held onto all her kitchenware and cutlery from Manhattan. I ate with the same worn silverware I had used growing up.

There were no phones to interrupt the serenity. Everything felt comfortable and secure, just the three of us together. I was back in the Highbridge section of Washington Heights, at 514.

After years of disappointment punctuated by episodic bursts of rage, Mom was resigned to the life she now had. My parents seemed to have found security in their new setting and relative comfort from decades spent with a familiar face. There was still no intimacy or passion between them, as they each had their own bedroom. But in the circumscribed world of the Puerto Rican deaf one is not likely to find a life partner that satisfies every need. They were so demonstrative and physical with their hands and arms and body language; how sad it was that these emotion-filled gestures had never carried over into expressions of love between them.

We visited the Ayalas often and also Pop's brother Miguel who lived in the beautiful countryside around Cayey. I was "reunited" with many relatives, including the three children of Miguel. Aidita, Blanca, and Mickey Jr. were the only Torres cousins who had not been born in New York City. Aside from the warm affection they always shared with me, they were strangely important to me because they validated my identity. Knowing I had cousins still living on the Island made me feel like a more "authentic" Puerto Rican.

To reach Tío Miguel's house we had to traverse the *Cordillera Central*, the central highlands. Even then, in my late twenties, I didn't drive so it was always Andrés Sr. driving Mom and me around, in his flashy used, two-door Camaro. Pop seemed unaware of the irony: a man in his sixties cautiously maneuvering his amber sports car through the tricky twists and turns of an old mountain roadway. Every five minutes we were confronted with a speeding truck careening around a turn right at us. One miscue and the three of us would have plummeted into an abyss. An automotive illiterate, I was blissfully ignorant of the danger. It was only years later, when I was behind the steering wheel and dodging maniacal truck drivers, that I could nervously laugh in retrospect.

Pop showed me off to his friends and neighbors. "Explain what you do in the PSP," he'd say when socializing with an *independentista* friend.

"Talk about your work in the New York City government," he'd prompt, alluding to my position as a policy analyst at the Community Service Society (CSS). This was a "straight" job I took when Vivian and

Pop working with sign language interpreters in Puerto Rico, 1981.

My parents in retirement, early 1980s.

I, both full-time PSP cadre, realized we were broke—so broke, in fact, that we had fled one of our apartments in the middle of the night to escape our rental debts. I tried to explain the difference between government and nonprofit groups, but it didn't matter. As far as Pop was concerned I was "an official in the government," and he wanted his friends to know that his hearing son was an "important person."

It was embarrassing enough when Pop boasted to a deaf friend. But relaying his words to *hearing* friends put me in the uncomfortable role of tooting my own horn. I would be lying, though, if I said it didn't make me feel good.

Pop proudly reported on his activities as a trainer of sign language interpreters. The Puerto Rican government created a program to turn out people who could educate deaf children and interpret for deaf people in the courts. He was one of the first deaf persons to work as a teacher, for which he received a small stipend.

One of his trainees became a daily TV presence. Each evening her miniaturized face appeared on the lower right corner of the screen, interpreting for the broadcasters. Pop said that aside from deaf people, who for the first time could follow the events of the day, children also loved watching the woman making signs.

"I taught that woman how to sign," Pop beamed as we watched over dinner.

I reminisced silently to myself, recalling apartment 43, when watching the TV news became such drudgery, having to interpret every night for Pop and Mom. Now Pop, the teacher, could follow the newscaster on his own.

Mom also watched the interpreter on the screen, but she never broke the dependency on her life-long teacher. After each broadcast, she queried Pop on bits and pieces of the interpreter's message that were unintelligible to her. Mostly though, Mom was just double-checking, seeking confirmation from Pop that the TV lady was saying what she thought she was saying.

My parents asked for reports on how my marriage with Vivian was going and how Rachel was. I could give them good news on both fronts. Rachel, now seven, stayed with us frequently and Vivian was a great second mother. They wanted to know if Vivian and I would have our own children, Pop saying it would be nice to have a boy some day. (A few years later I sent a telegram congratulating them on the arrival of Orlando, their new grandson.)

Unlike the last few years in New York, when I just hopped on a bus or subway back to Highbridge, these visits were long-distance affairs, and the plane flights accentuated the feel of migratory passage. But these travels were not just about changing geographies and climates. Entering, then exiting, then re-entering and re-exiting their lives had a different quality. Now, reflecting on that time, I realize that the first thirty years of my life had been a series of border crossings between the Deaf and hearing worlds.

In the first years it was my parents and Deaf culture that claimed my allegiance. Sign language and Deaf behaviors were building blocks of my personality and psyche. Then I loosened the ties to Deaf culture, as I gradually worked my way into the hearing world. But which hearing world would I settle into? The Puerto Rican, where my family's roots lie, or the American world of the Block, of schooling, of work? And later, as I re-encountered my Boricua roots through political activism, there were crossings between the often contradictory spaces of the Puerto Rican and American hearing worlds.

I could try to be free to chart my own life, but true independence is not possible without a stable sense of self. I had to figure out a personal identity that was consonant with a life in three overlapping and at times conflicting worlds: Deaf, Puerto Rican, and American.

My parents had clear expectations of me: to be their messenger, interpreter, negotiator, and advocate, and implicitly, to be in these ways available to them for the rest of their days. I felt these demands were somehow to be passed off. But to whom? Later I could see that some of these demands became *resources* for dealing with life. The ability to see the world from another's vantage point; the awareness of another's discomfort and uneasiness; the sense of power that comes from being embedded in another language and culture; the knowledge that comes from being a witness to routine injustice—now, I can choose to accept these as gifts.

Their greatest gift was unmediated by any ulterior motive. My parents loved me beyond anything a hearing person can understand. Strangely,

Mom or Pop never signed "I love you" directly to me. They had other ways to let me know this. I saw their love in the open-mouthed joy on their faces upon seeing me. I heard their love in the pinch-throated sigh that sounded like an infant's whisper of contentment. I felt their love when they greeted me, firmly grasping my body, hanging on to me as if seeing someone they thought was lost or dead.

To their way of thinking, Ahtay the hearing son had vindicated their very existence, had made them whole. This is not how most deaf people today think, and that is good. But it was so back then with Mom and Pop.

I visited again at the end of 1976, after the whirlwind political activities of that summer and fall. The back-to-back flurry of events and losses came to a quiet denouement in that final week of December that I spent with Mom and Pop. I remember the last evening.

How different was that night compared to the Friday evenings I rode with my parents on the A train downtown. Instead of Manhattan's frigid winds, I relaxed in Santurce's end-of-year breeze slipping through the metal slats of the second-floor social club. It was the annual Christmas affair of the Puerto Rico Society for the Deaf. The next day I would be on a flight back to New York.

Pop introduced me to new friends, as usual boasting of my accomplishments.

"He's the one who was on television in New York with the governor of Puerto Rico. Did you see the TV news?"

He was referring to my brief appearance on *Good Morning America* just a few weeks earlier. The election of 1976 had resulted in a change of government in Puerto Rico, installing a conservative, pro-statehood administration. Someone convinced ABC that this was worth a few minutes of discussion with David Hartman, the show's host. The event was a minor blip in network programming, but it had a big impact on the island when it was replayed on all of Puerto Rico's TV stations. My uncle Miguel had seen it, my Ayala relatives had seen it, and so had Pop. People wanted to know about that young man in the dark suit and tie and perfect American accent, and how he ended up representing the *Independentista* point of view. And what was a Nuyorican doing in the PSP?

I signed to Pop's friends that it was really no big deal, just a five-minute chat over a coffee table, interrupted by two commercials. I hardly got in any words in the competition for airtime.

Still, Pop's friends were impressed. They looked at me in amazement, and said they were proud of me. They signed in a combination of English and Spanish, and it took me time to get used to the Spanish signs. Pop had told me that many deaf Puerto Ricans resisted the American Sign Language, mostly because they couldn't then communicate with their parents. He said he understood where they were coming from but felt it was best they learned ASL. I reminded Pop that the same thing happened in the early twentieth century when the Americans tried to force all schools in Puerto Rico to teach in English. The plan backfired because it stirred nationalist sentiment, and eventually the Americans ended the English instruction policy.

Pop became something of an elder statesman in the Puerto Rico Society for the Deaf. Soon after arriving from New York, he had been drafted by the youngish members to be the president, but said he would do so only if he could get his old friend Félix de Jesús to help him. "Felito" had left the island with Pop to study at St. Rita School for the Deaf. Here they were, fifty years later, taking turns as leaders of the group.

Tonight the Society was having their annual Christmas meeting and party. There was a young man tending bar (a no-no in the Puerto Rican Society for the Catholic Deaf in New York!), some guys were playing dominoes, and salsa music was coming out of a jukebox. Percussive sounds filled the air, compliments of a few intruders, hearing friends who were checking out the young deaf beauties and offering them dance lessons. There were always some such outsiders at these affairs, looking to transgress the borderline between deaf and hearing worlds. The deaf *guys* didn't appreciate this.

Before the party got underway, it was the president's duty to address the forty or so members about the group's finances and upcoming activities. I sat next to Mom in the front row. Released from interpretation duties and surrounded by deaf people, I enjoyed a perfect view. I felt comfortably secure as a citizen of Deaf culture.

I could sit there hours watching Pop sign, under the spell of his looping arms and precisely expressive fingers. He wove his limbs through the air, a tai chi master, in wide, full circles. His face harmonized with the message emanating from his hands. When his sign vocabulary failed him, the crisp finger-spelling came to the rescue. The torso tightened or loosened, collaborating instinctively with the words. Humor was not foreign to him. He interjected a sly remark about someone's late dues, bringing forth a rattle of laughs and clapping hands. The signs: they had once been a source of embarrassment, a stigma. Now I could see their beauty, appreciate them as an art form. Now they were a treasured possession, a secret weapon that would accompany me on a life's journey.

His delivery was smooth and confident, interrupted here and there by hacking sounds from the throat. I was unaware they were signaling the forces that eventually would bring him down.

Toward the end, he proudly acknowledged my presence.

"I am happy my son Andrés Jr. is here from New York; tomorrow he goes back."

Then more information, more announcements. And he closed.

"Thank you."

"Finish. Have good time now."

Over the next decade my father battled with his health, with heart disease, diabetes, and the chronic pains he suffered from, until, in March of 1986, he passed away in his sleep from heart failure. But what survives is that night in the last days of 1976, seeing him settled in his retirement, back on the island of his youth, surrounded by friends and family, and the simple dignity with which he spoke.

Afterword

A FTER MY FATHER died in 1986, I brought Mom back to New York City and placed her in an apartment at Tanya Towers on Manhattan's Lower East Side. Tanya Towers was a rare gem of a place, offering housing to many low-income deaf and other disabled persons. Pop's passing pulled Mom out of his shadow and permitted her to flourish. She became much more self-reliant, participating in Tanya Towers' programs and taking an active role in the Puerto Rican Society for the Catholic Deaf. Among her other projects were storytelling sessions with children at the Lexington School for the Deaf. Our relationship thrived also, until late 1999, when she died after a harsh struggle with lymphoma. She wanted to be around for the new millennium, which fascinated her, but she fell short by a few months. My parents' remains rest in the soil of an old cemetery not far from Las Piedras.

Over the next few years the remaining deaf relatives passed on—Titi Olga, Titi Magdalena, Titi Carmela. The eight Torres and Ayala deaf, and all their spouses, are now gone. They were the core of my Deaf world.

In May of 2009 the Society celebrated its fiftieth anniversary. Since the 1970s it has been based at St. Elizabeth's Church on East 83rd Street, where Msgr. Patrick McCahill is the pastor, and it continues to sponsor various programs for the Deaf community. Besides social and religious activities the Society offers workshops for deaf teenagers, marriage counseling, and annual banquets. At the anniversary celebration the Society was honored with a Proclamation from the City Council of New York City that described it as "one of the oldest ethnic minority groups of deaf on the East Coast [that] . . . has served as an extraordinary resource for the deaf in our City . . . and is worthy of the esteem of all New Yorkers."

The Society is no longer dominated by Puerto Ricans. Other Latinos—Dominicans, Mexicans, Central Americans, and others—and all varieties of Caribbeans have made a home for themselves. This is as it should be. The city and the country diversify and the need for organizations that work with the Latino deaf will only grow. As the Latino demographic expands, no doubt will the Latino deaf population. Already, estimates are that from 15 to 25 percent of deaf and hard of hearing students in the U.S. are Hispanic.

Deaf people are no longer reluctant to reveal themselves in public, as was the case when I was growing up in the 1950s and 1960s. This is a major social advance. Every so often I observe people signing. In an airport, a restaurant, on the street, and, of course, on the subway. If I see an opening to engage them I do, and invariably their eyes light up (especially young people) and the conversation takes off. They pose one question after another at me:

"What's your name?" "Where do you come from?" "Where do you live?" "Oh, you're not deaf?" "How did you learn Sign?" "Who are your parents?"

I like to say, if the appropriate moment presents itself:

"I am not deaf, but I am your son."

Today deaf people are crossing new frontiers. Innovations such as the cochlear implant can help deaf people hear better than ever before. Other technological changes allow many deaf children to be placed in mainstream school settings. Will these developments undermine Deaf culture? Will they eliminate sign language? Why do deaf children nevertheless prefer being with deaf children? I am fascinated by these issues and not just because they remind me of my parents.

In July of 2002 I attended my first CODA conference. CODA is an organization of children of deaf adults (CODAs), founded in the mid-1980s. Growing up, neither I nor my own CODA cousins (Jimmy, Mary, Tony, Johnny, Elizabeth, Victor, Willie and the others) ever dwelt on our peculiar situation. We just did what we had to do. In the CODA network (several hundred active members across the country, and more around the world), I discovered a community that reflects on its special upbringing. It continues to be a source of tranquility and solidarity for me. The CODA stories we share are intriguing, hilarious, and heartbreaking. Our lives are quilted from such varying materials and colors, yet the common thread keeps us woven together. My CODA brothers and sisters help me make sense of my life.

During the years since the time covered in this memoir, the bonds that had been formed in youth and in young adulthood have largely been preserved. That is a fortune I treasure. As far as I am concerned, reunions steeped in nostalgia and sentimentality can't be overrated. The re-encounters of my extended family, of friends from the Block, and of activists from political involvements are important to me. These enduring relationships somehow shelter me against the randomness and uncertainty of life.

On one of these occasions a few years ago, Vivian and I celebrated our wedding anniversary. Family and friends joined us to inaugurate the fourth decade of our marriage. Mom and Pop would have enjoyed the night of familiar faces, and they would have insisted on being introduced to the unfamiliar ones. Titi Olga and Titi Madelina were there, so my parents wouldn't have been the only deaf in a sea of hearing people.

Finally, I know it would give my parents immense joy to know that their grandchildren, Rachel and Orlando, will be guardians of their memory. And that yet another generation, already of four great-grandchildren, follows.